D0410788

Bryson's Dictionary for Writers and Editors

Also by Bill Bryson

The Lost Continent
Mother Tongue
Troublesome Words
Neither Here Nor There
Made in America
Notes from a Small Island
Notes from a Big Country
Down Under
African Diary
A Short History of Nearly Everything
The Life and Times of the Thunderbolt Kid
Shakespeare (Eminent Lives Series)

Bryson's Dictionary for Writers and Editors

Bill Bryson

Doubleday

LONDON · TORONTO · SYDNEY · AUCKLAND · JOHANNESBURG

TRANSWORLD PUBLISHERS
61–63 Uxbridge Road, London W5 5SA
A Random House Group Company
www.rbooks.co.uk

First published in Great Britain in 1991 by Viking,
as *The Penguin Dictionary for Writers and Editors*
This revised edition first published
in 2008 by Doubleday
an imprint of Transworld Publishers

A CIP catalogue record for this book
is available from the British Library.

ISBN 9780385610445

Addresses for Random House Group Ltd companies outside the UK
can be found at: www.randomhouse.co.uk
The Random House Group Ltd Reg. No. 954009

The Random House Group Limited supports The Forest Stewardship Council
(FSC), the leading international forest-certification organization. All our titles that
are printed on Greenpeace-approved FSC-certified paper carry the FSC logo.
Our paper procurement policy can be found at
www.rbooks.co.uk/environment

Typeset in 11/14pt Minion by
Falcon Oast Graphic Art Ltd.

Printed and bound in Great Britain by
Clays Limited, Bungay, Suffolk.
2 4 6 8 10 9 7 5 3 1

Contents

Preface

This book is intended as a quick, concise guide to the problems of English spelling and usage most commonly encountered by writers and editors. How do you spell *supersede* and *broccoli* and *accessible*? Do I write *archaeology* or *archeology*? What's the difference between a cardinal number and an ordinal number? Is it *Capital* Reef National Park or *Capitol* Reef National Park? What did Belize use to be called? Doesn't Calcutta have a new name now? (It does – Kolkata.) What do we now call the Chinese river that I knew in my schooldays as the Hwang-Ho? In short, what are the answers to all those points of written usage that you kind of know or ought to know but can't quite remember?

It is a personal collection, built up over thirty years as a writer and editor in two countries, and so inevitably – inescapably – it reflects my own interests, experiences and blind spots. You may not need, as I do, to be reminded that it is Anjelica Huston but Whitney Houston, or have occasion at any point in your life to write the name of the district of Sydney known gloriously and unimprovably as Woolloomooloo. But I very much hope that what follows is broad enough and general enough to be frequently useful to nearly everyone.

To keep it simple, I have freely resorted to certain short cuts. Pronunciations have been simplified. I have scorned the

International Phonetic Alphabet, with its dogged reliance on symbols such as θ, i: and ʊ on the grounds that hardly anyone readily comprehends them and instead have attempted to convert tricky pronunciations into straightforward phonetic equivalents. Often these are intended as no more than rough guides – anyone who has ever heard the throat-clearing noise that is a Dutchman pronouncing ''s-Gravenhage' (the formal name of The Hague) will realize what a feebly approximate thing my suggested version is – and I unhesitatingly apologize for any shortcomings in this respect. Where pronunciation guidance is given – for instance, for the Spanish poet Vicente Aleixandre – the stress mark (´) appears after the stressed syllable: *ah-lay-hahn´-dray*.

I have also been forced on occasion to be arbitrary over spelling. Dictionaries are sometimes remarkably out of step with the rest of the world on certain matters of usage and orthography – in this respect I can cite no better example than the *Oxford English Dictionary*'s interesting but lonely insistence that Shakespeare should be spelled Shakspere – but there is usually a rough consensus, which I have sought to follow, though I try always to note alternatives when they are freely accepted.

I have tried also to keep cross-references to a minimum. In my view one of the more grating irritants of research is to hunt through several pages looking for 'Khayyám, Omar' only to be told: 'See Omar Khayyám'. So I have frequently put such information not only where it should be but also where a hurried reader might mistakenly look for it. The price for this is a certain repetition, for which I additionally apologize.

Some issues of style – whether you should write shopkeeper or shop-keeper, for instance – have been deliber-ately excluded. Such matters often are so overwhelmingly a question of preference, house style or fashion that my choices would be simply that: my choices. I would suggest that in such instances you should choose what seems most sensible, and strive to be consistent.

In the updating and typing of this new edition, I am hugely indebted to Meghan Bryson and Felicity Bryson Gould, respectively my daughter-in-law and daughter, for their unstinting and good-natured help. I am also much indebted to my editors Marianne Velmans and Deborah Adams for a thousand improvements to the text and countless errors caught. As always, my most special thanks to my dear wife, Cynthia, for her patience and support throughout.

Dictionary

a, an Errors involving the indefinite articles *a* and *an* are almost certainly more often a consequence of haste and carelessness than of ignorance. They are especially common when numbers are involved, as here: 'Cox will contribute 10 per cent of the equity needed to build a £80 million cable system' or 'He was assisted initially by two officers from the sheriff's department and a FBI agent.' When the first letter of an abbreviation is pronounced as a vowel, as in 'FBI', the preceding article should be *an*, not *a*.

Aachen, Germany in French, **Aix-la-Chapelle**

Aalto, Alvar (1898–1976) Finnish architect and designer

Aarhus city in Denmark. In Danish, **Århus**

abacus, pl. **abacuses**

abaft towards the stern, or rear, of a ship

abattoir

Abbas, Mahmoud (1935–) President of Palestinian National Authority 2005–

Abbot's Salford, Warwickshire

ABC American Broadcasting Companies (note plural), though the full title is no longer spelled out. It is now part of the Walt Disney Company. The television network is ABC-TV.

abdomen, but **abdominal**

Abdulaziz International Airport, King, Jeddah, Saudi Arabia

Aberdonian of or from Aberdeen

Aberfan coal-mining village in Mid-Glamorgan, scene of 1966 landslide in which 144 people died

Abergavenny, Gwent pronounced *ab-er-guh-ven´-nee* for the town, but *ab-er-ghen´-nee* for the Marquess of Abergavenny

aberrant departing from the normal standard; the noun is **aberration**

Aberystwyth, Ceredigion

abhorrent

Abidjan capital of Ivory Coast

ab incunabulis (Lat.) from the cradle

abiogenesis the concept that living matter can arise from non-living matter; spontaneous generation

abjure solemnly renounce. See also ADJURE.

-able In adding this suffix to a verb, the general rule is to drop a silent *e* (livable, lovable) except after a soft *g* (manageable) or sibilant *c* (peaceable). When a verb ends with a consonant and a *y* (justify, indemnify) change the *y* to *i* before adding -able (justifiable, indemnifiable). Verbs ending in *-ate* drop that syllable before adding *-able* (appreciable, demonstrable).

-able/-ible There are no reliable rules for knowing when a word ends in *-able* and when in *-ible*; see the Appendix for a list of some of the more frequently confused spellings.

ab origine (Lat.) from the beginning

abracadabra

abridgement/abridgment

abrogate to abolish, do away with

Absalom in the Old Testament, third son of David

Absalom, Absalom! novel by William Faulkner (1936)

Absaroka Range, Rocky Mountains, North America

abscess

abseil to descend a rockface by means of a rope; the North American term is **rappel**

absinthe an aniseed-flavoured liqueur

absquatulate (mock Lat.) to depart in haste

abstemious

Abu Dhabi capital city of and state in the United Arab Emirates

Abuja capital of Nigeria

Abu Simbel, Egypt site of temples built by Rameses II

abyss, abyssal, but **abysmal**

Abyssinia former name of Ethiopia

acacia

Académie française French literary society whose 40 members act as guardians of the French language; in English contexts, *Française* is usually capitalized

Academy of Motion Pictures Arts and Sciences institution responsible for the Oscars

a cappella singing without instrumental accompaniment

Acapulco, Mexico officially, Acapulco de Juárez

ACAS Advisory, Conciliation and Arbitration Service (UK)

Accademia della Crusca Italian literary academy

accelerator

accessible

accessory

acciaccatura grace note in music

accidentally, not -*tly*

accolade

accommodate very often misspelled: note -*cc*-, -*mm*-

accompanist, not -*iest*

accoutrement (US **accouterment**)

Accra capital of Ghana

Accrington, Lancashire

Acheson, Dean (1893–1971) American diplomat and politician, Secretary of State 1949–53

Achilles King of the Myrmidons, most famous of the Greek heroes of the Trojan War

Achilles heel, Achilles tendon

Achnashellach Station, Highland

acidulous, assiduous *Acidulous* means tart or acid; *assiduous* means diligent.

acknowledgement/acknowledgment

Acland, Sir Antony (1930–) British diplomat

acolyte, not -*ite*

Aconcagua, Cerro mountain in the Andes in Argentina, highest peak (at 22,835 feet/6,960 metres) in the western hemisphere

Açores Portuguese spelling of Azores

acoustics As a science, the word is singular ('Acoustics was his line of work'). As a collection of properties, it is plural ('The acoustics in the auditorium were not good').

acquiesce, acquiescence

acquit, acquittal, acquitted

acre a unit of land measuring 43,560 square feet, 4,840 square yards; equivalent to 4,047 square metres, 0.405 hectare

acronym is a word formed from the initial letter or letters of a group of words, as in NATO (North Atlantic Treaty Organization).

acrostic writing in which the first, and sometimes the last, letter of each line spells a word when read vertically; a type of word game based on the same principle

Actaeon in Greek mythology, a hunter who is turned into a stag by Artemis (the Roman Diana) after he spies her bathing

activity often a sign of prolixity, as here: 'The warnings followed a week of earthquake activity throughout the region.' Just make it 'a week of earthquakes'.

acute, chronic These two are sometimes confused, which is a little odd as their meanings are sharply opposed. *Chronic* pertains to lingering conditions, ones that are not easily overcome. *Acute* refers to those that come to a sudden crisis and require immediate attention. People in the Third World may suffer from a chronic shortage of food. In a bad year, their plight may become acute.

AD *anno domini* (Lat.) 'the year of the Lord'. AD should be written before the year (AD 25) but after the century (4th century AD) and is usually set in small caps. See also ANNO DOMINI and BC.

adage Even the most careful users of English frequently, but unnecessarily, refer to an 'old adage'. An adage is by definition old.

adagio slowly; slow movement; pl. **adagios**

adapter, adaptor The first is one who adapts, e.g., a book for theatrical presentation; the second is the device for making appliances work abroad and so on.

Addams, Charles (1912–88) American cartoonist, long associated with the *New Yorker*

Addams, Jane (1860–1935) American social activist and reformer; Nobel Peace Prize 1931

Addenbrooke's Hospital, Cambridge

addendum, pl. **addenda**

Addis Ababa capital of Ethiopia

adduceable capable of being proved

Adenauer, Konrad (1876–1967) West German Chancellor 1949–63

adenoid, adenoidal

ad hoc (Lat.) towards this, for a particular purpose

ad infinitum (Lat.) without limit, to infinity

Adirondack Mountains, US

adjudicator

adjure solemnly urge. See also ABJURE.

ad lib., *ad libitum* (Lat.) 'at will'. Note full stop after *lib*. To *ad-lib* is to speak in public without preparing in advance.

ad loc., *ad locum* (Lat.) 'at the place'. Note full stop after *loc.*

administer not *administrate*

Admiral's Cup series of yachting races held every two years

admissible, but **admittable**

admit to is nearly always wrong. You admit a misdeed, you do not admit to it.

ad nauseam (Lat.) not *-um*; to the point of nausea

ado, without further a cliché; best avoided

adrenalin is the preferred spelling, but **adrenaline** is accepted.

advance planning is common but always redundant. All planning must be done in advance.

adverse, averse *Averse* means reluctant or disinclined (think of *aversion*). *Adverse* means hostile and antagonistic (think of *adversary*).

adviser, but **advisory**

advocaat a liqueur

Aeaea in Greek mythology, the island inhabited by Circe

Aegean Sea area of the Mediterranean between Greece, Turkey and Crete

Aegina town and island off the south-eastern coast of Greece

Aeneid epic poem by Virgil

Aeolian Islands group of islands off north-eastern Sicily; also called Lipari Islands

Aeolus Greek god of winds

aeon (US **eon**)

aerate

Aer Lingus Irish airline

Aerolíneas Argentinas

AeroMéxico

aerosol

aerospace

Aérospatiale French aviation company

aerosphere one of the lower levels of the atmosphere

Aeschylus (c. 525–c. 450 BC) Greek playwright

Aesculapius (Lat.)/**Asclepius** (Grk) Roman and Greek god of medicine

aesthetic is normally the preferred spelling, though **esthetic** is acceptable in the US.

Afars and Issas, French Territory of former name of Djibouti

affaire de coeur (Fr.) love affair

affaire d'honneur (Fr.) a duel

affect, effect As a verb, *affect* means to influence ('Smoking may affect your health') or to adopt a pose or manner ('He affected ignorance'). *Effect* as a verb means to accomplish ('The prisoners effected an escape'). As a noun, the word needed is almost always *effect* (as in 'personal effects' or 'the damaging effects of war'). *Affect* as a noun has a narrow psychological meaning to do with emotional states (by way of which it is related to *affection*).

affenpinscher breed of dog

affettuoso in music, play with feeling

affidavit

affinity denotes a mutual relationship. Strictly, one should not speak of someone or something having an affinity for another, but rather with or between.

affrettando in music, speeding up

affright Note -*ff*-.

aficionado, pl. **aficionados**

AFL-CIO American Federation of Labor and Congress of Industrial Organizations

à fond (Fr.) thoroughly

a fortiori (Lat.) with even stronger reason, all the more so

Afrikaans, Afrikaners The first is a language; the second a group of people.

Afwerki, Issaias (or **Isaias**) (1946–) president of Eritrea

Ag *argentum* (Lat.) chemical symbol for silver

AG, *Aktiengesellschaft* (Ger.) roughly equivalent to *Inc.*

Agamemnon in Greek mythology, king of Argos and commander of the Greek army in the Trojan War; also the title of a play by Aeschylus, the first part of the Oresteian trilogy

Agassiz, (Jean) Louis (Rodolphe) (1807–73) Swiss-born American naturalist

à gauche (Fr.) to the left

ageing

agent provocateur, pl. **agents provocateurs**

aggravate, strictly, means to make a bad situation worse. If you walk on a broken leg, you may aggravate the injury. People can never be aggravated, only circumstances.

aggression, aggressiveness *Aggression* always denotes hostility. *Aggressiveness* can denote hostility or merely boldness.

aggrieve

Agincourt, Battle of (1415)

agoraphobia fear of open spaces

AGR advanced gas-cooled reactor, a type of nuclear power station

Agra, India site of Taj Mahal

agreeable

Aguascalientes city and state in central Mexico

Aguilera, Christina (1980–) American singer

Agusta, not *Aug*-; formally, Gruppo Agusta; Italian helicopter company

Ahmadinejad, Mahmoud (1956–) President of Iran 2005–

à huis clos (Fr.) behind closed doors

Ah, Wilderness! comedy by Eugene O'Neill (1933)

aid and abet A tautological gift from the legal profession. The two words together tell us nothing that either doesn't say on its own. The only distinction is that *abet* is normally reserved for contexts involving criminal intent. Thus it would be careless to speak of a benefactor abetting the construction of a church or youth club.

aide-de-camp, pl. **aides-de-camp**

aide-mémoire, pl. **aides-mémoire**

AIDS is not correctly described as a disease. It is a medical condition. The term is short for *acquired immune deficiency syndrome*.

aiguillette ornamental braid worn on the shoulder of a uniform

Ailesbury, Marquess of, but the town in Buckinghamshire is **Aylesbury**

Aintree, Merseyside site of the Grand National racecourse

airborne

Airbus Industrie   European aircraft manufacturer, now called **Airbus SAS**; it is a subsidiary of EADS NV

Airedale (cap.) a breed of terrier, named after the valley in Yorkshire

Air France-KLM   Franco-Dutch airline formed from merger of two national carriers in 2004

Air Line Pilots Association for the group that looks after the interests of American commercial pilots. **BALPA** performs the same function in the UK.

Airy, George Biddell (1801–92) English astronomer

Aix-en-Provence (hyphens), France

Aix-la-Chapelle (hyphens)   French name for Aachen, Germany

Aix-les-Bains (hyphens), France

Ajaccio capital of Corsica and birthplace of Napoleon

AK postal abbr. of Alaska

AL postal abbr. of Alabama

à la The adjectival forms of proper nouns in French do not take capital letters after *à la*: à la française, à la russe, à la lyonnaise.

alabaster

Aladdin

Alamein, El Egyptian village that gave its name to two battles of the Second World War

Alamogordo, New Mexico   site of first atomic bomb explosion

Alanbrooke, Alan Francis Brooke, Viscount (1883–1963) British field marshal

A la recherche du temps perdu novel by Marcel Proust, published in English as *Remembrance of Things Past*

Alaska Airlines, not *Alaskan*

'Alas! poor Yorick! I knew him, Horatio,' is the correct version of the quotation from *Hamlet*

Albigenses, Albigensians religious sect during 11th to 13th centuries, also known as Cathars

Albright, Madeleine (1937–) Czech-born American diplomat and academic

albumen, albumin *Albumen* is the white of an egg; *albumin* is a protein within the albumen.

Albuquerque, New Mexico

Alcaeus (*fl.*c. 600 BC) Greek poet

Alcatraz island, former prison, in San Francisco Bay

Alcibiades (c. 450–404 BC) Athenian statesman and general

Alcock, Sir John William (1892–1919) British aviator who with **Sir Arthur Whitten Brown** (1886–1948) was the first to fly non-stop across the Atlantic (1919)

Alcott, Louisa May (1833–88) American writer

Aleixandre, Vicente (1898–1984) Spanish poet, awarded Nobel Prize for Literature 1977; pronounced *ah-lay-hahn´-dray.*

Aleutian Islands, Alaska

alfalfa

Alfa-Romeo for the Italian make of automobile

Al-Fatah Palestinian political organization. Drop *Al-* when it is preceded by an article ('a Fatah spokesman', 'the Fatah organization').

Alfredsson, Daniel (1972–) Swedish ice hockey player

Alfredsson, Helen (1965–) Swedish professional golfer

alfresco (one word)

algae is plural; a single organism is an **alga**.

Algonquin Hotel, New York; **Algonquin** Indians

algorithm

Ali, Muhammad (1942–) born Cassius Marcellus Clay; American heavyweight boxer, three times world champion

à l'italienne (Fr., no caps) 'in the Italian style'

alkali, pl. **alkalis, alkalies**

al-Khwarizmi, Muhammad ibn-Musa (c. 780–850) Arab mathematician, often called the father of algebra

Allahabad city in Uttar Pradesh, India

allege, allegedly, allegation

Allegheny Mountains and **Allegheny River**, but **Alleghany Corporation** and **Allegany** for the town, county, Indian reservation and state park in New York. The plural of the mountains is **Alleghenies**. In short, there is huge variation in the spelling from place to place, so double-check.

Allenby, Edmund Henry Hynman, Viscount (1861–1936) British general

Allende, Salvador (1908–73) President of Chile 1970–3

All God's Chillun Got Wings play by Eugene O'Neill (1924)

Allhallowmass (one word) alternative name for All Saints' Day, 1 November

Allhallows, Kent

all intents and purposes is a tautology; use just 'to all intents'.

All Nippon Airways, not -*lines*

allophone in Canadian usage, someone who does not speak French

allot, allotted, allotting, allottable

all right, not *alright*

All Saints' Day 1 November

All Souls College, University of Oxford

All Souls' Day 2 November

all time Many authorities object to this expression in constructions such as 'She was almost certainly the greatest female sailor of all time' (*Daily Telegraph*) on the grounds that *all time* extends to the future as well as the past and we cannot possibly know what lies ahead. A no less pertinent consideration is that such assessments, as in the example just cited, are bound to be hopelessly subjective and therefore have no place in any measured argument. (There is a similar problem with futurity in the use of 'ever'.)

allusion 'When the speaker happened to name Mr Gladstone, the allusion was received with loud cheers' (cited by Fowler). The word is not, as many suppose, a more impressive synonym for *reference*. When you allude to something, you do not specifically mention it, but leave it to the reader to deduce the subject. Thus it would be correct to write, 'In an allusion to the President, he said: "Some people make better oil men than politicians." ' The word is closer in meaning to *implication* or *suggestion*.

Allyson, June (1917–2006) American film actress, real name Ella Gleisman

Almaty largest city in Kazakhstan. The capital is Astana.

Al Manāmah/Al Manama capital of Bahrain

Almodóvar, Pedro (1951–) Spanish film-maker

Alnwick, Northumberland pronounced *ann´-ick*

Alpes-de-Haute-Provence *département* of France

Al Qaeda (from the Arabic *al-qā'ida*) is the most common spelling in English for the terrorist group, but there are many variants, including commonly *Al Qaida*, *al-Qaeda* and *al-Qaida*.

Al Qahirah/El Qahira Arabic name for Cairo

alright is never correct; make it **all right**.

ALS amyotrophic lateral sclerosis, muscle-wasting disease. Also known as motor neurone disease. In the US it is called Lou Gehrig's disease, after the baseball player who suffered from it.

Alsatian (cap.) common UK name for breed of dog officially called German Shepherd

altar, alter The first is a table used in worship, the second means to change.

altercation is a heated exchange of words. If blows are traded or shoving is involved, it is not properly an altercation.

Althing parliament of Iceland

although, though The two are interchangeable except as an adverb placed after the verb, where only *though* is correct, and in the expressions *as though* and *even though*, where idiom precludes *although*.

altocumulus, altostratus (one word) for types of cloud

aluminium (US **aluminum**)

alumnae, alumni *Alumni* is the masculine plural for a collection of college graduates. In the context of an all-female institution, the correct word is *alumnae*. The singular forms are **alumna** (fem.) and **alumnus** (masc.).

alyssum border plant

Alzheimer's disease, but in formal medical contexts the non-possessive form **Alzheimer disease** is increasingly used instead

a.m./AM, *ante meridiem* (Lat.) before midday

Amalienborg Palace, Copenhagen residence of the Danish royal family

amanuensis one who takes dictation; pl. **amanuenses**

amaretto liqueur; pl. **amarettos**

Amarillo, Texas

amaryllis plant with trumpet-shaped flowers

Ambassadors Theatre, London (no apos.)

ambergris substance used in the manufacture of perfumes
ambience
ambiguous, equivocal Both mean vague and open to more than one interpretation. But whereas an *ambiguous* statement may be vague by accident or by intent, an *equivocal* one is calculatedly unclear.
ambidextrous, not -*erous*
Amenhotep name of four kings in the 18th dynasty of ancient Egypt
America's Cup yacht races
americium (not cap.) chemical element
AmeriCorps voluntary service organization
AmerisourceBergen (one word) US pharmaceutical supply company
Améthyste, Côte d', France
Amharic Semitic language; official tongue of Ethiopia
amicus curiae (Lat.) 'friend of the court'; pl. *amici curiae*
amid, among *Among* applies to things that can be separated and counted, *amid* to things that cannot. Rescuers might search among survivors, but amid wreckage.
amniocentesis the withdrawing of amniotic fluid from a pregnant woman's uterus
amoeba, pl. **amoebas/amoebae** (US **ameba**, pl. **amebas/amebae**)
à moitié (Fr.) in part, halfway
amok is generally the preferred spelling, but **amuck** is an accepted alternative.
among, between A few authorities insist that *among* applies to more than two things and *between* to only two. But by this logic you would have to say that St Louis is among California, New York and Michigan, not between them. In so far as the two words can be distinguished, *among*

should be applied to collective arrangements (trade talks among the members of the European Union) and *between* to reciprocal arrangements (a treaty between the UK, the US and Canada).

amoral, **immoral**   *Amoral* describes matters in which questions of morality do not arise or are disregarded; *immoral* applies to things that are evil.

amour-propre (Fr.) self-respect

Ampère, André Marie (1775–1836) French physicist; the unit of electricity named after him is the ampere (no cap., no accent)

amphetamine

amphibian, amphibious

Amphitryon In Greek mythology, a Mycenaean king whose wife, Alcmene, gave birth to Hercules after Zeus tricked her into sleeping with him

amphora, pl. **amphorae** (or **amphoras**)

ampoule is the preferred spelling; **ampule** is also accepted.

Amtrak   American passenger railway company. The company's formal designation is the National Railroad Passenger Corporation, but this is almost never used, even on first reference.

Amundsen, Roald (1872–1928) Norwegian explorer, first person to reach the South Pole (1911)

Anacreon (c. 563–c. 478 BC) Greek poet

anaesthesia, anaesthetic (US **anesthesia, anesthetic**) The doctor who administers anaesthetics is an **anaesthetist** in the UK, an **anesthesiologist** in the US.

analogous comparable in some way

analyse (US **analyze**)

anathema, pl. **anathemas**

Anaxagoras (c. 500–428 BC) Greek philosopher

Anaximander (c. 611–c. 547 BC) Greek philosopher
ancien régime (Fr.) the old order
ancillary
Andalusia region of Spain. In Spanish, **Andalucía**
Andersen, Hans Christian (1805–75)   Danish writer of
    children's tales. Not -*son*
Anderson, Marian (1897–1993) celebrated contralto
Andorra is a principality; the capital is **Andorra la Vella**.
Andra Pradesh Indian state
Andrejewski, Jerzy (1909–83) Polish novelist
Andretti, Mario (1940–) American racing driver
Andrewes, Lancelot (1555–1626) English scholar and prelate,
    one of the principal translators of the King James Bible
Andrews Air Force Base (no apos.), Maryland
androgenous, **androgynous**   The first applies to the
    production of male offspring; the second means having
    both male and female characteristics.
Andromache in Greek mythology, the wife of Hector
Androscoggin county, river and lake in Maine, US
aneurysm
Anfinsen, Christian B. (for **Boehmer**) (1916–95) American
    biochemist, awarded Nobel Prize for Chemistry 1972
anfractuosity having many turns
Angelico, Fra (1387–1455) Florentine painter, also known as
    Fra Giovanni da Fiesole
Angkor   complex of ruins in Cambodia. **Angkor Wat** is a
    single temple within the compound.
Angleterre French for England
anglicize (lower case)
Anglo American PLC South African mining conglomerate
    now based in London; Anglo American is spelled as two
    words, no hyphen

angora, Angora The first is a type of wool; the second is the
former name of Ankara, Turkey.

Angostura bitters

angstrom/ångström abbr. Å; unit used to measure wave-
lengths of light, and equal to one ten-billionth of a
metre; named for Anders Ångström (1814–74), Swedish
physicist

Anheuser-Busch US brewery

Anhui Chinese province, formerly spelled *Anhwei*

Aniakchak National Monument and Preserve, Alaska

animus, but **animosity** Both mean hostility, but *animosity* is
stronger than *animus.*

aniseed a flavourful seed

anisette a drink flavoured with aniseed

Ankara capital of Turkey

Annabessacook, Lake, Maine

Annapolis capital of Maryland

Annapurna a cluster of mountains in the Himalayas, of
which the highest peak is Annapurna I (26,545
feet/8,091 metres)

Ann Arbor, Michigan home of the University of Michigan

Anne Arundel County, Maryland

Anne of Cleves (1515–57) fourth wife of Henry VIII

annex, annexe In the UK, the first is the verb and the second
the noun. In the US, both noun and verb are spelled
annex.

Annieopsquotch Mountains, Newfoundland, Canada

annihilate

Ann-Margret (1941–) American actress, born Ann-Margret
Olsson; note hyphen and irregular spelling *Margret*

anno domini (Lat.) 'the year of the Lord'; see also AD

annus mirabilis (Lat.) remarkable year

anomaly, anomalous

anonymous, anonymity

Anouilh, Jean (1910–87)   French playwright; pronounced *an'-oo-ee*

anorak

Anschluss (Ger.)   a union; particularly applied to that of Germany and Austria in 1938

Antananarivo   capital of Madagascar

Antassawamock Neck, Massachusetts

ante bellum (Lat.)   'before the war'; especially applied to the period before the American Civil War

antecedence, antecedents   *Antecedence* means precedence; *antecedents* are ancestors or other things that have gone before.

antediluvian   antiquated, primitive

ante meridiem (Lat.)   'before midday', abbr. a.m./AM; not to be confused with **antemeridian** (one word), meaning of or taking part in the morning

antennae, antennas   Either is correct as the plural of *antenna*, but generally *antennae* is preferred for living organisms ('a beetle's antennae') and *antennas* for man-made objects ('radio antennas made possible the discovery of quarks').

anticipate   To *anticipate* something is to look ahead to it and prepare for it, not to make a reasonable estimate. A tennis player who anticipates his opponent's next shot doesn't just guess where it is going to go, he is there to meet it.

Anti-Defamation League

Antigone   in Greek mythology, the daughter of Oedipus; also the title of a play by Sophocles

Antigua and Barbuda   Caribbean state; capital St John's

antipasto (It.) appetizer, hors-d'oeuvre; pl. **antipasti**

Antipodean of Australia or New Zealand

antirrhinum note -*rr*-; a flower, also known as snapdragon

Antofagasta, Chile

Antonioni, Michelangelo (1912–2007) Italian film director

Antony and Cleopatra, not *Anthony* play by Shakespeare (c. 1606)

Antwerpen the Flemish name for Antwerp, Belgium; the French name is **Anvers**

anxious Since *anxious* comes from *anxiety*, it should contain some connotation of being worried or fearful and not merely eager or expectant.

any A tricky word at times, as here: 'This paper isn't very good, but neither is any of the others.' A simple and useful principle is to make the verb always correspond to the complement. Thus: 'neither is any other' or 'neither are any of the others'.

anybody, **anyone**, **anything**, **anywhere** *Anything* and *anywhere* are always one word. The others are normally one word except when the emphasis is on the second element (e.g., 'He received three job offers, but any one would have suited him'). *Anybody* and *anyone* are singular and should be followed by singular pronouns and verbs. A common fault – so common, in fact, that some no longer consider it a fault – is seen here: 'Anyone can relax so long as they don't care whether they or anyone else ever actually gets anything done.' The problem, clearly, is that a plural pronoun ('they') is being attached to a singular verb ('gets'). Such constructions may in fact be fully defensible, at least some of the time, though you should at least know why you are breaking a rule when you break it.

any more, any time Both are always two words.

ANZAC Australian and New Zealand Army Corps

ANZUS Pact 1951 security treaty between Australia, New Zealand and the United States

AONB area of outstanding natural beauty (UK)

à outrance (Fr.), not *à l'outrance*; to the very last, to the death

Apalachicola Florida river

Apeldoorn, Netherlands

Apennines for the Italian mountain range. Note -*nn*- in middle. In Italian, Appennini

aperitif, pl. **aperitifs**

apfelstrudel (Ger.) apple strudel

aplomb

apocalypse, apocalyptic

apogee the highest or most distant point, usually in reference to orbiting bodies. Its opposite is **perigee**.

Apollinaire, Guillaume (1880–1919) born Wilhelm Apollinaris de Kostrowitzky; French writer and critic

Apollo Greek god of light, son of Zeus

'Apologie for Poetrie, An' title of an essay by Sir Philip Sidney, also published as 'The Defence of Poesie' (1595)

aposiopesis, pl. **aposiopeses** the sudden breaking off of a thought or statement

apostasy, pl. **apostasies** the abandoning of one's faith

apostatize renounce a belief

a posteriori (Lat.) 'from what is after'; in logic, moving from effect to cause, reasoning from experience

apothegm a witty or pithy maxim; the *g* is silent

apotheosis, pl. **apotheoses** deification (generally used figuratively)

Appalachian Mountains, eastern US

Appaloosa breed of horse

apparatchik party functionary, especially of the Communist Party

apparel

apparition

appellant, **appellate** The first is a person who appeals against a court ruling; the second describes a court at which appeals are heard.

appendices, **appendixes** Either is correct.

Apple Mac

applicator

appoggiatura in music, an accented non-harmonized note that precedes a harmonized note

Appomattox town in Virginia where the Confederacy surrendered to the Union to end the American Civil War (9 April 1865)

appraise, **apprise** *Appraise* means to assess or evaluate. *Apprise* means to inform. An insurance assessor appraises damage and apprises owners.

appreciate has a slightly more specific meaning than writers sometimes give it. If you *appreciate* something, you value it ('I appreciate your concern') or you understand it sympathetically ('I appreciate your predicament'). But when there is no sense of sympathy or value (as in 'I appreciate what you are saying, but I don't agree with it') *understand* or *recognize* or the like would be better.

apprehensible

après-midi (Fr.) afternoon

après-ski (Fr., hyphen) the period after a day's skiing

April Fool's Day (UK)/**April Fools' Day** (US)

a principio (Lat.) from the beginning

a priori (Lat.) from what is before; in logic, an argument proceeding from cause to effect

apropos in French, *à propos*

Apuleius, Lucius (*fl.* 2nd c. AD) Roman satirist

Apulia region of Italy known in Italian as Puglia

Aqaba, Gulf of an arm of the Red Sea. Aqaba is also the name of a town in Jordan.

aqua vitae (Lat.) water of life; used to describe whiskies and other alcoholic spirits

aqueduct, but **aquifer** The first is a bridge carrying water across a valley, the second a mass of rock capable of holding water.

aquiline like an eagle

Aquinas, St Thomas (1225–74) Italian theologian, canonized 1323

à quoi bon? (Fr.) what for? what's the point?

AR postal abbr. of Arkansas; not Arizona, which is **AZ**

arabic numerals (no cap.)

Arafat, Yassir (1929–2004) born Mohammed Abed Ar'ouf Arafat; leader of the Palestine Liberation Organization 1969–2004, awarded Nobel Peace Prize 2004

Aramaic Semitic language

Aran Island and **Aran Islands** (Ireland) but **Isle of Arran** (Scotland) The sweater is spelled *Aran*.

Arc de Triomphe, Paris officially, Arc de Triomphe de l'Étoile

arc-en-ciel (Fr.) rainbow; pl. *arcs-en-ciel*

archaea type of unicellular organisms

archaeology is normally preferred, but **archeology** is accepted (and is standard in the US).

archaic, archaism

archetype

Archilochus of Paros (c. 714–c. 676 BC) Greek poet

Archimedes (c. 287–212 BC) Greek mathematician and engineer

archipelago, pl. **archipelagos**

Arctic Circle, **Arctic Ocean**, but **arctic fox** (no cap.)

Ardennes wooded plateau in southern Belgium, north-eastern France and Luxembourg

Ardizzone, Edward Jeffrey Irving (1900–79) British illustrator

Arezzo, Italy

arguable

Århus (Dan.)/**Aarhus** city in Denmark

Aristides (c. 530–c. 468 BC) Athenian statesman

Aristophanes (c. 448–c. 380 BC) Greek dramatist

armadillo, pl. **armadillos**

Armageddon

armament

armature

Armenia formerly part of Soviet Union, capital Yerevan

armour (US **armor**)

aroma applies only to agreeable smells; there is no such thing as a bad aroma.

Aroostook River, Maine and New Brunswick

Arran, Isle of Scotland. See also ARAN ISLAND.

arrière-pensée (Fr.) ulterior motive, mental reservation

arrivederci (It.) goodbye

arriviste disagreeably ambitious person

Arrol-Johnston British automobile of early 1900s

arrondissement principal division of French *départements* and some larger cities

Arrows of the Chace, not *Chase* letters by John Ruskin (1881)

artefact (US **artifact**) The word should be applied only to things fashioned by humans, not to animal bones, fossils or other naturally occurring objects.

Artemis Greek goddess of the moon, associated with

hunting. The Roman equivalent is Diana.

arteriosclerosis

Arthur Andersen, not -*son* accountancy firm

artichoke

Aruba Caribbean island, a self-governing dependency of the Netherlands; capital Oranjestad

Asahi Shimbun Japanese newspaper

as . . . as 'A government study concludes that for trips of 500 miles or less . . . automotive travel is as fast or faster than air travel, door to door' (George Will, syndicated columnist). The problem here is what is termed an incomplete alternative comparison. If we remove the 'or faster than' phrase from the sentence, the problem becomes immediately evident: 'A government study concludes that for trips of 500 miles or less . . . automotive travel is as fast air travel, door to door.' The writer has left the 'as fast' phrase dangling uncompleted. The sentence should say 'as fast as or faster than air travel'.

ascendancy, ascendant

ASCII short for American Standard Code for Information Interchange; computer terminology

Asclepius Use *Aesculapius.*

Asea Brown Boveri Swedish-Swiss electrical equipment company, now **ABB**

ASEAN Association of South East Asian Nations, formed 1967; members are Brunei, Cambodia, Indonesia, Laos, Malaysia, Myanmar/Burma, the Philippines, Singapore, Thailand and Vietnam

aseptic

as far as is commonly misused, as here: 'As far as next season, it is too early to make forecasts' (*Baltimore Sun*). The error here has been exercising authorities since at least Fowler's heyday and shows no sign of abating, either as a problem or as something that exercises authorities. The trouble is that 'as far as' serves as a conjunction and as such requires a following verb. The solution is either to remove the conjunction ('As for next season, it is too early to make forecasts') or to supply the needed verb ('As far as next season goes, it is too early to make forecasts').

Ashbery, John (1927–) American poet and critic

Ashby de la Zouch, Leicestershire (no hyphens)

Asheville, North Carolina

Ashgabat capital of Turkmenistan; also sometimes spelled **Ashkhabad**

Ashkenazi an East or Central European Jew; pl. **Ashkenazim**

Ashkenazy, Vladimir (1937–) Russian-born Icelandic pianist and conductor

Ashmolean Museum, Oxford

Ashuapmuchuan River, Quebec, Canada

Asimov, Isaac (1920–92) American biochemist and prolific science-fiction writer

asinine

ASLEF Associated Society of Locomotive Engineers and Firemen, a UK trade union

Asmara (formerly *Asmera*) capital of Eritrea

asparagus

Assad, Bashar (1965–) President of Syria 2000– ; succeeded his father, Hafez Assad (1928–2000)

assagai, **assegai** Either spelling is correct for the African spear.

assailant

assassin

Assateague Island, Maryland and Virginia

assault, battery They are not the same in law. *Assault* is a threat of violence; *battery* is actual violence.

assessor

asseverate to declare

Assiniboine River, Manitoba, Canada

assiduous, acidulous *Assiduous* means diligent; *acidulous* means tart or acid.

Assisi town in Umbria, birthplace of St Francis

assonance words that rhyme in consonants but not vowels (e.g., cat and kit) or in vowels but not consonants (e.g., bun and sponge)

assuage, assuaging

assume, presume The two words are often so close in meaning as to be indistinguishable, but in some contexts they do allow a fine distinction to be made. *Assume*, in the sense of 'to suppose', normally means to put forth a realistic hypothesis, something that can be taken as probable ('I assume we will arrive by midnight'). *Presume* has more of an air of sticking one's neck out, of making an assertion that may be arguable or wrong ('I presume we have met before?'). But in most instances the two words can be used interchangeably.

as to whether *Whether* alone is sufficient.

AstraZeneca pharmaceutical company

AstroTurf (one word) is a trademark.

Asunción capital of Paraguay

asymmetry, asymmetric, asymmetrical

Atatürk, Mustapha Kemal (1881–1938) Turkish leader and President 1923–38

Atchafalaya Louisiana river and bay

Athenaeum London club and other British contexts, but

Atheneum for the US publisher
Athene Greek goddess of wisdom
Athinai Greek spelling of Athens
ATM automated teller machine
à tout prix (Fr.) at any price
attaché
Attawapiskat Canadian river
Attenborough, Richard, Lord (1923–) British film actor and director; brother of **Sir David Attenborough** (1926–), zoologist and TV presenter
Attila (c. 405–53) king of the Huns
Attlee, Clement (1883–1967) British Prime Minister 1945–51; later appointed Earl Attlee
attorney-general, pl. **attorneys-general**
attributable
Atwater, (Harvey) Lee (1951–91) US Republican political adviser
Atwood, Margaret (1939–) Canadian novelist
Au *aurum* (Lat.) chemical symbol for gold
aubergine (US **eggplant**)
au besoin (Fr.) if need be
aubrietia flowering plant named after Claude Aubriet (1655–1742), French painter
Auchincloss, Louis (Stanton) (1917–) American novelist
Auchinleck family name of James Boswell; pronounced *aff-leck*
Auden, W. H. (for **Wystan Hugh**) (1907–73) Anglo-American poet
audible
Audubon, John James (1785–1851) American artist and naturalist
au fait (Fr.) to be in the know

au fond (Fr.) basically, at the bottom

auf Wiedersehen (Ger.) goodbye, until we meet again

auger, **augur** An *auger* is a tool for boring holes in wood or soil; an *augur* is a prophet or soothsayer. The two words are not related.

'**Auld Lang Syne**' (Scot.) literally 'old long since'; traditional end-of-year song with words by Robert Burns

Auld Reekie (Scot.) Old Smoky; nickname for Edinburgh

Aumann, Robert J. (1930–) Israeli-American academic; awarded Nobel Prize for Economics 2005

au mieux (Fr.) for the best, at best

au naturel (Fr.) in the natural state

Ausable River, **Ausable Chasm**, New York State

Au Sable River, **Au Sable Point**, Michigan

Auschwitz German concentration camp in Poland during the Second World War. In Polish, **Oświęcim**

au secours (Fr.) a cry for help

Ausländer (Ger.) foreigner

auspicious does not mean simply special or memorable. It means propitious, promising, of good omen.

Austral (adj.) of or relating to Australia or Australasia

austral (adj.) southern

austral (noun) former currency of Argentina, pl. **australes**

Australia, Commonwealth of, is divided into six states (New South Wales, Queensland, South Australia, Tasmania, Victoria, Western Australia) and two territories (Australian Capital Territory, Northern Territory). The latter two should not be referred to as states.

autarchy, **autarky** The first means absolute power, an autocracy; the second denotes self-sufficiency. However, neither word is well known, and in almost every instance an English synonym would bring an improvement in comprehension, if not in elegance.

Auteuil, Daniel (1950–) prolific French actor

autobahn (Ger.) express motorway. The English plural is **autobahns**; the German is **Autobahnen**.

auto-da-fé execution of heretics during the Inquisition; pl. *autos-da-fé*

autostrada (It.) express motorway; pl. **autostrade**

Auvergne region of France

auxiliary, not -*ll*-

avant-garde

avenge, revenge Generally, *avenge* indicates the settling of a score or the redressing of an injustice. It is more dispassionate than *revenge*, which indicates retaliation taken largely for the sake of personal satisfaction.

Avenue of the Americas, New York City. Often still referred to as Sixth Avenue, its former name

avocado, pl. **avocados**

avocation work done for personal satisfaction rather than need, usually in addition to a normal job

avoirdupois weights the system of weights traditionally used throughout the English-speaking world, based on one pound equalling 16 ounces

Avon former county of England, abolished 1996; also the name of several rivers in England, and the title of the former Prime Minister Anthony Eden (Earl of Avon)

à votre santé (Fr.) to your health

a while, awhile To write 'for awhile' is wrong because the idea of 'for' is implicit in 'awhile'. Write either 'I will stay here for a while' (two words) or 'I will stay here awhile' (one word).

awoke, awaked, awakened Two common problems are worth noting:

1. *Awoken*, though much used, is generally considered not standard. Thus this sentence from an Agatha Christie novel (cited by Partridge) is wrong: 'I was awoken by that rather flashy young woman.' Make it *awakened*.

2. As a past participle, *awaked* is preferable to *awoke*. Thus, 'He had awaked at midnight' and not 'He had awoke at midnight.' But if ever in doubt about the past tense, you will never be wrong if you use *awakened*.

axel, axle An *axel* is a jump in ice skating; an *axle* is a rod connecting two wheels.

Axelrod, George (1922–2003) American screenwriter and film director

ayatollah Shiite Muslim religious leader

Ayckbourn, Sir Alan (1939–) prolific British playwright

Ayer, Sir Alfred Jules (1910–89) English philosopher

Ayers Rock (no apostrophe) for the Australian eminence. However, the formal and now usual name is *Uluru*.

Aykroyd, Dan (1952–) Canadian-born actor and screen-writer

Aylesbury, Buckinghamshire, but the **Marquess of Ailesbury**

Ayres, Gillian (1930–) British artist

AZ postal abbr. of Arizona; the traditional abbreviation is **Ariz**

Azerbaijan former republic of the Soviet Union; capital Baku

B

Baader-Meinhof Gang German underground group named after Andreas Baader (1943–77) and Ulrike Meinhof (1934–76); also called the Red Army Faction

Baath Party formally **Baath Arab Socialist Party**

Babbitt novel by Sinclair Lewis (1922)

Babington conspiracy a plot to assassinate Queen Elizabeth I, named for its principal conspirator, Antony Babington (1561–86)

Babi Yar site near Kiev where Nazis massacred Russian Jews in 1941; also the title of a poem by Yevgeny Yevtushenko and a novel by Anatoly Kuznetsov

babushka a Russian grandmother; also a kind of scarf

Bacardi a brand of rum

baccalaureate

baccarat a casino game. In French, *baccara*

Bacchae, The play by Euripides

Bacchus Roman god of wine; the Greek equivalent was Dionysus. Words derived from Bacchus are usually not capitalized but do retain -*cch*- spelling: bacchanalian, bacchic, bacchantic.

Bach, Johann Sebastian (1685–1750) German composer and father of four others: **Wilhelm Friedemann** (1710–84), **Carl Philipp Emanuel** (1714–88), **Johann**

Christoph Friedrich (1732–95) and **Johann Christian** (1735–82)

bacillus, pl. **bacilli**

Bacon, Francis, Baron Verulam of Verulam, Viscount St Albans (1561–1626) English philosopher and essayist

Bacon, Francis (1909–92) Irish artist

BACS abbr. of banks' automated clearing system; a bank payment system

bacteria is plural. The singular is *bacterium*. Bacteria should not be confused with viruses, which are much smaller and cause different diseases.

Baden-Powell, Robert Stephenson Smyth, Lord (1857–1941) founder of Boy Scouts (1908) and, with his sister **Agnes Baden-Powell** (1858–1945), Girl Guides (1910)

Baden-Württemberg German state; capital Stuttgart

Baedeker famous series of travel guides first published in Germany by Karl Baedeker (1801–59)

Baekeland, Leo Hendrik (1863–1944) Belgian-born American chemist, invented Bakelite

bagatelle a trifle

Bagehot, Walter (1826–77) English economist, journalist and authority on the English Constitution; pronounced *badge´-ut*

bahadur a title of respect in India

Bahai a religion; the cognate forms are **Bahaist** and **Bahaism**

Bahamian of or from the Bahamas

Bahnhof (Ger.) railway station

Bahrain island state in the Persian Gulf; capital Al Manama

bail, bale *Bail* is a prisoner's bond, the pieces that rest atop the stumps in cricket and the act of scooping water. *Bale* is a bundle, as of cotton or hay. You bail out a boat, but bale out of an aircraft. A malicious person wears a baleful expression.

Baile Atha Cliath Gaelic for Dublin

Baird, John Logie (1888–1946) Scottish pioneer of television

baited breath is wrong; breath is *bated* (as in *abated*).

Bakelite (cap.) type of plastic

Bakunin, Mikhail (Aleksandrovich) (1814–76) Russian revolutionary

balaclava knitted hat named after the Ukrainian town where a battle was fought (1854) during the Crimean War

balalaika stringed instrument

Balanchine, George (1904–83) Russian-born American choreographer

baldechin/baldaquin a canopy over a throne or altar, pronounced *bald´-a-kin*; in Italian, *baldacchino*

Baldrige, Malcolm (1922–87), not *-ridge* American statesman

bale, bail *Bail* is a prisoner's bond, the pieces that rest atop the stumps in cricket and the act of scooping water. *Bale* is a bundle, as of cotton or hay. You bail out a boat, but bale out of an aircraft. A malicious person wears a baleful expression.

Balearic Islands cluster of Spanish islands in the Mediterranean; in Spanish, *Islas Baleares*

Balfour, Arthur (James), Earl of (1848–1930) British Prime Minister 1902–6; issued Balfour Declaration (1917) calling for creation of a Jewish state in Palestine. It should be noted that there are or have been three separate Lord Balfours – the Earl of Balfour, Lord Balfour of Inchrye and Lord Balfour of Burleigh – and care must be taken in distinguishing between them.

Balladur, Édouard (1929–) Prime Minister of France 1993–5

Ballesteros, Severiano (1957–) nickname 'Seve'; Spanish golfer

Balliol College, Oxford University

Balmoral Castle royal residence near Braemar, Grampian

BALPA British Air Line Pilots Association

Baluchistan region in Pakistan bordered by Iran and Afghanistan

Band-Aid (hyphen) is a trademark.

bandanna Note -*anna*, not -*ana*.

bandicoot type of marsupial

banister handrail on a staircase

banjos

Banjul capital of Gambia; formerly called Bathurst

BankAmerica Corporation is now **Bank of America**

Bankers Trust (no apos.)

Bankhead, Tallulah (1903–68) American actress

bank holiday (no caps)

Ban Ki-moon (1944–) South Korean diplomat, Secretary General of United Nations 2007– ; on second reference, Mr Ban

Bannister, Sir Roger (Gilbert) (1929–) first person to run a mile in less than four minutes (3 minutes 59.4 seconds, 1954)

banns notice in church of intended marriage

banshee evil spirit; in Gaelic *bean sídhe*

Bantustan South African black homeland

banzai, bonsai The first is a Japanese war cry or a greeting; the second is a type of Japanese gardening centred on miniature trees.

baptistery

Barabbas in the New Testament, the condemned thief

released instead of Jesus by Pilate

Barbadian of or from Barbados. The slang term *Bajan* is also sometimes used.

barbaric, barbarous *Barbaric*, properly used, emphasizes crudity and a lack of civilizing influence. A sharpened stick might be considered a barbaric implement of war. *Barbarous* stresses cruelty and harshness and usually contains at least a hint of moral condemnation, as in 'barbarous ignorance' or 'barbarous treatment'.

Barbarossa, not *-rosa* nickname of Frederick I (c. 1123–90), Holy Roman Emperor; German code name for the invasion of the USSR in 1941

barbecue is the only acceptable spelling in serious writing.

Barbirolli, Sir John (1899–1970) British conductor

Barbizon School group of French landscape painters, among them Millet, Daubigny and Rousseau

Barclays Bank, UK (no apos.)

Barents Sea

bar mitzvah religious coming-of-age ceremony for Jewish boys; the ceremony for girls is a **bat mitzvah**. The plural is *mitzvoth* or *mitzvahs*.

Barnard, Christiaan (1922–2001) South African heart surgeon; note *-aa-* in first name

Barnes & Noble (ampersand)

Barneys New York (no apos.) clothing retailer

Barnstable, town and county, Cape Cod, Massachusetts, but **Barnstaple**, England

Barnum, Phineas T(aylor) (1810–91) American showman

baron, baroness, baronet A *baron* is the lowest rank in the British nobility. A baronage can be either hereditary or non-hereditary. Holders of the latter are called life peers. A *baroness* is a woman who is the wife or widow of a baron, or a peer in her own right. In British contexts, Lord or Lady can be substituted for Baron or Baroness, e.g., Baron Baden-Powell is called Lord Baden-Powell. A *baronet* is not a peer; a baronetcy is a hereditary title ranking below a peer but above a knight. See also PEERS.

Barons Court, London (no apos.)

barracuda

Barrie, J. M. (formally **Sir James Matthew Barrie**) (1860–1937) Scottish writer, creator of Peter Pan

Barroso, José Manuel (1956–) Portuguese politician, president of the European Commission 2004–9

Barrow-in-Furness, Cumbria (hyphens)

Bartholdi, Frédéric Auguste (1834–1904) French sculptor; designed Statue of Liberty

Bartholomew Day, 24 August, but the **St Bartholomew's Day Massacre** (1572) and **St Bartholomew's Hospital**, London (familiarly known as **Bart's**)

Bartók, Béla (1881–1945) Hungarian pianist and composer

Bartolommeo, Fra (1475–1517) Florentine painter

Baryshnikov, Mikhail (1948–) Russian-born ballet dancer

Basel/Basle/Bâle third largest city in Switzerland. Basel is the usual spelling in Switzerland, the US and Germany; Basle is the usual spelling in Britain; Bâle is the usual spelling among French speakers.

Băsescu, Traian (1951–) President of Romania 2004–

Bashkortostan Russian republic

BASIC short for Beginner's All-purpose Symbolic Instruction Code; computer programming language

basically The trouble with this word, basically, is that it is almost always unnecessary.

Basilicata region of southern Italy

basis More often than not, a reliable indicator of wordiness, as here: 'Det. Chief Supt Peter Topping . . . said he would review the search on a day-to-day basis' (*Independent*). Why not make it 'would review the search daily' and save five words?

Basotho the people of Lesotho

bas-relief

Basse-Normandie region of France, capital Caen

Basseterre capital of St Kitts and Nevis

basset hound

Bastille Day 14 July (1789)

Bataan peninsula of the Philippines, famous for a long forced march ordered by the Japanese during which many thousands of Allied soldiers died in the Second World War

bated breath, not *baited* *Bated* is a cousin of *abated* and so implies something that is withheld.

bathos From the Greek word for 'depth', *bathos* can be used to indicate the lowest point or nadir, or triteness and insincerity. But its usual use is in describing an abrupt descent from an elevated position to the commonplace. It is not the opposite of *pathos*, which is to do with feelings of pity or sympathy.

Bathsheba in the Old Testament, the wife of Uriah and then of David, and mother of Solomon

bathyscaphe research submarine

Batista (y Zaldivar), Fulgencio (1901–73) Cuban President 1940–4 and dictator 1952–9

Baton Rouge capital of Louisiana; pronounced *batt'-un roojzhe*

battalion

Battelle Memorial Institute, Columbus, Ohio

Battenberg cake (cap.)

Baudelaire, Charles (Pierre) (1821–67) French poet

Baudouin, (Albert Charles Léopold Axel Marie Gustave) (1930–93) King of the Belgians 1951–93

Bauhaus German school of arts and architecture, founded by Walter Gropius (1883–1969)

Baum, L. (for **Lyman**) **Frank** (1856–1919) American writer of children's stories; author of *The Wizard of Oz*

Bausch & Lomb US eye-care company

Bayern German for Bavaria

Bayonne name of cities in France and New Jersey

Bayreuth, Bavaria

BC (before Christ) always goes after the year (e.g., 42 BC); usually set in small caps; see also AD.

BCE before the Common Era

be (with a participle) Almost always a wordy way of getting your point across, as here: 'He will be joining the board of directors in March.' Quicker to say, 'He will join the board of directors in March.'

Beachy Head, East Sussex

Beaconsfield, Buckinghamshire; the model village at Beaconsfield is **Bekonscot**

Beardsley, Aubrey (1872–98) British artist

béarnaise sauce

Bearwardcote, Derbyshire pronounced *bear´-a-kot*

Beauchamp Place, London pronounced *bee-chum*

Beaufort scale measures wind velocity on a scale of 0 to 12, with 0 representing dead calm and 12 representing a hurricane.

Beaufort, South Carolina pronounced *bew-furt*

Beaujolais French region and wine

Beaulieu, Hampshire pronounced *bew´-lee*

Beaumarchais, Pierre Augustin Caron de (1732–99) French playwright whose works inspired the operas *The Barber* of *Seville* and *The Marriage of Figaro*

beau monde (Fr.) the fashionable world; pl. *beaux mondes*

Beauregarde, Pierre (Gustave Toutant de) (1818–93) Confederate general in the American Civil War

Beauvoir, Simone (Lucie Ernestine Maria Bertrand) de (1908–86) French author

beaux arts (Fr.) the fine arts

Beaverbrook, Max (William Maxwell Aitken), Lord (1879–1964) Canadian-born British press baron

béchamel sauce

Becher's Brook celebrated jump on the Grand National racecourse

Bechuanaland former name of Botswana

Beckenbauer, Franz (1945–) German footballer; winner of World Cup as both player and manager

Becket, St Thomas (à) (1118–70) Archbishop of Canterbury, murdered by followers of Henry II

Beckett, Samuel (1906–89) Irish poet, playwright and novelist

becquerel unit of radioactivity, named after Antoine Henri Becquerel (1852–1908), French physicist

Bede (c. 673–735) British clerical scholar, known as the Venerable Bede

Bedloe's Island former name of Liberty Island, New York; site of the Statue of Liberty

bedouin, for nomadic Arab desert-dwellers, is both singular and plural. An alternative is *Bedu.*

Beecher, Henry Ward (1813–87) American preacher

Beelzebub Satan

Beene, Geoffrey (1927–2004) American fashion designer

Beerbohm, Sir (Henry) Max(imilian) (1872–1956) British writer and critic

Beethoven, Ludwig van (1770–1827) German composer

before, prior to There is no difference between these two except length and a certain inescapable affectedness on the part of *prior to*. To paraphrase Theodore Bernstein, if you would use 'posterior to' instead of 'after', then by all means use 'prior to' instead of 'before'.

Beggar's Opera, The, not *Beggars'* by John Gay (1728)

Begin, Menachem (1913–92) Polish-born Israeli Prime Minister 1977–83; awarded Nobel Peace Prize 1978

behalf A useful distinction exists between *on behalf of* and *in behalf of*. The first means acting as a representative, as when a lawyer enters a plea on behalf of a client, and often denotes a formal relationship. *In behalf of* indicates a closer or more sympathetic role and means acting as a friend or defender. 'I spoke on your behalf' means that I represented you when you were absent. 'I spoke in your behalf' means that I supported you or defended you.

Behn, Aphra (1640–89) English writer

behove (US **behoove**) An archaic word, but still sometimes a useful one. Two points need to be made:

1. The word means being necessary or contingent, but is sometimes wrongly used for 'becomes', particularly with the adverb *ill*, as in 'It ill behoves any man responsible for policy to think how best to make political propaganda' (cited by Gowers).

2. It should be used only impersonally and with the subject *it*. 'The circumstances behove us to take action' is wrong. Make it 'It behoves us in the circumstances to take action.'

Beiderbecke, Bix (1903–31) born Leon Bismarck Beiderbecke; jazz musician

Beijing (Pinyin)/**Peking**

Bekaa Valley, Lebanon

Belarussian (or **Belarusian**) for someone or something from Belarus. The language is also Belarussian.

beleaguered, not -*ured*

Belém Brazilian city, formerly Pará

Belisha beacon flashing amber light at pedestrian crossings

Belize Central American republic, formerly British Honduras

belladonna deadly nightshade

Belleek type of porcelain, named for a town in Northern Ireland

belle époque (no caps) the period just before the First World War

Belleisle, County Fermanagh, Northern Ireland, and New Brunswick, Canada; **Belle-Île**, Brittany, France; **Belle Isle**, Florida; **Strait of Belle Isle**, Newfoundland, Canada

Bellerophon in Greek mythology, a warrior who killed the Chimera and was crippled trying to fly Pegasus over Mount Olympus

belles-lettres writing that has a literary or aesthetic, as opposed to purely informational, value. The word is usually treated as a plural, but may be used as a singular. For reasons unconnected to logic, the hyphen is lost and the word itself contracted in the related terms *belletrist*, *belletrism* and *belletristic*.

bellicose warlike

bellwether, not -*weather* *Wether* is an Old English word for a castrated sheep. A *bellwether* is a sheep that has a bell hung from its neck, by which means it leads the herd from one pasture to another. In general use, it signifies something that leads or shows the way. A *bellwether* *stock* is one that is customarily at the head of the pack. It does not mean a harbinger or foreteller of events.

Belsen full name Bergen-Belsen; concentration camp in Lower Saxony, Germany, during the Second World War

beluga is a type of sturgeon, and not a manufacturer or producer of caviar, as is sometimes thought, so the word should not be capitalized.

Belvoir Castle, **Vale of Belvoir**, Leicestershire both pronounced *beaver*

Ben Ali, Zine El Abidine (1936–), President of Tunisia 1987–

Bendl, Karel (1838–97) Czech composer

Benedick character in *Much Ado About Nothing* by William Shakespeare (1598–9)

beneficence

Benelux short for Belgium, the Netherlands and Luxembourg

Beneš, Eduard (1884–1948) Czechoslovakian Prime Minister 1921–2 and President 1935–8, 1939–45 (in exile) and 1945–8

Benét, Stephen Vincent (1898–1943) American writer, brother of **William Rose Benét** (1886–1950), also a writer

Bene't Street, Cambridge

Benetton Italian clothing company

Benghazi Libyan city

Ben-Gurion, David (1886–1973) born David Grün; Israeli Prime Minister 1948–53, 1955–63

benignancy/benignity Both mean kindliness and, in medicine, the opposite of malignancy.

Bening, Annette (1958–) American actress

benison a blessing

Bennet family in Jane Austen's *Pride and Prejudice* (1813)

Bentsen, Lloyd (1921–2006) American Democratic politician, Secretary of the Treasury 1993–4; ran for Vice-President in 1988

benvenuto (It.) welcome

benzene, **benzine** Both are liquid hydrocarbons commonly used as solvents. *Benzene* is primarily associated with the production of plastics, while *benzine* is most often encountered as a solvent used in dry-cleaning establishments. They are quite different substances and not merely alternative spellings of a single compound.

Beograd Serbian for Belgrade

Beowulf, not -*wolf* Anglo-Saxon epic

Berchtesgaden, not -*garden* Bavarian tourist centre where Hitler had a country retreat

bereft To be *bereft* of something is not to lack it but to be dispossessed of it, to lose it. A spinster is not bereft of a husband, but a widow is. (The word is the past participle of *bereave*.)

Bérégovoy, Pierre (1925–93) Prime Minister of France 1992–3

Berenson, Bernard (or **Bernhard**) (1865–1959) Lithuanian-born American art critic

Beretta Italian manufacturer of handguns

Bergdorf Goodman New York department store

Bergman, Ingrid (1915–82) Swedish film actress; wife of **Ingmar Bergman** (1918–2007), Swedish film director

berk a boorish or foolish person; rhyming slang derived from Berkshire or Berkeley Hunt

Berkeleian of or from the philosophy of George Berkeley (1685–1753)

Berkeley, California, and **Berkeley Square**, London   The latter is pronounced *barkly*.

Berkeley, Busby (1895–1976) Hollywood choreographer

Berkeley, Sir Lennox (1903–89) British composer

berkelium chemical element

Berklee Performance Center, Boston, Massachusetts

Berlin, Irving (1888–1989) born Israel Baline; Russian-born American composer

Berlin, Sir Isaiah (1909–97)   Latvian-born British philosopher

Bermudan, not *-ian*

Bern is the normal English spelling for the capital of Switzerland, though **Berne** is also accepted.

Bernabéu Stadium, Madrid   formally Santiago Bernabéu Stadium, home of Real Madrid football team

Bernanke, Ben (1953–) American economist, chairman of the US Federal Reserve Board 2006–

Bernhardt, Sarah (1844–1923)   born Henriette Rosine Bernard, French actress, called 'the Divine Sarah'

Bernini, (Giovanni) Lorenzo (1598–1680) Italian sculptor and architect

Bertelsmann German media group

Bertolucci, Bernardo (1940–) Italian film director

beryllium chemical element

Besant, Sir Walter (1836–1901) British novelist and critic; brother-in-law of **Annie Besant**, birth control advocate

beseech

besides means *also* or *in addition to*, not *alternatively*. Partridge cites this incorrect use: '. . . the wound must have been made by something besides the handle of the gear-lever.' Make it 'other than'.

besiege, not *-ei-*

Bessarabia former name of Moldova

Bessemer process steelmaking method named after Sir Henry Bessemer (1813–98), British metallurgist

bestseller, **bestsellerdom** (one word), but **best-selling** (hyphen)

Betelgeuse star in Orion constellation

bête noire (Fr.) something much disliked; pl. *bêtes noires*

Betjeman, Sir John (1906–84) British poet; Poet Laureate 1972–84

Bettelheim, Bruno (1903–90) Austrian-born American child psychologist

bettor one who bets

between, **among** A few authorities continue to insist that *between* applies to two things only and *among* to more than two, so that we should speak of dividing some money between the two of us but among the four of us. That is useful advice as far as it goes, but it doesn't always go very far. It would be absurd, for instance, to say that Chicago is among New York, Los Angeles and Houston. More logically, *between* should be applied to reciprocal arrangements (a treaty between the US, the UK and Canada) and *among* to collective arrangements (trade talks among the members of the European Union).

between you and I is always wrong. Make it 'between you and me'. The object of a preposition should always be in the accusative. More simply, we don't say 'between you and I' for the same reason that we don't say 'give that book to I'.

Betws-y-coed, Gwynedd proounced *bet´ toos-a-koyd*

Bevan, Aneurin (1897–1960), but **Ernest Bevin** (1881–1951) British politicians

Beveridge, William Henry, Lord (1879–1963) British economist, best known as the author of the Beveridge Report (formally *A Report on Social Insurance and Allied Services*, 1942) which led to the setting-up of a comprehensive social security system in Britain

Beverley, Humberside, but **Beverly Hills**, California

Bevin, Ernest See BEVAN, ANEURIN, above.

Bexleyheath, Kent

Bhagavadgita sacred Hindu text, part of the Sanksrit epic *Mahabharata*

Bhumibol (Adulyadej) (1927–) King of Thailand 1946–

Bhutan Asian kingdom; capital Thimphu. Natives are Bhutanese (sing. and pl.).

biannual, biennial *Biannual* means twice a year; *biennial* means every two years.

Biarritz French resort

biased

biathlon sport in which competitors ski across country and shoot set targets

Bible (cap.), but **biblical** (no cap.)

biceps (sing. and pl.)

Big Ben, strictly speaking, is not the famous clock on the Houses of Parliament in London, but just the great hour bell, so a passing visitor will hear Big Ben but never see it. The formal name of the clock, for what it is worth, is the clock on St Stephen's Tower on the Palace of Westminster.

Bildungsroman (Ger.) novel dealing with a character's early life and psychological development

Biletnikoff Award American sporting award

bilharzia parasitic disease of the tropics; also known as **schistosomiasis**

billabong Australian backwater; literally 'dead stream'

Billericay, Essex pronounced *bill-a-rik´-ee*

billet-doux (Fr.) love letter; pl. *billets-doux*

Billingsgate historic London fish market; when lower-cased it denotes foul or abusive speech of the type once heard there

bimonthly, **biweekly** and similar designations are almost always ambiguous. It is far better to say 'every two months', 'twice a month', etc., as appropriate.

biped two-legged animal

Birds Eye Walls frozen food company named after Clarence Birdseye (1886–1956), American who invented methods of quick-freezing food

biretta hat worn by Catholic priests

biriani/biryani Indian rice dish

Bishkek capital of Kyrgyzstan

Bishops Cannings, Wiltshire; **Bishops Sutton**, Hampshire; **Bishop's Castle**, Shropshire; **Bishop's Caundle**, Dorset; **Bishop's Cleeve**, Gloucestershire; **Bishop's Clyst**, Devon; **Bishop's Frome**, Hereford and Worcester; **Bishop's Hull**, Somerset; **Bishop's Itchington**, Leicestershire; **Bishop's Lydeard**, Somerset; **Bishop's Nympton**, Devon; **Bishop's Offley**, Staffordshire; **Bishop's Stortford**, Hertfordshire; **Bishop's Tachbrook**, Warwickshire; **Bishop's Tawton**, Devon

Bishopsgate, London

Bishop Sutton, Somerset

Bismarck, Prince Otto (Eduard Leopold) von (1815–98) German Chancellor 1871–90

bivouac, bivouacked, bivouacking

BlackBerry communications device

Blackfeet Native American tribe or a member thereof; never *Blackfoot*

Blackfriars (no apos.), London, but **Black Friars** for members of the Dominican order

Blackley, Greater Manchester pronounced *blake´-lee*

Blackmoor, Hampshire, but **Blackmore**, Essex

Blackmore, R. D. (for **Richard Doddridge**) (1825–1900) English novelist

Black Rod formally Gentleman Usher of the Black Rod; the officer of the House of Lords who summons Members of the Commons to hear the Queen's speech at the opening of Parliament and to hear her assent to bills, etc.

Black Watch nickname of the Scottish Royal Highland Regiment

Blagojevich, Rod (1956–) US politician, governor of Illinois 2003–

blameable (US **blamable**)

blatant, flagrant The words are not quite synonymous. Something that is *blatant* is glaringly obvious and contrived ('a blatant lie') or wilfully obnoxious ('blatant commercialization') or both. Something that is *flagrant* is shocking and reprehensible ('a flagrant miscarriage of justice'). If I tell you that I regularly travel to the moon, that is a *blatant* lie, not a *flagrant* one. If you set fire to my house, that is a *flagrant* act, not a *blatant* one.

Blatter, Sepp (1936–) Swiss sports administrator; president of FIFA 1998–

blazon means to display or proclaim in an ostentatious manner. Trails are blazed, not blazoned.

Bleecker Street, New York City

Blériot, Louis (1872–1936) French aviator

blitzkrieg (Ger.) 'lightning war', an overwhelming attack

Blixen, Karen, Baroness (1885–1962) Danish writer, who used the pseudonym Isak Dinesen

Bloemfontein, South Africa capital of Orange Free State

blog, **blogger** A *blog* is an online journal; a *blogger* is a writer of a blog.

Bloomberg, Michael (1942–) American businessman and politician, mayor of New York City 2002–

blueprint, as a metaphor for a design or plan, is much overworked. At least remember that a *blueprint* is a completed plan, not a preliminary one.

Blumberg, Baruch S. (for **Samuel**) (1926–) American scientist, joint winner of 1976 Nobel Prize for Physiology or Medicine

Blu-Tack

bmi, **bmibaby** (not cap.) airlines operated by British Midland Airways

BMW short for Bayerische Motoren Werke

B'nai B'rith Jewish organization

Boadicea (d. AD 62) traditional spelling of the queen of the Iceni, a British Celtic tribe, but now more often spelled **Boudicca**

Boboli Gardens, Florence

Boccaccio, Giovanni (1313–75) Italian writer

bocce (It.) bowling game

Bodensee German name for Lake Constance

Bodhisattva in Buddhism, an enlightened one

Bodleian Library, Oxford University pronounced *bodd-lee-un*

Boeotia region of ancient Greece, centred on Thebes

Boethius, Anicius Manlius Severinus (c. 480–c. 524) Roman statesman and philosopher

Boettcher Concert Hall, Denver

boffo hugely successful

Bofors gun (cap.) named for a town in Sweden

Bogdanovich, Peter (1939–) American film director

bogey, bogie, bogy *Bogey* (pl. *bogeys*) is the usual spelling for contexts involving golf strokes, malevolent spirits and nasal deposits. *Bogie* is used to describe parts of wheels or tracks on mechanical conveyances. *Bogy* is an alternative spelling for either of the first two words.

Bogotá capital of Colombia

Bohème, La opera by Giacomo Puccini (1896)

Bohr, Niels (1885–1962) Danish physicist, won Nobel Prize for Physics 1922

Bois de Boulogne Paris park

bok choi US spelling of **pak choi**, a Chinese vegetable

Bokhara, a river in Australia, but **Bukhara**, a town in Uzbekistan

Boleyn, Anne (c. 1507–36) second wife of Henry VIII

Bolingbroke, Henry St John, Viscount (1678–1751) English statesman

bolívar monetary unit of Venezuela, named for Simón Bolívar (1783–1830), Venezuelan-born revolutionary

Bolivia South American republic; the seat of government is La Paz, but the official capital is Sucre

Böll, Heinrich (1917–85) German writer, awarded the Nobel Prize for Literature 1972

bollito misto, pl. *bolliti misti* an Italian meat stew

bollix US spelling of **bollocks**

Bombay now known as Mumbai

bon appétit (Fr.) eat well, enjoy your food

Bonhams (no apos.) London auction house

bonhomie (Fr.) good nature

Bonnard, Pierre (1867–1947) French painter

bonne nuit (Fr.), good night, but *bonsoir* for good evening

Bonington, Sir Chris (1934–), not *Bonn-* English mountaineer

Bonington, Richard Parkes (1802–28) English painter

bonsai, banzai *Bonsai* is the Japanese art of growing dwarf shrubs; *banzai* is a Japanese battle cry, or a greeting that means 'May you live 10,000 years.'

bonsoir (Fr.), good evening, but *bonne nuit* for good night

bon vivant, bon viveur The first is a person who enjoys good food, the second a person who lives well.

Book-of-the-Month Club

Boonyaratglin, General Sonthi (1946–) leader of military coup in Thailand in 2006; on second reference he is General Sonthi

Boorstin, Daniel (1914–2004) American historian

Bophuthatswana former South African black homeland, capital Mmabatho; reintegrated into South Africa in 1994

bordellos

Borders Books and Music (no apos.)

bored with, not *bored of*

Borghese noble Italian family

Borgia, Rodrigo (1431–1503) Pope Alexander VI, father of **Cesare Borgia** (1476–1507) and **Lucrezia Borgia** (1480–1519)

Borglum, Gutzon (1871–1941) American sculptor, designer of the presidential memorial at Mount Rushmore; full name John Gutzon de la Mothe Borglum

Bormann, Martin (1900–45) Nazi politician

born, borne Both are past participles of the verb *bear*, but by convention they are used in slightly different ways. *Born* is limited to the idea of birth ('He was born in December'). *Borne* is used for the sense of supporting or tolerating ('She has borne the burden with dignity'), but is also used to refer to giving birth in active constructions ('She has borne three children') and in passive constructions followed by 'by' ('The three children borne by her . . .')

Borodin, Alexander (Porfiryevich) (1833–87)   Russian composer

Bosch, Hieronymus (c. 1450–1516)   Dutch painter; born Hieronymus van Aken

borscht

Börse, **Borsa**, **Bourse**   respectively German, Italian and French for stock exchange

bo's'n, bosun, bo'sun all abbrs of boatswain, a ship's officer; not to be confused with **boson**, a type of subatomic particle

Bosnia and Herzegovina/Bosnia-Herzegovina Serbian republic, formerly part of Yugoslavia; capital Sarajevo

Bosporus, not *Bosph-*, for the strait separating Europe and Asia

BOSS   Bureau for (not *of*) State Security; former South African intelligence department

both   Three small problems to note:

1. *Both* should not be used to describe more than two things. Partridge cites a passage in which a woman is said to have 'a shrewd common sense . . . both in speech, deed and dress'. Delete *both*.

2. Sometimes it appears superfluously: '. . . and they both went to the same school, Charterhouse' (*Observer*). Either delete *both* or make it '. . . they both went to Charterhouse'.

3. Sometimes it is misused for *each*. To say that there is a supermarket on both sides of the street suggests that it is somehow straddling the roadway. Say either that

there is a supermarket on each side of the street or that there are supermarkets on both sides. See also EACH.

both . . . and 'He was both deaf to argument and entreaty' (cited by Gowers) is incorrect. The rule involved here is that of correlative conjunctions, which states that in a sentence of this type *both* and *and* should link grammatically similar entities. If *both* is followed immediately by a verb, *and* should also be followed immediately by a verb. If *both* immediately precedes a noun, then so should *and*. In the example above, however, *both* is followed by an adjective (*deaf*) and *and* by a noun (*entreaty*). The sentence needs to be recast, either as 'He was deaf to both argument [noun] and entreaty [noun]' or as 'He was deaf both to argument [preposition and noun] and to entreaty [preposition and noun].' The rule holds true equally for other such pairs: 'not only . . . but also', 'either . . . or' and 'neither . . . nor'.

Botswana southern African republic, formerly known as Bechuanaland; capital Gaborone; the people are Batswana (sing. and pl.)

Botticelli, Sandro (c. 1445–1510) Italian painter; born Alessandro di Mariano di Vanni Filipepi

Boucicault, Dion (1822–90) Irish playwright; pronounced *boo´-see-ko*

Boudicca (d. AD 62) is now the more common spelling for the Celtic queen traditionally known as Boadicea. Queen of the Iceni, she led an unsuccessful revolt against the Romans.

bougainvillea
bouillabaisse, not -*illi*-
bouillon, not -*ion* broth

bourgeois, bourgeoisie

Bourgogne the French name for Burgundy

Bourn, Cambridgeshire, but **Bourne**, Lincolnshire

Bournville, greater Birmingham   home of Bournville chocolate

boustrophedon writing in which alternate lines go from right to left and left to right

boutonnière flower for buttonhole

Boutros-Ghali, Boutros (1922–) Egyptian politician and civil servant; Secretary-General of the United Nations 1992–6

Bouygues Group French construction company

bouzouki Greek stringed musical instrument

Bow Bells (caps) were located in the Church of St Mary-le-Bow, Cheapside, London. Those born within their sound are said to be Cockneys.

Bowes Lyon (no hyphen) family name of the late Queen Elizabeth the Queen Mother

boyfriend, girlfriend (one word)

boysenberry

Brady, Mathew (1823–96) American Civil War photographer; note irregular spelling of first name

braggadocio hollow boasting, after the character Braggadochio in Spenser's *Faerie Queene*

Brahman/Brahmin The first is a member of a Hindu caste; the second is used to describe long-established socially exclusive people ('Boston Brahmins'). The breed of cattle is spelled Brahman.

Brahmaputra Asian river

Brahms, Johannes (1833–97) German composer

Braille, Louis (1809–52) French inventor of the embossed reading system for the blind

Bramante, Donato di Pasuccio d'Antonio (1444–1514) Italian architect and artist

Brancusi, Constantin (1876–1957) Romanian sculptor

Brandeis, Louis D. (for **Dembitz**) (1856–1941) American jurist; Brandeis University is named for him

Brandywine creek in Pennsylvania and Delaware, site of a battle in the Revolutionary War (1777)

Braque, Georges (1882–1963) French Cubist painter

Brasenose College, Oxford University

Brasília capital of Brazil

Braun, Wernher von (1912–77) German-born American space scientist

bravado should not be confused with *bravery*. It is a swaggering or boastful display of boldness, often adopted to disguise an underlying timidity. It is, in short, a false bravery and there is nothing courageous about it.

bravura skill and daring (in performance)

BRD abbr. of Bundesrepublik Deutschland (Federal Republic of Germany)

breach, **breech** Frequently confused. *Breach* describes an infraction or a gap. It should always suggest *break*, a word to which it is related. *Breech* applies to the rear or lower portion of things. The main expressions are *breach of faith* (or *promise*), *breech delivery*, *breeches buoy*, *breechcloth* and *breech-loading gun*.

Breakspear, Nicolas (c. 1100–59) Pope Adrian IV

Brearley, Mike (1942–) English cricketer

Breathalyser a trademarked device that analyses exhaled breath to determine the amount of alcohol in the body

Brest-Litovsk, Treaty of (1918) treaty that ended Russian involvement in the First World War

Bretagne French for Brittany

Bretton Woods mountain resort in New Hampshire, site of 1944 conference that led to the establishment of the International Monetary Fund and World Bank

Breuer, Marcel (1902–81) Hungarian-born American architect and designer

Breugel/Breughel Use **Brueghel**.

Brezhnev, Leonid (Ilyich) (1906–82) leader of the Soviet Union 1977–82

bric-a-brac

Bridge of San Luis Rey, The novel by Thornton Wilder (1927)

Bridgwater, Somerset, but **Bridgewater**, Nova Scotia, the **Earl of Bridgewater** and the **Bridgewater Treatises**

brie (not cap.) cheese

Brillat-Savarin, Anthelme (1755–1826) French gastronome

Bristol-Myers Squibb US pharmaceuticals company

Britannia, **Britannic**, not -*tt*-. The song is 'Rule, Britannia', with a comma. See also BRITTANY.

British aristocracy, or **peerage**, comprises, in descending order, the ranks duke, marquess, earl/countess, viscount and baron/baroness. Male peers below the rank of duke may be referred to as Lord (i.e., the Earl of Avon may be called Lord Avon), and peeresses below the rank of duchess may be referred to as Lady. However, not every lord is a peer. The eldest son of a duke, marquess or earl, for instance, may use one of his father's minor titles as a courtesy title and call himself the Marquess of X or Earl of Y, but he is not a peer and would not be eligible to sit in the House of Lords. Younger sons of dukes and marquesses may put Lord in front of their names: Lord John X. Their wives are then called Lady John X. Daughters of dukes, marquesses and earls will similarly put Lady before their names: Lady Mary Y. Wives of peers, and of knights and baronets, are referred to as Lady X or Lady Y; that is, their first names are not used. Sir John Bloggs's wife is simply Lady Bloggs, not Lady Mary Bloggs. Life peers are people of distinction who are elevated to the peerage but whose titles die with them.

British Guiana former name of the South American country now known as Guyana

British Honduras former name of Belize

British Indian Ocean Territory group of 2,300 scattered islands in the Indian Ocean run as a British colony; principal island Diego Garcia

Brittain, Vera (1893–1970) British feminist and writer, mother of politician Shirley Williams (1930–)

Brittan, Sir Leon (1939–) British politician

Brittany/Bretagne (Fr.) region of France; see also Britannia, Britannic.

Britten, (Edward) Benjamin, later Lord Britten of Aldeburgh (1913–76) English composer

Broackes, Sir Nigel (1934–99) British businessman

Brobdingnag, not -*dig*- place inhabited by giants in *Gulliver's Travels*

broccoli

Bronfman, Edgar M. (for **Miles**) (1929–) Canadian businessman

Brontë, Anne (1820–49), **(Patrick) Branwell** (1817–48), **Charlotte** (1816–55) and **Emily (Jane)** (1818–48) English literary family. Among their best-known works are Emily's *Wuthering Heights*, Charlotte's *Jane Eyre*, and Anne's *The Tenant of Wildfell Hall*.

brontosaurus, not *bronta*- type of dinosaur

Brooke, Rupert (Chawner) (1887–1915) English poet

Brookings Institution, not *Institute*, Washington, DC named after Robert Somers Brookings (1850–1932), American philanthropist

brouhaha an uproar

Brown v. Board of Education 1954 landmark civil rights case in which the US Supreme Court ruled that segregated schools were illegal; see also *Plessy v. Ferguson*

brucellosis disease of cattle

Brueghel, Pieter, the Elder (c. 1520–69), not *-eu-* Flemish painter and father of two others: **Pieter Brueghel the Younger** (1564–1638) and **Jan Brueghel** (1568–1625)

Bruges (Fr.)/**Brugge** (Flemish)   historic city in northern Belgium

Brummell, (George Bryan) Beau (1778–1840) celebrated English dandy

Brundtland, Gro Harlem (1939–)   Norwegian Prime Minister 1981, 1986–9, 1990–6

Bruneau-Jarbidge site of historic supervolcano, Idaho

Brunei independent oil-rich state on Borneo; capital Bandar Seri Begawan. A native is a Bruneian.

Brunel, Isambard Kingdom (1806–59) British engineer; son of **Sir Marc Isambard Brunel** (1769–1849), also an engineer

Brunelleschi, Filippo (c. 1377–1446) Renaissance architect and sculptor

Brunhild In Scandinavian sagas, she is a Valkyrie, or priestess, in a deep sleep. In Wagner's *Ring* cycle, the name is spelled **Brünnhilde**.

Brussels   capital of Belgium. In French, **Bruxelles**; in Flemish, **Brussel**

brussels sprouts (no cap., no apos.)

Brzezinski, Zbigniew K. (1928–) Polish-born American academic and statesman

BSE bovine spongiform encephalopathy, more commonly known as mad cow disease

BST bovine somatotropin, genetically engineered hormone used to increase milk production in cows

BTU British thermal unit, the amount of heat required to raise the temperature of one pound of water by one degree Fahrenheit

Buccleuch ancient Scottish dukedom; pronounced *buck-loo'*

Bucharest capital of Romania; in Romanian, **Bucureşti**

Buddenbrooks novel by Thomas Mann (1901)

Buddha, Buddhist, Buddhism

buddleia genus of shrub attractive to butterflies

budgerigar parakeet

buenos dias (for good day or hello in Spanish), but *buenas* (not *-os*) *noches* (good night) and *buenas tardes* (good afternoon)

buffalo The plural can be either **buffalo** or **buffaloes**.

Bugatti sports car

Bujumbura capital of Burundi

Bulfinch's Mythology subtitle of *The Age of Fable* by Thomas Bulfinch (1796–1867)

bull's-eye in the sense of a target

Bulwer-Lytton, Edward (1803–73) also Lord Lytton, English writer and politician, celebrated for penning the classically bad opening line 'It was a dark and stormy night' in his novel *Paul Clifford* (1830). The annual Bulwer-Lytton Fiction Contest, for a mock bad opening line, is named in his honour.

bumf assorted papers

Bumppo, Natty note *-pp-*; hero of James Fenimore Cooper stories

Bunche, Ralph (Johnson) (1904–71) American statesman; one of the founders of the United Nations; awarded Nobel Peace Prize 1950

Bundesbank central bank of Germany

Bundesrat/Bundestag The *Bundesrat* (Federal Council) is the upper house of the German parliament; the *Bundestag* (Federal Assembly) is the lower house.

Bundesrepublik Deutschland abbr. BRD, Federal Republic of Germany

Bundeswehr German armed forces

Bunsen burner (one cap.)

buoy is pronounced *boy*, not *boo-ee*. Think of *buoyant*.

BUPA British United Provident Association; private medical insurance company

Burdett-Coutts, Angela Georgina, Baroness (1814–1906) British philanthropist

burgeon does not mean merely to expand or thrive. It means to bud or sprout, to come into being. For something to burgeon, it must be new. Thus it would be correct to talk about the burgeoning talent of a precocious youth, but to write of 'the burgeoning population of Cairo' is wrong. Cairo's population has been growing for centuries.

bürgermeister (Ger.) mayor

Burges, William (1827–81) English architect and designer

Burgess, Anthony (1917–93) British writer

Burgess, (Frank) Gelett (1866–1951) American humorist

Burghley (or **Burleigh**), **William Cecil, Lord** (1520–98) English statesman, confidant of Elizabeth I

burglar, not *-ler*

Burgundy region of eastern France. In French, **Bourgogne**. The wine is **burgundy** (lower case).

Burke and Hare bodysnatchers and murderers in Edinburgh in the early 19th century; they were both named William.

Burke's Peerage formally *A Genealogical and Heraldic History of the Peerage, Baronetage and Knightage of the United Kingdom*

Burkina Faso landlocked west African state, formerly Upper Volta; capital Ouagadougou. Natives are Burkinabe (sing. and pl.).

Burma, **Myanmar** The first is the former official name of the south-east Asian nation and the one now preferred by many publications and other informed users outside Burma. *Myanmar* was for a time used by many publications, but now its use is mostly confined to the country's government and institutions under its influence. Some authorities write *Burma/Myanmar*. The United Nations uses just *Myanmar.*

Burne-Jones, Sir Edward Coley (1833–98) British painter and designer

Burnet, Sir Alastair (1929–) British journalist and broadcaster

burnous (US also **burnoose**) a hooded Arab cloak

Burnt-Out Case, A novel by Graham Greene (1960)

burnt sienna, not *siena*

burqa (also spelled **burkha**, **burka**, **burqua**) type of enveloping dress worn by Muslim women when in public to preserve their modesty

Burrell Collection, Glasgow

Burton upon Trent, Staffordshire (no hyphens)

Burtts Corner, New Brunswick, Canada

Burundi African republic, capital Bujumbura

Buryatiya Russian republic

Bury St Edmunds, Suffolk (no apos.)

bus, **buses**, **bused**, **busing** are words relating to a form of transportation and should not be confused with **buss**, **busses**, etc., meaning kiss(es).

Bushey, Hertfordshire, but **Bushy Park**, London

Bustamante, Sir (William) Alexander (1884–1977) Jamaican politician; Prime Minister 1962–7

but used negatively after a pronoun presents a problem that has confounded careful users for generations. Do you say, 'Everyone but him had arrived' or 'Everyone but he had arrived'? The authorities themselves are divided.

Some regard *but* as a preposition and put the pronoun in the accusative – i.e., *me, her, him* or *them*. So just as we say, 'Give it to her' or 'between you and me', we should say, 'Everyone but him had arrived.'

Others argue that *but* is a conjunction and that the pronoun should be nominative (*I, she, he* or *they*), as if the sentence were saying, 'Everyone had arrived, but he had not.'

The answer perhaps is to regard *but* sometimes as a conjunction and sometimes as a preposition. Two rough rules should help.

1. If the pronoun appears at the end of the sentence, you can always use the accusative and be on firm ground. Thus, 'Nobody knew but her'; 'Everyone had eaten but him.'

2. When the pronoun appears earlier in the sentence, it is almost always better to put it in the nominative, as in 'No one but he had seen it.' The one exception is when the pronoun is influenced by a preceding preposition,

but such constructions are relatively rare and often clumsy. Two examples might be 'Between no one but them was there any bitterness' and 'To everyone but him life was a mystery.' (See also THAN (3).)

Buthelezi, Mangosuthu (1928–) South African politician, founder of Inkatha Freedom Party

by-election, not *bye-*

by-law, not *bye-*

byte in computing, a unit of information storage; a set of eight bits

c., *circa* (Lat.) 'about' or 'approximately'; it is customary to put a full stop after it

CABE   Commission for Architecture and the Built Environment (UK)

cacao   the tree from whose seed cocoa and chocolate are made

Cadbury Schweppes (no hyphen)

caddie, caddy   A *caddie* is a golfer's assistant; a *caddy* is a container or small casket. The affectionate term for a Cadillac is *Caddy*.

Cadmean victory   one that leaves the victor ruined. See also PYRRHIC VICTORY.

caduceus   staff with two winged serpents wrapped around it

Cadw   Welsh historic monuments organization; pronounced *cad-doo*

Caedmon (*fl.* 7th c.)   English poet

Caernafon/Caernarvon, Gwynedd   See also CARNARVON.

Caerphilly cheese   in Welsh, *Caerffili*

Caesarean, not *-ian*, remains the preferred spelling for the form of childbirth properly known as a *Caesarean section*, as well as for references to Roman emperors named Caesar.

caesar salad (not cap.)

Cage, Nicolas (1964–)   American actor; not *Nicholas*. His

— 67 —

birth name was Nicholas Coppola.

cagey (pref.), **cagy** (alt.)

Caius, the Cambridge college, is formally Gonville and Caius College. Caius is pronounced *keys*.

Cajun (cap.) native of traditionally French-speaking region of Louisiana; derived from *Acadian*

calamine lotion

Calaveras County, California scene of the Mark Twain story 'The Celebrated Jumping Frog of Calaveras County'

Calcutta, the Indian city, is now officially **Kolkata**; until the new name is fully established, the use of both on first reference is advisable.

Calderón, Felipe (1962–) President of Mexico 2006–

Calderón de la Barca (y Henao), Pedro (1600–81) Spanish playwright

calico, pl. **calicoes**

Callaghan, (Leonard) James, Lord (1912–2005) British Prime Minister 1976–9

Callicrates (*fl.* 5th c. BC) Greek architect, co-designer (with Ictinus) of the Parthenon

calligraphy is an art. The study of handwriting and written symbols is graphology.

Callimachus (*fl.* 3rd c. BC) Greek scholar

calliope fairground steam-organ, named after Calliope, the Greek muse of epic poetry

calliper (US **caliper**) instrument for measuring the thickness or diameter of objects

callous, callus The first is an adjective meaning insensitive, the second is a noun that refers to a thickening of the skin.

Calmann-Lévy French publisher

Caltech (one word) is the common name for the California Institute of Technology in Pasadena.

Calypso nymph who delayed Odysseus for seven years on his way home from Troy

camaraderie

Cambodia has been variously known in recent decades as the Khmer Republic, Democratic Kampuchea and the People's Republic of Kampuchea, but in 1989 it resumed its historical name of Cambodia.

Cambridge University colleges: Christ's, Churchill, Clare, Clare Hall, Corpus Christi, Darwin, Downing, Emmanuel, Fitzwilliam, Girton, Gonville and Caius, Homerton, Hughes Hall, Jesus, King's, Lucy Cavendish, Magdalene, New Hall, Newnham, Pembroke, Peterhouse, Queens', Robinson, St Catharine's, St Edmund's, St John's, Selwyn, Sidney Sussex, Trinity, Trinity Hall, Wolfson

Cambs abbr. of Cambridgeshire

camellia, not *camelia* flower

Camembert (cap.) soft French cheese and the village in Normandy for which it is named

Cameroon/Cameroun The first is the English spelling, the second is the French (and local) spelling for the west African republic formerly called The Cameroons. Capital Yaoundé

Camisards French Calvinists disaffected by the revocation of the Edict of Nantes (1703)

camisole

Camorra Mafia-type secret society of Naples

Campagna di Roma countryside around Rome

Campaign to Protect Rural England, not *to Preserve, for the Preservation of*, etc.

campanile bell tower

Campbell-Bannerman, Sir Henry (1836–1908) British Prime Minister 1905–8

Camp Nou   FC Barcelona football stadium commonly referred to as the Nou Camp

can, may   *Can* applies to what is possible and *may* to what is permissible. You *can* drive your car the wrong way down a one-way street, but you *may* not. Despite the simplicity of the rule, errors are common, even among experts. Here is William Safire writing in the *New York Times* on the pronunciation of 'junta': 'The worst mistake is to mix languages. You cannot say *joonta* and you cannot say *hunta.*' But you can and quite easily. What Mr Safire meant was that you *may not* or *should not* or *ought not.*

Canada   is a dominion, comprising 10 provinces (Alberta, British Columbia, Manitoba, New Brunswick, Newfoundland and Labrador, Nova Scotia, Ontario, Prince Edward Island, Quebec and Saskatchewan) and three territories (Yukon, Northwest and Nunavut); capital Ottawa.

Canaletto   (1697–1768)   Venetian artist, real name Giovanni Antonio Canal

Canandaigua Lake, New York

canard   a ridiculous story or rumour. 'Gross canard' is a cliché. The French satirical magazine is *Le Canard Enchaîné.*

Canary Islands   island group off north-west Africa. They are not a colony but are part of Spain; in Spanish, *Islas Canarias.*

Cancún   Mexican resort

candelabrum   (or **candelabra**), pl. **candelabra** (or **candelabras**) not *candle-*

Candlemas   the Feast of the Purification of the Virgin Mary; 2 February

Canetti, Elias (1905–94)   Bulgarian-born British writer; awarded Nobel Prize for Literature 1981

canine

canister

cannabis

Cannae   site of battle in southern Italy where Hannibal routed the Romans in 216 BC

cannelloni

Cannizzaro, Stanislao (1826–1910)   Italian chemist

cannon, canon   A *cannon* is a gun. *Canon* is an ecclesiastical title, a body of religious writings or the works of a particular author.

cannonball (one word)

cannot help but   is an increasingly common construction, and perhaps now may be said to carry the weight of idiom, but it is also worth noting that it is both unnecessarily wordy and a little irregular. 'You cannot help but notice what a bad name deregulation has with voters' would be better (or at least more conventionally) phrased as either 'You cannot help noticing . . .' or 'You cannot but notice . . .'

canoodle

canopy

Canova, Antonio (1757–1822)   Italian sculptor

cant, jargon   Both apply to words or expressions used by particular groups. *Cant* has derogatory overtones and applies to the private vocabulary and colloquialisms of professions, social groups and sects. *Jargon* is a slightly more impartial word and usually suggests terms used in a particular profession.

Cantab   abbr. of *Cantabrigiensis* (Lat.), of Cambridge University

cantaloupe

Canton, China, is now normally referred to by its Pinyin name, Guangzhou. It is the capital of Guangdong Province, formerly Kwantung. **Cantonese** is still used to describe the food of the region, however.

Canute (c. 995–1035) King of England, Norway and Denmark; sometimes spelled Cnut

canvas, **canvass** The first is the fabric; the second is a verb meaning to solicit, especially for votes.

Cape Canaveral, Florida called Cape Kennedy from 1963 to 1973

Čapek, Karel (1890–1938) Czech author

Cape Town (two words), South Africa

Cape Verde Atlantic island nation off African coast; capital Cidade de Praia

capital, **capitol** *Capitol* always applies to a building, usually the place where legislatures gather in the United States. It is always capitalized when referring to the domed building in Washington, DC, that houses the US Congress. The rise on which the US Capitol stands is Capitol Hill. In all other senses, *capital* is the invariable spelling.

Capitol Reef National Park, Utah, not -*al*

Capodichino Airport, Naples

cappuccino, pl. **cappuccinos**

carabinieri, not *cari-*, for the Italian security force roughly equivalent to the French *gendarmerie*. Like gendarmes, *carabinieri* are soldiers employed in police duties. They are separate from, and not to be confused with, the state police (*polizia statale* in Italian), who also deal with criminal matters. *Carabinieri* is a plural; a single member of the force is a *carabiniere*. See also GENDARMES.

Caracalla, Marcus Aurelius Antoninus (186–217) Roman emperor

carafe a container, especially for wine or water

Caraqueño a person from Caracas, Venezuela

Caravaggio, Michelangelo Merisi/Amerighi da (c. 1569–1609) Italian painter

carat, caret, karat *Carat* is the unit of measurement used by jewellers; *caret* is an insertion mark (∧) associated with proofreading; *karat* is the American spelling for a measure of the purity of gold (UK *carat*).

caraway seeds

carbon dioxide, carbon monoxide *Carbon dioxide* is the gas people exhale; *carbon monoxide* is the highly poisonous gas associated with car exhausts.

carburettor (US **carburetor**)

carcass

Carcassonne walled city in southern France

cardamom a spice

cardinal numbers, ordinal numbers *Cardinal numbers* are those that denote size but not rank: 1, 2, 3, etc. *Ordinal numbers* are those that denote position: first, second, third, etc.

CARE international charity, short for Cooperative for American Relief Everywhere; originally the R stood for Remittances and the E for Europe

careen, career occasionally confused when describing runaway vehicles and the like. *Careen* should convey the idea of swaying or tilting dangerously. If all you mean is uncontrolled movement, use *career.*

caret, not *carat*, for the insertion mark (∧) associated with proofreading. See also CARAT, CARET, KARAT.

Carey Street, London To 'go to Carey Street' is to become bankrupt, as the entrance to the London bankruptcy courts was on Carey Street.

cargoes

Caribbean

Cariboo Mountains, Canada part of the Rockies

caricature

CARICOM short for Caribbean Community, regional trade organization

carillon

Carioca (cap.) colloquial name for a person or persons from Rio de Janeiro, Brazil

Carisbrooke Castle, Isle of Wight

Carl XVI Gustaf (1946–) King of Sweden 1973–

Carlyle, Thomas (1795–1881) Scottish historian

Carlyle Group investment company

Carlyle Hotel, New York City

Carmichael, Hoagy (1899–1981) American songwriter; full name Hoagland Howard Carmichael

Carnarvon, Lord (formally George Edward Stanhope Molyneux Herbert, Earl of Carnarvon) (1866–1923) English archaeologist, co-discoverer with Howard Carter of the famous tomb of Tutankhamun in Egypt

Carnegie Institute, Pittsburgh, but **Carnegie Institution**, Washington, DC

Carnoustie, Angus site of famous golf course

Carolina, North and **South** They are separate states. There is no state of Carolina in the US.

carom cannon shot in billiards or pool

Carothers, Wallace (Hume) (1896–1937) American scientist and inventor of nylon

carotid arteries

carpaccio thinly sliced raw beef or fish, named for Vittore

Carpaccio (c. 1460–c. 1526), Italian painter

carpal tunnel syndrome pain in the hand when a nerve is compressed

carpe diem (Lat.) seize the day, make the most of the present

Caracci, Lodovico (1555–1619), **Agostino** (1557–1602) and **Annibale** (1560–1609) family of Italian painters

Carpentaria, Gulf of, Australia

Carrantuohill highest mountain in Ireland (3,414 feet, 1,050 metres), in Macgillicuddy's Reeks, County Kerry

Carrington, Peter Alexander Rupert Carington, Baron (1919–) Note -*r*- in the family name and -*rr*- in title; British Conservative politician; Secretary-General of Nato 1984–8

Carrara town in Tuscany, and the fine white marble quarried nearby

Carrefour French supermarkets group

Carroll, Diahann (1935–) American singer and actress

Carroll, Lewis pen name of Charles Lutwidge Dodgson (1832–98)

cartel describes not just any alliance of businesses but one designed to maximize prices; unless a negative connotation is desired, avoid the word.

Carter Barron Amphitheatre, Washington, DC Note that Amphitheatre is spelled -*re*.

Carthusian

Cartier-Bresson, Henri (1908–2004) French photographer

cartilage

Carton, Sydney principal character in Dickens's *A Tale of Two Cities* (1859)

Caruso, Enrico (1874–1921) Italian tenor

Cary, Joyce (1888–1957) British author; full name Arthur Joyce Lunel Cary

caryatid in architecture, a female form used as a supporting pillar

Casablanca, Morocco

Casals, Pablo (1876–1973) Spanish cellist

Casamassima, The Princess novel by Henry James (1886)

Casanova (de Seingalt), Giovanni Jacopo/Giacomo (1725–98) Italian sexual adventurer

cashmere

Cassandra In Greek mythology, she was given the power of prophecy by Apollo but doomed never to be believed. The name is now used as a synonym for any prophet of doom.

Cassatt, Mary (1845–1926) American Impressionist painter

cassava root crop widely grown in Africa and parts of Asia and South America; also known as **manioc**, **yuca** or **tapioca**

Cassavetes, John (1930–89) American actor and director

cassette

Cassiopeia a constellation in the northern hemisphere named after the mother of Andromeda in Greek mythology

cassowary flightless bird

castanets Spanish rhythm instruments

caster, castor The first is a person who casts something, or fine sugar; the second is the oil, the bean or wheel on a chair.

Castile area of northern Spain; in Spanish, **Castilla**. The name appears in two Spanish regions: Castilla-La Mancha and Castilla-Léon.

Castlereagh, Robert Stewart, Viscount (1769–1822) British statesman

castrato a male singer castrated as a child so that he retains a high-pitched voice; pl. **castrati**

casus belli (Lat.) act that gives rise to war

catalyst is not just any agent of change, but one that hastens change without becoming changed itself.

catamaran

catarrh

cater-corner (US), not *catty-corner* diagonally opposite

Catharine's College, St, Cambridge University, but **St Catherine's College**, Oxford

Cathays Park, Cardiff (no apos.) pronounced *cat´-tays*

CAT scan short for computerized axial tomography; in medicine, a diagnostic tool

Catullus, Gaius Valerius (c. 84–c. 55 BC) Roman poet

Caudillo (Sp.) Leader, title assumed by General Francisco Franco of Spain

cauliflower

cause célèbre

caveat emptor (Lat.) let the buyer beware

caviar

Cawley, Evonne Goolagong (1951–) Australian tennis star

Cayenne, capital of French Guiana, but **cayenne pepper**

CBC Canadian Broadcasting Corporation

CBI Confederation of British Industry

CBS Columbia Broadcasting System

CCCP abbr. in the Cyrillic alphabet of Soyuz Sovyetskikh Sotsialistcheskikh Respublik (Union of Soviet Socialist Republics), former USSR

ceanothus blue-flowered shrub

Ceauşescu, Nicolae (1918–89) pronounced *chow-shess´-coo*, President of Romania 1967–89

Cecil, William See BURGHLEY.

cedilla mark [ ] placed under a *c* to indicate that it is pronounced in French as an *s*, in Turkish as *ch* and in Portuguese as *sh*

Ceefax teletext system used by the BBC

ceilidh (Gaelic) a gathering for music and dancing; pronounced *kay'-lee*

Cela, José Camilo (1916–2002) Spanish novelist; awarded Nobel Prize for Literature 1989

celebrant, celebrator The first is the term for persons taking part in religious ceremonies. Those who gather for purposes of revelry are celebrators.

celibacy does not, as is generally supposed, indicate abstinence from sexual relations. It means only to be unmarried, particularly if as a result of a religious vow. A married person cannot be celibate, but he may be chaste.

Cellini, Benvenuto (1500–71) Italian sculptor, goldsmith and author

Celsius, centigrade abbr. C; interchangeable terms referring to the scale of temperature invented by Anders Celsius (1701–44), a Swedish astronomer. To convert Celsius to Fahrenheit, multiply the Celsius temperature by 1.8 and add 32, or use the table in the Appendix.

cement, concrete The two are not interchangeable. *Cement* is a constituent of *concrete*, which also contains sand, gravel and crushed rock.

cemetery, not *-ary*

Cenozoic era the present geological era, beginning about 65 million years ago. In earlier periods it was sometimes also spelled *Caenozoic* or *Cainozoic*.

centavo a monetary unit in many countries of South and Central America equivalent to one one-hundredth of the country's main unit of currency; pl. **centavos**

Centers for Disease Control and Prevention, Atlanta US federal institution that deals with matters of public health. Note the plural 'Centers'. It is part of the Department of Health and Human Services.

Central Criminal Court formal title of the Old Bailey, London

centrifugal/centripetal force *Centrifugal force* is to pull away from; *centripetal force* is to draw towards.

Cephalonia Greek island in the Ionian chain; in Greek, **Kephallonia**

Cerberus in Greek mythology, a three-headed dog that stood guard over the gates to the underworld

Ceres Roman goddess of grain, identified with the Greek goddess Demeter

CERN originally Conseil Européen de Recherches Nucléaires, now the Organisation Européenne de Recherches Nucléaires, the European Organization for Nuclear Research, based in Geneva

Cervantes, (Saavedra) Miguel de (1547–1616) Spanish author

c'est la guerre (Fr.) 'that's the way of war'; by extension, 'what can you do?'

Cévennes mountains in southern France

Ceylon former name of Sri Lanka

Cézanne, Paul (1839–1906) French Impressionist painter

cf., *confer* (Lat.) 'compare'; used in cross-references

Chablais region of Haute-Savoie, France

Chablis French village and white burgundy wine (also cap.)

chacun à son goût (Fr.) each to his own taste

chacun pour soi (Fr.) everyone for himself

chador large piece of cloth worn by some Muslim women which is wrapped around the body to leave only the face exposed; pl. **chadors**

chaebol Korean business conglomerate; pl. same

chafe, **chaff** To *chafe* means to make sore or worn by rubbing (or, figuratively, to annoy or irritate). To *chaff* means to tease good-naturedly.

chaffinch type of bird

Chagall, Marc (1889–1985) Russian-born French artist

chagrined ashamed, annoyed

chaise-longue, pl. *chaises-longues*

Chakvetadze, Anna (1987–) Russian tennis player

Chaliapin, Feodor (Ivanovich) (1873–1938) Russian opera singer

challah (or **chalah** or **hallah**) type of Jewish bread

Chalon-sur-Sâone, **Châlons-en-Champagne**, **Chalonnes-sur-Loire**, France

Chamberlain, Sir (Joseph) Austen (1863–1937) British politician, awarded Nobel Peace Prize 1925; son of **Joseph Chamberlain** (1836–1914), also a politician; half-brother of **(Arthur) Neville Chamberlain** (1869–1940), British Prime Minister 1937–40

Chambers's Encyclopaedia

chameleon

chamois The plural is also *chamois*, for both the antelope and the cloth for wiping cars.

Champagne region of France, formally Champagne-Ardenne; the wine is champagne (no cap.)

Champaign, Illinois

champaign an open plain

Champaigne, Philippe de (1602–74) French painter

Champigny-sur-Marne suburb of Paris

Champlain, Samuel de (1567–1635) founder of Quebec

Champollion, Jean François (1790–1832) French Egyptologist who helped decipher the hieroglyphics on the Rosetta Stone

Champs-Élysées, Paris

Chancellor of the Duchy of Lancaster Cabinet post that has no formal duties, enabling the holder to take up special assignments for the Prime Minister

Chancellorsville, Battle of Note -*orsv*-; battle in the American Civil War

Chandigarh Indian city laid out by Le Corbusier

Chang Jiang (Pinyin)/**Yangtze River** If you use the Pinyin spelling (as many writers now do) you should make at least passing reference to the Yangtze, as that name is much more widely known in the English-speaking world.

Channel Islands They are not formally part of the United Kingdom, but are Crown dependencies. The principal islands are Jersey, Guernsey, Alderney, Brechou, Sark, Herm and Jethou.

Chanukkah Use **Hanukkah** for the Jewish festival of lights.

chaparral scrubby thicket of the American west

chapatti type of unleavened bread from India

chaperone

Chappaquiddick island off Martha's Vineyard, Massachusetts, made internationally famous in 1969 when Senator Edward Kennedy drove a car off a bridge following a party and his passenger, Mary Jo Kopechne, died

CHAPS clearing house automated payments system; a bank payment system

chargé d'affaires an ambassador's deputy; pl. **chargés d'affaires**

Charlemagne Charles I (742–814), first Holy Roman Emperor (800–814)

Charleston, South Carolina, not to be confused with

Charleston, West Virginia, or Charlotte, North Carolina. The Charleston (cap.) is a dance named after the city in South Carolina.

Charlestown, Massachusetts, and Nevis Island, St Kitts-Nevis

Charlotte Amalie capital of US Virgin Islands

Charlottenburg suburb of Berlin

Charolais cattle

chary, doubtful, cautious, but **chariness**

Charybdis in Greek mythology, a whirlpool off the coast of Sicily. It is often paired metaphorically with Scylla, a six-headed monster who lived nearby. In this sense *Scylla and Charybdis* signifies any highly unattractive – and unavoidable – dilemma.

chastise, not -*ize*

chasuble priest's garment

Châteaubriand, François-René, Vicomte de (1768–1848) French statesman and writer. The steak dish named for him is usually not capitalized.

Châteaubriant, France

Château Lafite, **Château Margaux** French red wines

Chatham House Rule (not *Rules*) is a rule of confidentiality formulated in 1927 at the Royal Institute of International Affairs, or Chatham House, London. Under it, information learned at a meeting may be used, but the source may not be disclosed.

Chattahoochee River, Georgia and Alabama

Chattanooga, Tennessee

Chatto & Windus British publisher, now an imprint of Random House UK

chauffeur

Chávez, Hugo (1954–) President of Venezuela 1999– ; full name Hugo Rafael Chávez Frías

Chayefsky, Paddy (1923–81)   American playwright and
   screenwriter
cheap, cheep The first means inexpensive, the second refers
   to the sound birds make.
cheddar cheese, but Cheddar (cap.) for the place in England
   whence it originated
Cheeryble brothers characters in Charles Dickens's *Nicholas
   Nickleby* (1838–9)
Chelyabinsk, Siberia
Chemnitz, Germany formerly Karl-Marx-Stadt
Chennai is the new official name for Madras, India, but until
   it is fully established both names should probably be
   used on first reference.
Chennault, Claire (1890–1958) American general; organized
   Flying Tigers air corps in the Second World War
Chequers   official country home of the British Prime
   Minister, near Princes Risborough, Buckinghamshire
Chernenko, Konstantin (1911–85) President of the Soviet
   Union 1984–5
Chernobyl   Ukrainian site of the world's worst known
   nuclear accident, 1986
Cherokee North American Indian people
Chery Chinese car manufacturer; not *Cherry*
Chesapeake Bay between Maryland and Virginia
Chesebrough-Pond's US cosmetics and household products
   company
Chesil Beach, Dorset
Chester-le-Street, County Durham
Chevalier, Maurice (1888–1972) French entertainer
Cheviot Hills   on the border between England and
   Scotland
ChevronTexaco (one word) oil company

Chevy diminutive form of Chevrolet

Chevy Chase, Maryland

Cheyenne North American Indian people, river, and capital of Wyoming

Chhatrapati Shivaji International Airport, Mumbai, India Note *Chh-*.

Chiang Kai-shek (1887–1975) leader of Nationalist Republic of China 1928–49 and first President of Taiwan 1950–75

chiaroscuro interplay of light and shade

Chicano an American of Mexican origin; pl. **Chicanos**

Chichén Itzá Mayan ruins in Mexico

Chickamauga, Georgia; not *-magua* site of American Civil War battle (1863)

chickenpox (one word)

chicory herb

Chihuahua city and state in Mexico and breed of dog

chilblain, not *chill-*

Childe Harold's Pilgrimage, not *Child* poem by Lord Byron (1812–18)

Childers, (Robert) Erskine (1870–1922) Irish nationalist and writer, and father of **Erskine Childers** (1905–74), President of Ireland 1973–4

children's is the only possible spelling of the possessive form of *children*.

chilli, pl. **chillies** (US **chili**, pl. **chilies**)

Chiltern Hundreds Because British MPs are not permitted to resign, they must apply to become stewards of the Chiltern Hundreds – effectively a non-existent position – which disqualifies them from Parliament.

chimera a wild or fanciful creation, taken from Chimera (sometimes Chimaera), a mythological beast with the head of a lion, body of a goat and tail of a serpent

China, Republic of official name of Taiwan, used almost nowhere except in Taiwan itself. The mainland country is **the People's Republic of China**.

chinchilla

Chincoteague bay, island and town in Virginia or Maryland

Chinese names The system now used almost everywhere for transliterating Chinese names into English is Pinyin (which means transcription). This has occasioned many striking changes in the rendering of Chinese names: Mao Tse-tung is now Mao Zedong; Peking is now Beijing. In some cases, particularly where long-established names are concerned, older forms continue to be used: Confucius, Hong Kong, Shanghai. But even many of these are slowly changing. If uncertain, or where confusion is likely, it is a courtesy to give both names: 'Chang Jiang River, formerly known as the Yangtze'.

Chingachgook character in James Fenimore Cooper's novel *The Deerslayer* (1841)

chinook warm dry wind that blows off the Rocky Mountains

chipmunk, not -*monk*

chipolata a small sausage

Chippendale, Thomas (c. 1718–79) English furniture designer and manufacturer

Chipping Campden, Gloucestershire pronounced C*hipping Camden*

Chişinău capital of Moldova

chitterlings is the formal name of the southern American dish made from pig's intestines, but it is often more informally spelled **chitlins**

chivvy to hurry or harass

chlorophyll

chockfull (or **chock-full**) The US brand of coffee and restaurants is **Chock full o'Nuts**.

chocolate

Choctaw native American group

cholesterol

Chomsky, Noam (1928–) American linguist and political activist

Chongqing city in Sichuan province, China; formerly referred to as **Chungking**

Chopin, Frédéric François (1810–49) Polish composer

chord, **cord** A *chord* is a group of musical notes or a type of arc in geometry; a *cord* is a length of rope or similar material of twisted strands, or a stack of wood. You speak with your *vocal cords*.

Chou En-lai (1898–1976) Prime Minister of China 1949–76. The name is now usually spelled **Zhou Enlai.**

Christ Church, **Christchurch** *Christ Church* is the spelling and full name of the Oxford college (i.e., not 'Christ Church College'). The communities in New Zealand and England are *Christchurch*.

Christiania former name of Oslo

Christie's London auction house; formally Christie, Manson & Woods, but the parent company styles itself **Christies International** (no apos.)

Christ's College, Cambridge University

Christy Minstrels

chromosome

chronic, **acute** *Chronic* means constant or long-standing; *acute* (when applied to an illness or situation) means approaching a crisis.

chrysalis The formal plural, and the one to use in scientific contexts, is **chrysalides**, but **chrysalises** is acceptable for more general writing.

chrysanthemum

chukka (US **chukker**) period of play in polo

Church of Christ, Scientist (with comma) is the formal name of the Christian Scientist Church.

Church of Jesus Christ of Latter-day Saints formal title of the Mormon Church

Churchs Ferry (no apos.), North Dakota

chutzpah (Yiddish) shameless audacity, brashness

Chuvashiya Russian republic

ciao (It.) salutation meaning either hello or goodbye

Ciba-Geigy Swiss pharmaceuticals company

Cicero, Marcus Tullius (106–43 BC) Roman orator and statesman

Ciechanover, Aaron (1947–) Israeli scientist, awarded Nobel Prize for Chemistry 2004

Cimoszewicz, Wlodzimierz (1950–) Prime Minister of Poland 1996–7

Cincinnati, Ohio

Cincinnatus, Lucius Quinctius (c. 519–c. 439 BC) Roman general

Cinderella

CinemaScope wide-screen film system

cinéma-vérité realistic style of film-making

cineraria, pl. **cinerarias** type of flower

cinnamon

cinquecento (It.) literally 'the five hundreds'; Italian name for the 16th century

Cinque Ports pronounced *sink*; originally Hastings, Romney, Hythe, Dover and Sandwich; later including Rye and Winchelsea

CIPFA Chartered Institute for Public Finance and Accountancy

cipher, not *cypher*

circadian, taking place in 24-hour cycles

Circe in Greek mythology, an enchantress on the island of Aeaea who detained Odysseus and his men, turning the latter into swine and bearing a son by the former

circumstances, in the and **under the** A useful distinction can be drawn between the two. *In the circumstances* should indicate merely that a situation exists: 'In the circumstances, I began to feel worried.' *Under the circumstances* should denote a situation in which action is necessitated or inhibited: 'Under the circumstances, I had no choice but to leave.'

cirrhosis

Citigroup Inc., the financial services corporation, has a habit of dazzling inconsistency with regard to capitalization and spacing when naming subsidiaries. Among its offshoots are Citibank, Citi Cards, CitiFinancial, CitiMortgage and Citi Private Bank. Take care.

Citlatépetl dormant Mexican volcano

C. Itoh Japanese trading company

Citroën French automobile manufacturer

city names Where cities have the same name as surrounding territory, it is normal to capitalize 'City' even when it is not formally part of the place name. Thus, New York City, Mexico City, Luxembourg City, Quebec City

Ciudad Trujillo former name of Santo Domingo, capital of the Dominican Republic

Civil List annual payment for expenses made to the Queen and other members of the royal family

civil servant, but **Civil Service**

Civitavecchia Italian coastal city and port for Rome

Clackmannanshire smallest Scottish county, principal town Alloa

clamour, but **clamorous**

Clare, County, Ireland

Claridge's Hotel, London, but **Hôtel Claridge**, Paris

clarinettist

Clarke, Arthur C. (for **Charles**) (1917–) English science-fiction writer

Clemenceau, Georges (Eugène Benjamin) (1841–1929) Prime Minister of France, 1906–9, 1917–20

Clemens, Samuel Langhorne (1835–1910) American author better known by his pen name, Mark Twain

clerestory upper part of the nave, choir and transepts of a church, containing a series of windows

clerihew four-line nonsense poem devised by Edmund Clerihew Bentley (1875–1956)

Cley, Norfolk pronounced *klye*

climactic, climatic, climacteric *Climactic* means appearing at a climax ('the climactic scene in a movie'); *climatic* means having to do with climate and weather ('the climatic conditions of the Brazilian rainforest'); *climacteric* is a noun signifying a time of important change and is most commonly applied to the menopause.

clitoris, pl. **clitorises** or **clitorides**

cloisonné a type of enamel work

close proximity is inescapably tautological. Make it 'near' or 'close to'. See also SCRUTINY.

Clouseau, Inspector fictional character mostly portrayed by Peter Sellers in *Pink Panther* films

Clwyd pronounced *kloo´-wid*; county of northern Wales

Clytemnestra in Greek mythology, the wife of Agamemnon

cnidarians members of the phylum of marine invertebrates that includes jellyfish, corals and sea anemones; also called coelenterates

Coahuila state in north-eastern Mexico

Cobh, County Cork, Ireland pronounced *Cove*

COBOL Common Business Oriented Language, early computer programming language

Coca-Cola (hyphen) The diminutive term Coke should always be capitalized.

coccyx tailbone; pl. **coccyxes**

cock-a-leekie soup

cockney (no cap.) a native of London's East End; pl. **cockneys**

coconut, but the Marx Brothers movie of 1929 is *The Cocoanuts*

cocoon

coelacanth ocean fish famed in scientific circles for its archaic qualities; pronounced *see-luh-kanth*

coequal is a pointless word; *co-* adds nothing to *equal* that *equal* doesn't already say alone.

Coetzee, J. M. (for **John Maxwell**) (1940–) South African-born Australian author, awarded Nobel Prize for Literature 2003

Coeur d'Alene, Idaho

Coeur de Lion, Richard (1157–99) Richard the Lionheart, Richard I of England

cogito, ergo sum (Lat.) I think, therefore I am; Descartes's aphorism

cognoscente a person who is well informed or of elevated taste; pl. ***cognoscenti***

Cohen-Tannoudji, Claude (1933–) French physicist, born in Algeria; awarded Nobel Prize for Physics 1997

COHSE Confederation of Health Service Employees, former British trade union, now part of UNISON

Cointreau liqueur

colander, not -*dar*; a perforated bowl

Coleg Prifysgol Cymru (Welsh) University College of Wales

coleus plant with variegated leaves

Colgate-Palmolive (hyphen) personal products company

colic, but **colicky**

coliseum, Colosseum The first applies to any large amphitheatre; the second describes a particular amphitheatre in Rome.

collapsible, not -*able*

collectable is the normal UK spelling, but **collectible** is an accepted alternative.

collectives Deciding whether to treat nouns of multitude – words like *majority, flock, variety, group* and *crowd* – as singulars or plurals is entirely a matter of the sense you intend to convey. Although some authorities have tried to fix rules, such undertakings are almost always futile. On the whole, Americans lean to the singular and Britons to the plural, often in ways that would strike the other as absurd (compare the American 'The couple was married in March' with the British 'England are to play Hungary in their next match'). A common fault is to flounder about between singular and plural. Even Samuel Johnson stumbled when he wrote that he knew of no nation 'that *has* preserved *their* words and phrases from mutability'. Clearly the italicized words should be either singular both times or plural both times. See also NUMBER and TOTAL.

collisions can occur only when two or more moving objects come together. If a car runs into a stationary object, it is not a collision.

Colman, Ronald (1891–1958) English actor

Colombey-les-Deux-Églises town east of Paris where Charles de Gaulle is buried

Colombia South American country; capital Bogotá

Colombo capital of Sri Lanka

Colón, Cristobál Spanish spelling of Christopher Columbus. In his native Italy, his name was Cristoforo Colombo.

colonnade

colossal

Colosseum, Rome

Colossus of Rhodes

colostomy

Colquhoun pronounced *ko-hoon'*; Scottish name

Columba, St (521–97) Irish saint associated with the Scottish island of Iona

Columbus Day US bank holiday, second Monday in October

Comaneci, Nadia (1961–) Romanian gymnast; winner of five Olympic gold medals

combatant, **combated**, **combating**

combustible capable of being burned

Comédie-Française national theatre of France; formally, the Théâtre Français

Comedy of Errors, The, not *A* play by William Shakespeare (1592–4)

comestible foodstuff

comic, **comical** Something that is *comic* is intended to be funny ('a comic performance'). Something that is *comical* is funny whether or not that was the intention ('a comical misunderstanding').

commedia dell'arte type of farcical Italian comedy

commence an unnecessary genteelism. What's wrong with 'begin'?

commingle to mix together; note -*mm*-

commiserate

committal

Commodus, Lucius Aelius Aurelius (161–92) Roman emperor 180–92

Comoros island state off Madagascar; capital Moroni

compact disc, not *disk*

comparatively 'Comparatively little progress was made in the talks yesterday' (*Guardian*). Compared with what? *Comparatively* should be reserved for occasions when a comparison is being expressed or at least clearly implied. If all you mean is *fairly* or *only a little*, choose another word. See also RELATIVELY.

compare to, compare with These two can be usefully distinguished. *Compare to* should be used to liken things, *compare with* to consider their similarities or differences. 'He compared London to New York' means that he felt London to be similar to New York. 'He compared London with New York' means that he assessed the two cities' relative merits. *Compare to* most often appears in figurative senses, as in 'Shall I compare thee to a summer's day?'

compatible

compatriot fellow countryman; not to be confused, in meaning or spelling, with *expatriate*

compel, impel Both words imply the application of a force leading to some form of action, but they are not quite synonymous. *Compel* is the stronger of the two and, like its cousin *compulsion*, suggests action undertaken as a result of coercion or irresistible pressure: 'The man's bullying tactics compelled us to flee.' *Impel* is closer in meaning to *encourage* and means to urge forward: 'The audience's ovation impelled me to speak at greater length than I had intended.' If you are compelled to do something, you have no choice. If you are impelled, an element of willingness is possible.

compendium No doubt because of the similarity in sound to *comprehensive*, the word is often taken to mean vast and all-embracing. In fact, a *compendium* is a succinct summary or abridgement. Size has nothing to do with it. It may be as large as *The Oxford English Dictionary* or as small as a memorandum. What is important is that it should provide a complete summary in a brief way. The plural can be either **compendia** or **compendiums**. The *OED* prefers the former, most other dictionaries the latter.

complacent, **complaisant** The first means self-satisfied, contented to the point of smugness. The second means affable and cheerfully obliging. If you are *complacent*, you are pleased with yourself. If you are *complaisant*, you wish to please others. Both words come from the Latin *complacere* ('to please'), but *complaisant* reached us by way of France, which accounts for the difference in spelling.

Compleat Angler, The book by Izaak Walton (1653)

complement, **compliment/complementary**, **complimentary** The words come from the same Latin root, *complere*, meaning to fill up, but have long had separate meanings. *Compliment* means to praise. *Complement* has stayed closer to the original meaning: it means to fill out or make whole. So a gracious guest compliments a host; an espresso after dinner complements a meal. In the adjectival forms *complementary* and *complimentary* the words retain these senses, but *complimentary* has the additional meaning of something given without charge: a complimentary ticket, for instance.

complete Partridge includes *complete* in his list of false comparatives – that is, words that do not admit of comparison, such as *ultimate* and *eternal* (one thing cannot be 'more ultimate' or 'more eternal' than another). Technically, he is right, and you should take care not to modify *complete* needlessly. But there are occasions when it would be pedantic to carry the stricture too far. As the Morrises note, there can be no real objection to 'This is the most complete study to date of that period.' Use it, but use it judiciously.

complete and unabridged Though blazoned across the packaging of countless audio books, part of the phrase is palpably redundant. If a work is unabridged, it must be complete, and vice versa. Choose one or the other.

compos mentis (Lat.) of sound mind

comprehensible

compressor

comprise 'Beneath Sequoia is the Bechtel Group, a holding company comprised of three main operating arms . . .' (*New York Times*). Not quite. It is composed of three main operating arms, not comprised of them. *Comprised of* is a common expression, but it is always wrong. *Comprise* means to contain. The whole comprises the parts and not vice versa. A house may comprise seven rooms, but seven rooms do not comprise a house – and still less is a house comprised of seven rooms. The example above should be either 'a holding company comprising three main operating arms' or 'composed of three main operating arms'.

conceived 'Last week, 25 years after it was first conceived . . .' (*Time*). Delete 'first'. Something can be conceived only once. Similarly with 'initially conceived' and 'originally conceived'.

Concertgebouw Orchestra, Amsterdam

condone The word does not mean to approve or endorse, senses that are often attached to it. It means to pardon, forgive, overlook. You can condone an action without supporting it.

Coney Island, New York

confectionery, not -*ary*

confidant (masc.)/**confidante** (fem.) a person entrusted with private information

Congo, confusingly, now applies to two neighbouring nations in Africa. The larger of the two, which was called Zaire until 1997, now styles itself the **Democratic Republic of the Congo**; its capital is Kinshasa. Bordering it to the west is the much smaller **Republic of the Congo**; capital Brazzaville.

Congonhas International Airport, São Paulo, Brazil

Congressional Medal of Honor, for the highest US military honour, is not strictly correct. It is awarded by Congress, but its correct title is simply the Medal of Honor.

Congreve, William (1670–1729) English playwright

Connacht province of Ireland comprising five counties: Galway, Leitrim, Mayo, Roscommon and Sligo

Connecticut US state; postal abbr. **CT**

Connemara, Galway, Ireland

connoisseur

ConocoPhillips oil company

consensus 'General consensus' is a tautology. Any consensus must be general. Equally to be avoided is 'consensus of opinion'. Above all, note that *consensus* is spelled with a middle *s*, like *consent*. It has nothing to do with *census*.

consols consolidated annuities, a stock market term

Constance, Lake/Bodensee (Ger.) lake bounded by Switzerland, Germany and Austria; the principal lakeside city is Constance in English and French, but Konstanz in German

Constantinople former name of Istanbul

Consumers' Association publisher of *Which?* and other consumer-interest magazines and books

consummate As a term of praise, the word is much too freely used. A consummate actor is not merely a very good one, but someone who is so good as to be unrivalled or nearly so. It should be reserved to describe only the very best.

contagious, infectious Diseases spread by contact are *contagious*. Those spread by air and water are *infectious*. Used figuratively ('contagious laughter', 'infectious enthusiasm'), either is fine.

contemptible, contemptuous *Contemptible* means deserving contempt. If someone is *contemptuous* he bestows contempt. A contemptible offer may receive a contemptuous response.

conterminous, coterminous sharing a common boundary

continual, continuous Although the distinction is not widely observed, or indeed always necessary, there is a useful difference between the two words. *Continual* refers to things that happen repeatedly but not constantly. *Continuous* indicates an uninterrupted sequence. However, few readers will be aware of this distinction, and the writer who requires absolute clarity will generally be better advised to use *incessant* or *uninterrupted* for continuous and *repetitive* for continual

contrary, converse, opposite, reverse *Contrary* describes something that contradicts a proposition. *Converse* applies when the elements of a proposition are reversed. *Opposite* is something that is diametrically opposed to a proposition. *Reverse* can describe any of these. For the statement 'I love you', the opposite is 'I hate you'; the converse is 'You love me'; the contrary would be anything that contradicted it: 'I do not love you', 'I have no feelings at all for you', 'I like you moderately'. The reverse could embrace all of these meanings.

conurbation does not describe just any urban area, but rather a place where two or more sizeable communities have sprawled together, such as Pasadena–Los Angeles–Long Beach in California or Amsterdam–Rotterdam–Haarlem–Utrecht in the Netherlands.

convener, not -*or* one who convenes

convince, persuade The words are not quite the same. You convince someone that he should believe, but persuade him to act. It is possible to persuade a person to do something without convincing him of the correctness or necessity of doing it. A separate distinction is that *persuade* may be followed by an infinitive, but *convince* may not. Thus the following is wrong: 'The Soviet Union evidently is not able to convince Cairo to accept a rapid cease-fire.' Make it either 'persuade Cairo to accept' or 'convince Cairo that it should accept'.

coolly

Cooper, James Fenimore (1789–1851) American writer

Cooper-Hewitt National Design Museum, New York

Copland, Aaron (1900–90) American composer
Copley, John Singleton (1737–1815) American painter
Coppola, Francis Ford (1939–) American film director
Corbière, (Édouard Joachim) Tristan (1845–75) French
　　poet
Corbusier, Le pseudonym of Charles Édouard Jeanneret
　　(1887–1965), Swiss architect and city planner
Corcoran Gallery of Art, Washington, DC
cord, **chord** A *cord* is a length of rope or similar material of
　　twisted strands; a *chord* is a group of musical notes. You
　　speak with your *vocal cords.*
corduroy
CORE Congress of (not *for*) Race Equality, US civil rights
　　organization
Coriolis effect the tendency of winds to deflect to the right
　　in the northern hemisphere and to the left in the
　　southern hemisphere as a consequence of Earth's spin
Corneille, Pierre (1606–84) French playwright
Cornouaille, Côte de, Brittany, France
Coronado, Francisco Vásquez de (c. 1500–54) Spanish
　　explorer of the New World
Corot, Camille (1796–1875) French painter
Corporation for Public Broadcasting, US
Correggio, Antonio Allegri da (1494–1534) Italian painter
corrigible capable of being corrected or improved
corruptible
cortege (no accents)
Cortes legislative assembly of Spain, but see next entry
Cortés/Cortéz, Hernando/Hernan (1485–1547) Spanish
　　conqueror of the Aztecs
coruscate, not -*rr*- glittering, dazzling, as in 'coruscating wit'
Così fan tutte opera by Mozart (1790)

cos lettuce
Costa Book Awards formerly Whitbread Literary Awards, 1971–2006
Costa-Gavras, (Henri) Constantin (1933–) film director
Côte d'Azur the French Riviera
coterminous/conterminous sharing a common boundary
cotoneaster type of shrub
Cotten, Joseph (1905–94) American film actor
Cottian Alps section of Alps between France and Italy
couldn't of ' "Couldn't of got it without you, Pops," Parker said . . .' (*New Yorker*). As a shortened form of 'couldn't have', *couldn't of* does unquestionably avoid the clumsy double contraction *couldn't've*, a form not often seen in print since J. D. Salinger stopped writing. However, I would submit that that does not make it satisfactory. Using the preposition *of* as a surrogate for *'ve* seems to me simply to be swapping an ungainly form for an illiterate one. If *couldn't've* is too painful to use, I would suggest simply writing *couldn't have* and allowing the reader's imagination to supply the appropriate inflection.
coulee ravine
council/counsel The first is a deliberative body (*city council*); the second applies to contexts involving the giving of advice or guidance (*marriage counsellor*).
Countess Cathleen, The, not *Kath-* play by William Butler Yeats (1899)
country, nation It is perhaps a little fussy to insist too strenuously on the distinction, but strictly *country* refers to the geographical characteristics of a place and *nation* to the political and social ones. Thus the United States is one of the richest nations, but largest countries.

coup de grâce a decisive blow

coup d'état, pl. **coups d'état**

coup de théâtre dramatic turn of events

couple The idea, fiercely adhered to in some quarters, that *couple* must always be singular is both pointless and unsupported by wider authority. When a couple are thought of as separate individuals ('The couple were apprehended in different counties'; 'The couple have been living apart since 1999') the plural is always to be preferred.

couple of The second word is required in sentences like 'Can I borrow a couple of dollars?' To drop the 'of' is a common but nonetheless grating illiteracy in any but the most casual writing.

courgette French and British name for the vegetable known to Americans as *zucchini*

Courmayeur Italian ski resort

court-martial (hyphen), pl. **courts-martial** Some authorities also accept *court-martials*.

Courtneidge, Dame Cicely (1893–1980) British actress, often paired theatrically with her husband, **Jack Hulbert**

Court of St James's, the the place to which ambassadors are posted in Great Britain. Note the apostrophe and second *s*.

Court of Session the supreme court of Scotland

Covarrubias, Miguel (1902–57) Mexican artist

Cowper, William (1731–1800) English poet; pronounced *cooper*

Cozzens, James Gould (1903–78) American author

CPRE Campaign to Protect Rural England

crackerjack, Cracker Jack The first is an old slang term for something good; the second is an American candied popcorn snack.

Cradock, Fanny (1909–94) British television cook, assisted by her husband, **Johnnie Cradock** (1904–87)

crass means stupid and grossly ignorant to the point of insensitivity and not merely coarse or tasteless. A thing must be pretty bad to be crass.

Cratchit, Bob character in Dickens's *A Christmas Carol* (1843)

crèche, pl. **crèches**

Crécy, Battle of (1346)

crème brûlée literally 'burnt cream'; custard dessert

creole, pidgin A *pidgin* is a simplified and rudimentary language that springs up when two or more cultures come in contact. If that contact is prolonged and generations are born for whom the pidgin is their first tongue, the language will usually evolve into a more formalized *creole* (from the French for 'indigenous'). Most languages that are commonly referred to as pidgins are in fact creoles.

crêpes suzette (not cap.) When *crepes* is used on its own, in most circumstances the circumflex may be dropped.

crescendo is not a climax or conclusion. It is the movement towards a climax. Properly, it should be used only to describe a gradual increase in volume or intensity.

Cressida, Troilus and play by Shakespeare (c. 1601). The poem by Geoffrey Chaucer is '**Troylus and Criseyde**'. In Boccaccio's *Il Filostrato* the spelling is **Criseida**.

crevasse, crevice A *crevasse* is a deep fissure, particularly in ice; a *crevice* is a narrow and generally shallow fissure.

Crèvecoeur, J. Hector St John (1735–1813) French-born American essayist, born Michel Guillaume Jean de Crèvecoeur

Criccieth, Gwynedd small Welsh resort; pronounced *crick´-ee-eth*

cri de coeur (Fr.) an impassioned plea

crime passionnel (Fr.) a crime motivated by sexual jealousy

crisis, pl. **crises**

criterion, pl. **criteria**

Croat/Croatian The first describes the people of Croatia; the second is a more general adjective ('a Croatian city').

Croce, Benedetto (1866–1952) Italian writer, philosopher and politician

crocheted, crocheting

Crockett, Davy (1786–1836) American frontiersman and politician

Croesus (reigned 560–546 BC) last king of Lydia, byword for wealth

Cro-Magnon early form of *Homo sapiens*, named after a hill in France

Crome Yellow, not *Chrome*, for the 1921 novel by Aldous Huxley

Cronos in Greek mythology, a Titan dethroned by his son Zeus; equivalent to the Roman god Saturn. Sometimes spelled *Kronos* (esp. in UK)

crony

Crosland, Anthony (1918–77) British politician and writer

cross-Channel ferry is a tautology; delete *cross-*.

Crossman, Richard (1907–74) British politician and diarist

Crowley, Aleister (1875–1947) English writer and diabolist

Crown Estate Commissioners, not *Estates*

Cruft's Dog Show

Cruikshank, George (1792–1878)   English cartoonist and illustrator

Cruyff, Johan (1947–)   Dutch footballer, originator of the 'Cruyff turn'

cruzeiro   principal unit of currency of Brazil; from 1986 to 1990 it was the cruzado

Cry, the Beloved Country   note comma; novel by Alan Paton (1948)

CSA Czech Airlines

C-Span, C-Span 2   US cable television networks; the initials are short for Cable-Satellite Public Affairs Network

CT   postal abbr. for Connecticut

Cucamonga   suburb of Los Angeles; now called Rancho Cucamonga

Cuchulain   warrior hero of Irish mythology; pronounced *koo-hoo´-lin*

cuckoo

cueing   signalling; not to be confused with **queueing/ queuing**, forming a line

cul-de-sac (hyphens); pl. **cul-de-sacs**

Culloden, Battle of (1746)

Culpeper, Nicholas (1616–54) apothecary and herbalist

Culpeper, Virginia

Culzean Castle, Ayrshire pronounced *kuh-lane´*

cumbrous, not *-erous*

cuneiform   wedge-shaped writing

cupful, pl. **cupfuls**

cupola

Curaçao   island in the Netherlands Antilles. The liqueur produced there is spelled the same but lower-cased.

curettage   a surgical scraping procedure using a curette

curette   a surgical instrument

Curie, Marie (1867–1934) born Marie Skłodowska; Polish-born French physicist; joint winner, with her husband, Pierre Curie, and Henri Becquerel, of the Nobel Prize for Physics in 1903; she was also awarded the Nobel Prize for Chemistry in 1911.

curlicue

Curragh Incident a near-mutiny in 1914 by British officers stationed at The Curragh, near Dublin, who refused to fire on civilians. A *curragh* is also a type of small boat.

current, currently When there is a need to contrast the present with the past, *current* has its place, but all too often it is merely an idle occupier of space, as in these two examples from a single article in *Time* magazine: 'The Government currently owns 740 million acres, or 32.7% of the land in the U.S. . . . Property in the area is currently fetching $125 to $225 per acre.' The notion of currency is implicit in both statements, as it is in most other sentences in which *current* and *currently* appear. *Currently* should be deleted from both. (The second sentence could be further improved by changing 'is fetching' to 'fetches'.)

curriculum vitae abbr. CV; summary of a job applicant's qualifications and experience

Curtiss aircraft named after Glenn Curtiss (1878–1930), American inventor and aviator

Curtiz, Michael (1888–1962) born Mihály Kertész; Hungarian-born American film director

curtsy, not -*ey*

curvaceous, not -*ious*

Cuthbertson, Iain (1930–) British actor

CV abbr. of **curriculum vitae**

Cwmbran, Gwent pronounced *koom-rahn*

Cwmtwrch, West Glamorgan pronounced *koom-toorch, ch* as in *loch*

cyanosis turning blue from lack of oxygen

cyclamen

cymbal percussion instrument

Cynewulf (*fl.* 8th c.) Anglo-Saxon poet

Cyrillic alphabet Alphabet widely used for Slavonic languages. It is named after St Cyril, who is popularly credited with its invention. Some of the characters vary slightly between Russian, Bulgarian and other languages.

cystic fibrosis genetic disease

cystitis

D

Dachau town near Munich, site of infamous concentration camp in the Second World War

Dadullah, Mullah (1966–2007) Afghan Taliban commander; sometimes called **Dadullah Akhund**

Daedalus in Greek mythology, the father of Icarus and builder of the Labyrinth; but the character in the works of James Joyce is **Stephen Dedalus** and the pseudonym used by the Italian author Umberto Eco is also **Dedalus**

Dafydd Welsh for David; not *Daffyd*

daguerreotype early photographic process, named after Louis Daguerre (1789–1851), French painter and photographer

Dahomey former name of the west African state of Benin

Dai-Ichi Kangyo Japanese bank

Dáil Éireann lower house of the Irish Parliament; pronounced *doyle air-ran*

DaimlerChrysler AG German car manufacturer, separated in 2007 into **Daimler AG** and **Chrysler Holding**

daiquiri

Dalai Lama the high priest of Tibet

d'Alembert, Jean le Rond (1717–83) French mathematician

Dallapiccola, Luigi (1904–75) Italian composer

Damariscotta town and lake in Maine

Danaë mother of Perseus in Greek mythology

Danegeld, Danelaw The *Danegeld* was a tax levied in England in the 10th–12th centuries initially to pay for defences against Viking incursions. The *Danelaw* was a section of England occupied by Danes in the 9th–11th centuries and the laws that prevailed there.

danke schön (Ger.) thank you very much

d'Annunzio, Gabriele (1863–1938) Italian writer and adventurer

danse macabre, not *dance* from the French for a dance of death. The plural is *danses macabres*.

Dante Alighieri (1265–1321) Italian poet; the adjective is Dantesque

Danzig former name of Gdańsk, the Polish city

Darby and Joan, not *Derby* after a couple in an 18th-century English song

Dardanelles the narrow channel linking the Aegean Sea and the Sea of Marmara, known in antiquity as the Hellespont

Dar es Salaam former capital of Tanzania. See also DODOMA.

Darjeeling tea, but **Darjiling** for the Indian city for which it is named

data is a plural. Although this fact is widely disregarded, you should at least be aware that 'The data was fed into a computer' is incorrect. It is also worth observing that the sense of *data* is generally best confined to the idea of raw, uncollated bits of information, the sort of stuff churned out by computers, and not used as a simple synonym for *facts* or *reports* or *information*.

Davenant (or **D'Avenant**), **Sir William** (1606–68) English poet and dramatist

Davies, Robertson (1913–95) Canadian novelist and playwright

Davies, Sharron (1962–) British swimmer; note *-rr-* in first name

da Vinci, Leonardo (1452–1519) Florentine artist. On second reference he is properly referred to as *Leonardo*, not as *da Vinci*.

Davy, Sir Humphry (1778–1829), not *Humphrey* English chemist

Dayan, Moshe (1915–81) Israeli general and politician

Day-Lewis, Cecil (1904–72) Irish-born British poet; father of actor **Daniel Day-Lewis** (1957–)

dB abbr. for **decibel**

DC District of Columbia, coextensive with the US capital, Washington

DCLG Department of Communities and Local Government, UK government department; now styles itself simply **Communities and Local Government**

DCMS Department for Culture, Media and Sport (UK)

DCSF Department for Children, Schools and Families (UK)

DDR Deutsche Demokratische Republik; German Democratic Republic, former East Germany

DDT dichlorodiphenyltrichloroethane; insecticide

DE postal abbreviation of Delaware; the traditional abbreviation is **Del.**

debacle a rout or ruin; in French, *débâcle*

DeBakey, Michael (1908–) American heart surgeon

de Beauvoir, Simone (1908–86) French author

De Benedetti, Carlo (1934–) Italian industrialist

debonair in French, *débonnaire*

Debrett's Peerage and Baronetage guide to British aristocracy

Debussy, (Achille-) Claude (1862–1918) French composer

débutante

decathlon   The ten events are long jump, high jump, pole vault, discus, shot put, javelin, 110 metre hurdles and 100, 400 and 1,500 metre races.

deceit, deceive

deci-   prefix meaning one-tenth

decimate   Literally the word means to reduce by a tenth (from the ancient practice of punishing the mutinous or cowardly by killing every tenth man). By extension it may be used to describe the inflicting of heavy damage, but it should never be used to denote annihilation, as in this memorably excruciating sentence cited by Fowler: 'Dick, hotly pursued by the scalp-hunter, turned in his saddle, fired and literally decimated his opponent.' Equally to be avoided are contexts in which the word's use is clearly inconsistent with its literal meaning, as in 'Frost decimated an estimated 80 per cent of the crops.'

De Clercq, Willy (1927–)   Belgian politician

décolletage   a plunging neckline on clothing

decry   denounce in public

Dedalus, Stephen   character in James Joyce's works. See also DAEDALUS.

de facto (Lat.)   existing in fact but not in law. See also DE JURE.

defective, deficient   When something is not working properly, it is *defective*; when it is missing a necessary part, it is *deficient*.

defence, but **defensive, defensible**

Defferre, Gaston (1910–86)   French Socialist politician and journalist

defibrillator

definite, definitive   *Definite* means precise and unmistakable. *Definitive* means final and conclusive. A definite offer is a clear one; a definitive offer is one that permits of no haggling.

Defoe, Daniel (1659–1731) British author

DEFRA Department for (not *of*, not *the*) Environment, Food and Rural Affairs; British government department

defuse, diffuse Occasionally confused. *Defuse* means to make less harmful; *diffuse* means to spread thinly.

de Gaulle, Charles (1890–1970) President of France 1944–6, 1959–69

de haut en bas (Fr.) with contempt

De Havilland aircraft

Deirdre of the Sorrows play by J. M. Synge (1910)

déjà vu

de jure (Lat.) according to law. See also DE FACTO.

Dekker, Thomas (c. 1570–c. 1640) English playwright

de Klerk, F. W. (for **Frederik Willem**) (1936–) President of South Africa 1989–94; co-winner with Nelson Mandela of the Nobel Peace Prize 1993

de Kooning, Willem (1904–97) Dutch-born American painter

Delacroix, Eugène (1789–1863) French painter

de la Mare, Walter (1873–1956) English novelist and poet

Delaney, Shelagh (1939–) English dramatist

De La Rue British security printing firm

de la Tour, Frances (1944–) British actress

de La Tour, Georges (1593–1652) French painter

De Laurentiis, Dino (1919–) Italian film producer; his formal first name is Agostino

delectable, not *-ible*

Deledda, Grazia (1871–1936) Italian novelist, awarded Nobel Prize for Literature 1926

deleterious

delftware (no cap.)

Delilah

DeLillo, Don (1936–) American novelist

Delius, Frederick (1862–1934) British composer

Deloitte Touche Tohmatsu (no commas) accountancy company

DeLorean automobile, named for John Z. DeLorean (1925–2005)

de los Angeles, Victoria (1923–2005) Spanish soprano

Delta Air Lines (note *Air Lines* two words)

Del Toro, Benicio (1967–) Puerto Rican actor

De Lucchi, Michele (1951–) Italian architect and designer

demagogue

de mal en pis, *de pis en pis* (Fr.) Both mean from bad to worse.

de Maupassant, (Henri René Albert) Guy (1850–93) French writer of short stories and novels

dementia praecox schizophrenia

Dementieva, Elena (1981–) Russian tennis player

demerara sugar (not cap.)

Demerol (cap.) type of medication

Demeter in Greek mythology, the goddess of agriculture and fertility; the Roman equivalent is Ceres

De Mille, Cecil B. (for **Blount**) (1881–1959) American film producer and director, noted for epics

demi-monde (Fr.) term loosely applied to prostitutes, kept women or anyone else living on the wrong side of respectability

demise does not mean decline; it means death.

de mortuis nil nisi bonum (Lat.) say nothing but good of the dead

Demosthenes (384–322 BC) Athenian orator and statesman
Denali National Park and Preserve, Alaska Denali is also an alternative name for Mount McKinley, North America's highest peak (20,320 feet/6,194 metres), which stands within the park.
Deng Xiaoping (1904–97) Chinese elder statesman
De Niro, Robert (1943–) American actor
dénouement outcome or solution
deodorant
Deo gratias (Lat.) thanks be to God
Deo volente (Lat.) God willing
De Palma, Brian (1941–) American film director
Department for Business, Enterprise and Regulatory Reform abbr. **BERR**; British government department, replaced the Department of Trade and Industry
Department for Children, Schools and Families abbr. DCSF; British government department, replaced the Department for Education
Department for Communities and Local Government British government department; it now styles itself simply **Communities and Local Government**
Department for (not *of*) **Culture, Media and Sport** abbr. DCMS; British government department
Department for (not *of*) **Environment, Food and Rural Affairs** abbr. DEFRA; British government department
Department for Innovation, Universities and Skills abbr. DIUS; British government department
dependant, dependent The first is a noun referring to a person, the second an adjective referring to a situation.
deplete, reduce Though their meanings are roughly the same, *deplete* has the additional connotation of

injurious reduction. As the Evanses note, a garrison may be reduced by administrative order, but depleted by sickness.

deplore Strictly, you may deplore a thing, but not a person. I may deplore your behaviour, but I cannot deplore you.

deprecate does not mean to play down or show modesty, as is often intended. It means to disapprove of strongly or to protest against.

de profundis (Lat.) from the depths; a heartfelt cry

De Quincy, Thomas (1785–1859) English writer

de rigueur Often misspelled. Note the two *us*.

derisive, **derisory** Something that is *derisive* conveys ridicule or contempt. Something that is *derisory* invites it. A derisory offer is likely to provoke a derisive response.

DERV abbr. of diesel-engined road vehicles

desalination, not *desalinization*

descendible

Deschamps, Didier (1968–) French footballer, captain of 1998 World Cup-winning team

Deschanel, Zooey (1980–) American actress

Deschutes River, Oregon

descry catch sight of

déshabillé (Fr.) untidily or incompletely dressed; sometimes rendered in English as **dishabille**

De Sica, Vittorio (1902–74) Italian film actor and director

desiccate

Des Moines capital of Iowa; pronounced *duh moyne*

de Soto, Hernando (c. 1496–1542) Spanish explorer

desperate

despite, **in spite of** There is no distinction between the two. A common construction is seen here: 'But despite the fall in sterling, Downing Street officials were at pains to play down any suggestion of crisis.' Because *despite* and *in spite of* indicate a change of emphasis, 'but' is generally superfluous with either. It is enough to say: 'Despite the fall in sterling, Downing Street officials . . .'

Des Plaines   Illinois river and suburb of Chicago; pronounced *dess plainz*

destroy is an incomparable – almost. If a house is consumed by fire, it is enough to say that it was destroyed, not that it was 'completely destroyed' or 'totally destroyed'. However, and illogical as it may seem, it is all right to speak of a house that has been partly destroyed. There is simply no other way of putting it without resorting to more circuitous descriptions. That is perhaps absurd and inconsistent, but ever thus was English.

destructible

detestable

de trop (Fr.) excessive

deus ex machina In drama, a character or event that arrives late in the action and provides a solution.

Deuteronomy the last book of the Pentateuch in the Old Testament

Deutschmark former currency of Germany. The euro is now used.

Deutsches Museum, Munich

de Valera, Éamon (1882–1975) US-born Prime Minister of Ireland 1919–21, 1932–48 and 1957–9, and President 1959–73

devilry/deviltry Either is acceptable.

Devil's Island, French Guiana site of infamous prison; in French, île du Diable

Devils Playground (no apos.) desert in California

Devils Tower National Monument, Wyoming (no apos.)

Devon, Earl of, but **Duke of Devonshire**

dexterous is preferred, but **dextrous** is acceptable.

Dhaulagiri Himalayan mountain, seventh highest in the world (26,810 feet/8,172 metres)

dhow Arab boat

DHTML short for Dynamic Hypertext Markup Language; computer terminology

diaeresis (US **dieresis**), the punctuation mark consisting of two dots above a vowel, as in Brontë or Chloë, is used to indicate that adjacent vowels are to be sounded separately. (It is a curiosity of English that the word *diaeresis* is entitled to, but never given, the mark it describes.) The diaeresis mark always goes above the second vowel in the pair. It should not be confused with the German *umlaut,* which also consists of two dots, as in Göring or Müller, but which signifies a phonetic shift rather than an elaboration into separate sounds.

Diaghilev, Sergei (Pavlovich) (1872–1929) Russian ballet impresario, founder of the Ballets Russes

diagnosis, **prognosis** To make a *diagnosis* is to identify and define a problem, usually a disease. A *prognosis* is a projection of the course and likely outcome of a problem. *Diagnosis* applies only to conditions, not to people. Thus 'Asbestos victims were not diagnosed in large numbers until the 1960s' (*Time*) is not quite right. It was the victims' conditions that were not diagnosed, not the victims themselves.

dialect, **patois** Both describe the form of language prevailing in a region and can be used interchangeably, though *patois* is normally better reserved for contexts involving French or its variants. 'He spoke in the patois of

Yorkshire' is at best jocular. The plural of *patois*, incidentally, is also *patois*.

Dial 'M' for Murder note quotation marks around *M*; drama by Frederick Knott and film by Alfred Hitchcock

dialysis

Diana Roman goddess of the moon and the hunt; identified with the Greek goddess Artemis

diaphragm

diarrhoea (US **diarrhea**)

Dickins & Jones London department store

Dickinson, Emily (Elizabeth) (1830–86) American poet

Diderot, Denis (1713–84) French encyclopaedist and philosopher

Diefenbaker, John George (1895–1979) Prime Minister of Canada 1957–63

Dien Bien Phu battle in 1954 that led the French to pull out of Indochina (later Vietnam)

Dieppe French port

diesel, not *deisel*

Diet Japanese parliament

dietitian

Diet of Worms an assembly concerned with Luther and the Protestant Reformation (1521)

Dietrich, Marlene (1904–92) German-born actress and singer; born Maria Magdalene von Losch

Dieu et mon droit (Fr.) God and my right, motto of the British royal family

different Often used unnecessarily as in 'It is found in more than 250 different types of plants.' In such constructions it can nearly always be deleted without loss.

different from, to, than Among the more tenacious beliefs of many writers and editors is that *different* may be followed only by *from*. In fact, the belief has no real basis. *Different from* is, to be sure, the usual form in most sentences and the only acceptable form in some, as when it precedes a noun or pronoun ('My car is different from his'; 'Men are different from women'). But when *different* introduces a clause, there can be no valid objection to following it with a *to* (though this usage is chiefly British) or *than*, as in this sentence by John Maynard Keynes: 'How different things appear in Washington than in London.' You may, if you insist, change it to 'How different things appear in Washington from how they appear in London,' but all it gives you is more words, not better grammar.

diffuse to spread out; not to be confused with *defuse*, meaning to make safe

digestible

dignitary, not -*tory*

dike/dyke Either is acceptable.

dilapidated, dilapidation

dilatory, not -*tary*

dildos

dilemma refers to a situation involving two courses of action, both unsatisfactory. A person who cannot decide what he wants for breakfast is not in a dilemma.

dilettante a lover of, or dabbler in, the fine arts; most often used with a hint of condescension; pl. **dilettantes** or **dilettanti**

diligence, diligent

dilly-dally

DiMaggio (no space) for the baseball players (and brothers) **Joe** (1914–99) and **Dom** (1917–)

Diners Club International (no apos.)

Dinesen, Isak   pen name of Karen Blixen (1885–1962), Danish writer and baroness

dingo   wild Australian dog; pl. **dingoes**

Dione   moon of Saturn

Dionysius the Elder (c. 430–367 BC)   tyrant of Syracuse who suspended the famous sword above the head of Damocles

Dionysus (or **Dionysos**), not -*ius*   Greek god of wine and revelry, corresponding to the Roman god Bacchus; the adjective is **Dionysian** or **Dionysiac**

diphtheria   Note that the first syllable is spelled *diph-*, not *dip-*, and is pronounced accordingly.

dirigible   capable of being guided; airship

dirigisme (Fr.)   dominance of the economy by the state; adjective is *dirigiste*

dirndl   full skirt or Alpine style of dress

disassemble, dissemble   The first means to take apart; the second means to pretend.

disassociate, dissociate   The first is not incorrect, but the second has the virtue of brevity.

disastrous

disc, disk   *Disc* generally is used for contexts involving music and entertainment (*compact disc, disc jockey*), machinery (*disc brakes*) and anatomy (*slipped disc*), and *disk* is used in contexts involving computers and memory storage (*hard disk, floppy disk*).

discernible, not -*able*

discomfit, discomfort   'In this she is greatly assisted by her husband ... who enjoys spreading discomfiture in a good cause as much as she does' (*Observer*). The writer here, like many before him, clearly meant *discomfort*, which has nothing in common with *discomfiture* beyond a superficial resemblance. *Discomfit* means to rout, overwhelm or completely disconcert. Some dictionaries now accept the newer sense of to perplex or induce uneasiness, but I would submit that the distinction is very much worth preserving. If *discomfort* is the condition you have in mind, why not use that word and leave *discomfiture* for less discriminating users?

discotheque

discreet, discrete The first means circumspect, careful, showing good judgement ('He promised to be discreet in his inquiries'). The second means unattached or unrelated ('The compound was composed of discrete particles').

dishabille variant of **déshabillé**; untidily or incompletely dressed

dishevelled

disinterested, uninterested The first means neutral, the second not caring. A *disinterested* person is one who has no stake in the outcome of an event; an *uninterested* person is one who doesn't care. As with DISCOMFIT and DISCOMFORT (see above), the distinction is an important one and worth observing.

dismissible

Disneyland, Disney World They are separate places. Disneyland is in Anaheim, California. Disney World is near Orlando, Florida. The European version is Disneyland Paris.

dispensable

disposal, disposition If you are talking about getting rid of, use *disposal* ('the disposal of nuclear weapons'). If you mean arranging, use *disposition* ('the disposition of troops on the battlefield').

Disprin (cap.)

Disraeli, Benjamin, Earl of Beaconsfield (1804–81) British Prime Minister 1868, 1874–80. The family name was spelled d'Israeli by his father, Isaac (1766–1848).

dissatisfy, dissatisfied, dissatisfaction Note -*ss*-.

dissect, dissection

dissemble, disassemble The first means to pretend; the second means to take apart.

dissent, but **dissension**

dissimilar

dissipate

dissociate/disassociate The first is preferred, but either is acceptable.

dissolvable

distrait, distraught The first means abstracted in thought, absent-minded; the second means deeply agitated.

disturb, perturb They can often be used interchangeably, but generally the first is better applied to physical agitation, the second to mental agitation.

DIUS Department for Innovation, Universities and Skills (UK)

dived, dove Either is acceptable.

diverge When two things diverge, they move farther apart (just as when they converge they come together). It should not be applied freely to any difference of opinion, but only to those in which a rift is widening.

divergences, not -*ies*

divertissement light diversion

Divina Commedia, La Dante's *Divine Comedy*

divvy to divide, especially equally, as with a jackpot

Dixie states that fought for the Confederacy in the American Civil War, now used loosely as a synonym for the South

Djakarta, Indonesia Use Jakarta.

Djibouti African republic, formerly French Somaliland and, briefly, French Territory of Afars and Issas; the capital is also called Djibouti

Djokovic, Novak (1987–) Serbian tennis player

DNA deoxyribonucleic acid

Dnieper river in Russia, Belarus and Ukraine

Dniester river in Ukraine and Moldova

Dobbs Ferry, New York

Dobermann pinscher (US **Doberman pinscher**) breed of dog. Ludwig Dobermann was the breeder for whom the dogs are named.

Dodecanese chain of twelve Greek islands, including Rhodes and Kos

Dodgson, Charles Lutwidge (1832–98) real name of Lewis Carroll

Dodoma capital of Tanzania

Dodsworth novel by Sinclair Lewis (1929)

doggerel

dogsbody a person given menial tasks to perform for a superior

doily, pl. **doilies**

Dolce & Gabbana Italian fashion firm

Dollfuss, Engelbert (1892–1934) Austrian Chancellor 1932–4, assassinated by Austrian Nazis

doll's house (US **dollhouse**)

dolour (US **dolor**), but **dolorous**

Domenichino (1581–1641) Italian painter

Domesday Book pronounced *doomsday*; census of England carried out in 1086

Dominica small (pop. 69,000) Caribbean island state, capital Roseau; not to be confused with the nearby **Dominican**

Republic, capital Santo Domingo

dominoes

Dom Pérignon champagne

Donatello (c. 1386–1466) Italian sculptor, real name Donato di Niccolò di Betto Bardi

Donegal, Irish county, but **Marquess of Donegall**

Don Giovanni opera by Mozart (1787)

Donizetti, Gaetano (1797–1848) Italian composer

Donleavy, J. P. (for **James Patrick**) (1926–) American-born Irish writer and artist

Donne, John (c. 1571–1631) English poet

doorjamb

doppelganger (Ger.) a person's ghostly double

Doppler effect the change that occurs in sound waves as the source and the hearer move closer together or further apart; named after Christian Johann Doppler (1803–53), Austrian physicist

dormouse for the small rodent, which isn't actually a mouse at all. The name is thought to be a corruption of the Norman French *dormeus*, meaning sleepy. The plural is *dormice.*

Dorneywood, Buckinghamshire country house used as official residence by any minister chosen by the Prime Minister

dos and don'ts, not *do's*

Dosewallips River, Washington

Dos Passos, John (1896–1970) American writer

Dostoyevsky, Fyodor, is the commonest spelling of the Russian novelist (1821–81), but there are many possible variants for both names.

Double Top Mountain, New York, but **Doubletop Peak**, Wyoming

doubt if, that, whether Idiom demands some selectivity in the choice of conjunction to introduce a clause after *doubt* and *doubtful.* The rule is simple: *doubt that* should be reserved for negative contexts ('There is no doubt that . . .'; 'It was never doubtful that . . .') and interrogative ones ('Do you have any doubt that . . . ?'; 'Was it ever doubtful that . . . ?'). *Whether* or *if* should be used in all others ('I doubt if he will come'; 'It is doubtful whether the rain will stop').

doubtless, undoubtedly, indubitably *Doubtless* usually suggests a tone of reluctance or resignation: 'You are doubtless right.' *Undoubtedly* carries more conviction: 'You are undoubtedly right.' *Indubitably* is a somewhat jocular synonym for either.

Douglas-Home, Alec (Alexander Frederick), Baron Home of the Hirsel (1903–95) British Prime Minister 1963–4; brother of **William Douglas-Home** (1912–92), playwright

Douglass, Frederick (1817–95) escaped American slave who became a leading abolitionist and statesman; born Frederick Augustus Washington Bailey

Dounreay nuclear power station, Caithness, Scotland

douse, dowse The first means to drench; the second means to search for water.

Douwe Egberts Koninklijke Tabaksfabriek-Koffiebranderijen-Theehandel NV full name of Dutch coffee and tea company; literally, Douwe Egberts Royal Tobacco Factory–Coffee Roasters–Tea Traders Limited

Dow Jones industrial average (no hyphen, last two words no caps)

Downers Grove (no apos.), Illinois

Down House, Charles Darwin's home, is in **Downe,** Kent.

Down syndrome congenital subnormality, formerly called mongolism; named after the British physician J. L. H. Down (1828–96). Sometimes still called **Down's syndrome,** but increasingly the convention in medical circles is to abandon the possessive in the names of diseases and syndromes (Parkinson disease, Hodgkin disease).

draft, draught *Draft* applies to military conscription, preliminary plans, rough sketches and money orders; *draught* applies to beer, chill winds, ships' displacement and working horses. A draftsman draws up documents; a draughtsman makes drawings. In the US, *draft* is the spelling used for all meanings.

dramatis personae cast of characters.

Drechsler, Heike (1964–) German sprinter and long jumper

Dreiser, Theodore (1871–1945) American writer

Dresdner Kleinwort Wasserstein investment bank

Dreyfus, Alfred (1859–1935) French officer whose wrongful imprisonment on Devil's Island became a celebrated controversy

Dreyfuss, Richard (1949–) American actor

Driberg, Tom, Lord Bradwell (1905–76) British politician and journalist

drier, dryer *Dryer* is an appliance for drying clothes and hair; *drier* is the condition of being more dry.

droit de seigneur a feudal lord's supposed right to spend the first night with a vassal's bride

drunkenness Note -*nn*-.

dual, duel *Dual* means twofold; *duel* describes a fight between two parties.

du Barry, Marie Jeanne Bécu, Comtesse (1743–93) mistress of Louis XV, beheaded during the French Revolution

Dubček, Alexander (1921–92)   First Secretary of the Communist Party (i.e., head of state) in Czechoslovakia 1968–9; his reforms led to the Soviet invasion of the country in 1968

dubiety the state of being dubious

Du Bois, W. E. B. (for **William Edward Burghardt**) (1868–1963) American political activist and civil rights leader

Duchamp, Marcel (1887–1968) French painter

dudgeon   resentment; *in high dudgeon*, resentful, feeling offended

duenna governess or chaperone; in Spanish, *dueña*

due to   Most authorities continue to accept that *due* is an adjective only and must always modify a noun. Thus 'He was absent due to illness' would be wrong. Make it either 'He was absent because of [or owing to] illness' or recast the sentence to give *due* a noun to modify, e.g., 'His absence was due to illness.' The rule is mystifyingly inconsistent – no one has ever really explained why 'owing to' used prepositionally is acceptable while 'due to' used prepositionally is not – but it should perhaps still be observed, at least in formal writing, if only to avoid a charge of ignorance.

duffel bag, **duffel coat** after the Belgian town of Duffel

Dufy, Raoul (1877–1953) French painter

Duisburg, Germany pronounced *doos-boork*

Dukakis, Michael (Stanley) (1933–) US presidential candidate 1988, governor of Massachusetts 1975–9, 1983–90

Duma Russian parliament

Dumas, Alexandre (1802–70) French novelist and dramatist, father of **Alexandre Dumas** (1824–95), known as **Dumas fils**, also a writer

du Maurier, Dame Daphne (1907–89) English writer

Dumbarton, West Dunbartonshire, Scotland; **Dumbarton Oaks**, Washington, DC; see also DUNBARTON

dumbfound, dumfound The first is preferred but both are acceptable.

dumdum bullet

Dummkopf (Ger.) a stupid person; not *dumb-*

Dum spiro, spero (Lat.) 'While I breathe, there is hope.'

Dun & Bradstreet Corporation provider of business credit information

Dunaway, Faye (1941–) American actress

Dunbarton former Scottish county, now comprising the unitary authorities of East Dunbartonshire and West Dunbartonshire. See also DUMBARTON.

Dunkin' Donuts

Dunkirk French port; in French, Dunkerque

Dun Laoghaire Irish port near Dublin; pronounced *dun-leery*. In the Gaelic spelling **Dún** has an accent.

Duns Scotus, Johannes (c. 1270–1308) Scottish philosopher and theologian

duomo (It.) cathedral; pl. *duomi*

Du Pont formally E. I. du Pont de Nemours & Company; US chemicals business. But on second or informal references it is normally spelled **DuPont** (one word). The place in Washington, DC, is **Dupont Circle**.

du Pré, Jacqueline (1945–87) British cellist

Dürer, Albrecht (1471–1528) German artist and engraver

duress coercion

Durrell, Gerald (1925–95) naturalist and writer; brother of **Lawrence Durrell** (1912–90), novelist

durum a type of wheat

Dushanbe capital of Tajikistan

Düsseldorf capital of North Rhine-Westphalia, Germany
Dutchess County, New York State
Dutch Guiana former name of Suriname
Dvořák, Antonín (1841–1904), Czech composer
dwarfs is generally preferred to *dwarves.*
dyeing, **dying** The first means adding colour; the second means becoming dead.
Dyfed Welsh county formed from the former counties of Pembrokeshire, Cardiganshire and Carmarthenshire
dysentery
dyslexia
dysprosium chemical element
dystrophy lacking adequate nutrition
Dzibilchaltún National Park, Mexico

each When *each* precedes the noun or pronoun to which it refers, the verb should be singular: 'Each of us was . . .' When it follows the noun or pronoun the verb should be plural: 'They each were . . .' *Each* not only influences the number of the verb, it also influences the number of later nouns and pronouns. In simpler terms, if *each* precedes the verb, subsequent nouns and pronouns should be plural (e.g., 'They each are subject to sentences of five years'), but if *each* follows the verb, the subsequent nouns and pronouns should be singular ('They are each subject to a sentence of five years').

each and every is hopelessly tautological. Choose one or the other.

each other, one another A few arbiters of usage continue to insist on *each other* for two things and *one another* for more than two. There is no harm in observing such a distinction, but also little to be gained from it, and, as Fowler long ago noted, the practice has no basis in historical usage. The possessive form is **each other's**, not *each others'*.

EADS short for European Aeronautic Defence and Space Company, maker of Airbus planes

Eagels, Jeanne (1890–1929) American actress

Earhart, Amelia (1897–1937)   American aviator who disappeared while trying to circumnavigate the globe

Earl's Court, London

Earnhardt, Dale (1951–) racing car driver

earring Note -*rr*-.

Earth, **earth** When considering it as a planet, particularly in apposition to other cosmic features, *Earth* is normally capitalized. In more general senses ('He shot the arrow and it fell to earth') lower case is usually favoured.

East Chester, New York, and **Eastchester**, New York (separate places)

easyJet low-fare airline

eau-de-vie, pl. **eaux-de-vie** French term for brandy from fruit other than grapes

eBay

Ebbets Field, Brooklyn, New York home of the Brooklyn Dodgers baseball team, 1913–57

EBITDA short for *earnings before interest, taxes, depreciation and amortization*; in finance, it is a measure of a company's profits before various deductions.

Eboracum Roman name for York

Ecce Homo (Lat.) 'behold the man'; in art, a painting of Christ wearing the crown of thorns

Ecclesiastes, **Ecclesiasticus** The first is a book in the Old Testament, the second a book in the Old Testament Apocrypha.

ECG electrocardiogram; records heart function

éclat brilliant display or effect, notable success, renown

Eco, Umberto (1932–) Italian academic and novelist

economic, **economical** If what you mean is cheap and thrifty, use *economical*. For every other sense use *economic*. An economic rent is one that is not too cheap for the landlord. An economical rent is one that is not too expensive for the tenant.

ecstasy

Ecuadorean is generally the preferred spelling for a person or product from Ecuador.

Eddy, Mary Baker (1821–1910) American religious leader, founder of the Christian Science Church, formally the Church of Christ, Scientist

Eddystone Lighthouse, Eddystone Rocks off Plymouth in the English Channel

Eden, (Robert) Anthony, Earl of Avon (1897–1977) British Prime Minister 1955–7

Edgbaston district of Birmingham, site of the famous cricket ground

Edgware Road street and Underground station in London

Edmonton capital of Alberta, Canada

Edmund Hall, St, Oxford, not to be confused with **St Edmund's College**, Cambridge

Edmund Ironside (c. 980–1016) English king

Education and Skills, Department for British government department that ceased to exist in June 2007, when most of its responsibilities were transferred to a new **Department for Children, Schools and Families**

Eduskunta Parliament of Finland

EEG electroencephalogram; records brain function

eerie, frighteningly strange; not to be confused with **eyrie**, an eagle's nest

effect, affect As a verb, *effect* means to accomplish ('The prisoners effected an escape'); *affect* means to influence ('Smoking may affect your health') or to adopt a pose or manner ('He affected ignorance'). As a noun, the word needed is almost always *effect* (as in 'personal effects' or 'the damaging effects of war'). *Affect* as a noun has a narrow psychological meaning to do with emotional states (by way of which it is related to *affection*).

effete does not mean effeminate and weak, as it is often used. It means exhausted and barren. An effete poet is not necessarily foppish, but rather someone whose creative impulses are spent.

e.g., i.e. The first is an abbreviation of *exempli gratia* and means 'for example', as in 'Some words are homonyms, e.g., *blew* and *blue*.' The second is the abbreviation for *id est* and means 'that is' or 'that is to say', as in 'He is pusil-lanimous, i.e., lacking in courage.'

eggplant (US) aubergine

Eglin Air Force Base, Florida

egoism, egotism The first pertains to the philosophical notion that a person can prove nothing beyond the existence of his own mind. It is the opposite of altruism and is better left to contexts involving metaphysics and ethics. If all you wish to suggest is inflated vanity or pre-occupation with the self, use *egotism.*

Eichmann, Adolf (1906–62) notorious Nazi war criminal, head of Gestapo; captured in Argentina by Israeli agents in 1960 and tried and executed in Israel

Eid Muslim festival that marks the end of Ramadan

Eiffel Tower, Paris, but **Eifel Mountains**, Germany

Eigg, Inner Hebrides, Scotland pronounced *egg*

Eilean common name among Scottish islands (e.g., Eilean Dubh, Eilean More); pronounced *ell´-en*

Eileithyia Greek goddess of childbirth

Eindhoven, Netherlands

Eisenbahn (Ger.) railway

Eisenhower, Dwight David (1890–1969)   US general and President 1953–61

Eisenstaedt, Alfred (1898–1995)   German-born American photographer

Eisenstein, Sergei (1898–1948)   Russian film-maker

eisteddfod   Welsh festival or competition of music or literature; pl. **eisteddfods** or (in Welsh) **eisteddfodau**

either   *Either* suggests a duality and is almost always better avoided when the context involves quantities of more than two, as in 'Decisions on Mansfield's economy are now made in either Detroit, Pittsburgh or New York.' Often in such constructions, *either* is unnecessary anyway; delete it and the sentence says no less. A separate problem with *either* is seen here: 'But in every case the facts either proved too elusive or the explanations too arcane to be satisfactory.' *Either* should be placed before 'the facts' or deleted; for a discussion, see BOTH . . . AND. For a discussion of errors of number involving *either*, see NEITHER.

eke   means to add to something in a meagre way or with difficulty, not to gain a close but favourable result. A hungry person might eke out a supply of food, but a football team does not eke out a victory.

El Alamein/Al Alamein   Egyptian village that gave its name to two battles in the Second World War

El Dorado   legendary Latin American city of gold

Electra   in Greek mythology, the daughter of Agamemnon and Clytemnestra, and the subject of plays by Sophocles, Euripides and Aeschylus. An *Electra complex* is an unnatural attachment to a father by a daughter. See also OEDIPUS COMPLEX.

electrolyte   a solution that conducts electricity

elegy, **eulogy** The first is a mournful poem; the second is a tribute to the dead.

elemental, **elementary** *Elemental* refers to things that are basic or primary: 'Physiology is an elemental part of a medical student's studies.' *Elementary* means simple or introductory: 'This phrase book provides an elementary guide to Spanish.'

elephantiasis condition of abnormal swelling caused by disease of the lymph nodes

Elgin Marbles, British Museum pronounced with a hard *g*: *el-gin*, not *el-jin*

El Guerrouj, Hicham (1974–) Moroccan middle-distance runner, nicknamed the 'King of the Mile'

elicit, **extract**, **extort** These three are broadly synonymous, but are distinguished by the degree of force that they imply. *Elicit*, the mildest of the three, means to draw or coax out, and can additionally suggest an element of craftiness: you can elicit information without the informant being aware that he has divulged it. *Extract* suggests a stronger and more persistent effort, possibly involving threats or importuning. *Extort* is stronger still and suggests clear threats of violence or harm.

Elien signature of the Bishop of Ely

Eli Lilly, not *Lilley* US pharmaceuticals company

Eliot, George pen name of Mary Ann (later Marian) Evans (1819–80), English author

Eliot, T. S. (for **Thomas Stearns**) (1888–1965) American-born British poet, critic and playwright; awarded Nobel Prize for Literature 1948

Elizabeth II (1926–) Queen of the United Kingdom 1952– In the UK her formal title is Elizabeth the Second, by the Grace of God, of the United Kingdom of Great Britain and Northern Ireland and of Her Other Realms and Territories, Queen, Head of the Commonwealth, Defender of the Faith. The title varies somewhat in other Commonwealth countries.

Ellesmere Port, Cheshire

Ellice Islands former name of Tuvalu; Pacific island group

Elliott, Denholm (1922–92) British actor

Elliott Bay, Seattle

Ellis Island site of the former immigration centre in New York

El Salvador Central American country; capital San Salvador. The people are Salvadorans.

Elstree film studios, England

Élysée Palace, Paris strictly speaking, not *the*; official home of French presidents

Elysium, Elysian Fields in Greek mythology, paradise

embalmment Note -*mm*-.

embarcadero (Sp.) wharf

embargoes

embarrass, embarrassment Both are misspelled more often than they should be. Note, however, that the French spelling is *embarras*, as in *embarras de richesses* ('an embarrassment of riches') and *embarras du choix* ('an embarrassment of choice').

Emerson, Ralph Waldo (1803–82) American poet and essayist

émigré an emigrant, particularly a political refugee

Emilia-Romagna region of Italy, capital Bologna

Emmanuel College, Cambridge University

Emmental a type of Swiss cheese with holes in it

empathy, sympathy *Empathy* denotes a close emotional understanding of the feelings or problems of another. It is thus similar in meaning to *compassion*. *Sympathy* is more general. It can denote a closeness of understanding, but it can equally suggest no more than an abstract or intellectual awareness of another's misfortune. *Empathy* generally applies only to serious misfortunes; *sympathy* can apply to any small annoyance or setback.

Empedocles (c. 495–c. 435 BC) Greek philosopher and poet

emphysema lung disease

empower, not *en-*

EMU In the context of the European Union, it stands for **Economic** (not *European*) **and Monetary Union**.

encomium a lavish tribute or eulogy; pl. **encomiums**

encumbrance, not -*erance*

encyclopedia, **encyclopedist**, but *Encyclopaedia Britannica*

endemic regularly found in a particular place. See EPIDEMIC.

Endymion in Greek mythology, a young man loved by the moon and condemned to eternal sleep

enfant terrible (Fr.) troublesome young person; anyone of embarrassingly indiscreet or unruly behaviour

Engels, Friedrich (1820–95) German social scientist and philosopher

Englischer Garten, Munich, Germany

English Nature now called **Natural England**; a conservation authority

Enniskillen, Northern Ireland site of infamous IRA bombing in 1987; the army regiment is the Inniskilling Dragoons

ennoble

ennui world-weariness

enormity does not, as is frequently thought, indicate size, but rather refers to something that is wicked, monstrous and outrageous ('The enormity of Hitler's crimes will never be forgotten'). If what you require is a word denoting large scale, try 'immensity' or 'vastness'.

en passant (Fr.) in passing

enquiry See QUERY.

enrol, enrolment (US **enroll, enrollment**)

ENSA Entertainments National Service Association; organization that provided entertainment for troops during the Second World War

ensure, insure In the UK, use *insure* in the sense of claiming compensation and *ensure* for the general sense of making sure.

entelechy the act of changing from potential to actual, or a kind of vital force for living things

entente cordiale term used to describe a long-standing amity between countries

Entertaining Mr Sloane, not *Sloan* comedy by Joe Orton (1964)

enthrall

entomology the study of insects; not to be confused with **etymology**, the study of words

entr'acte in the theatre an interval between acts or an entertainment performed then

entrecôte a boneless steak cut from sirloin of beef

entrepôt a trading place or storehouse

envelop (verb) to wrap up

envelope (noun) container for letters, or anything that envelops

envisage, envision Both words suggest the calling up of a mental image. *Envision* is slightly the loftier of the two. You might envision a better life for yourself, but if all you are thinking about is how the dining room will look when the walls have been repainted, *envisage* is probably the better word. If no mental image is involved, neither word is correct. A rough rule is that if you find yourself following either word with *that* you are using it incorrectly, as here: 'He envisaged that there would be no access to the school from the main road' (cited by Gowers).

Eocene geological epoch

EOKA Ethniki Organosis Kypriakou Agonos (National Organization for Cypriot Struggle); Greek Cypriot underground movement

E.On German utility company

epaulette (US **epaulet**) a decoration worn on the shoulder of a uniform; in French, *épaulette*

EPCOT Environmental Prototype Community of Tomorrow, Disney World, Florida

épée thin, flexible sword used in fencing

ephemera items of no lasting value

epicene of uncertain sex

epicurean person devoted to the pursuit of pleasure; when capitalized it refers to the philosophy of Epicurus (341–270 BC)

epidemic Strictly speaking, only people can suffer an epidemic (the word means 'in or among people'). An outbreak of disease among animals is *epizootic*. It is also worth noting that *epidemic* refers only to outbreaks. When a disease or other problem is of long standing, it is *endemic*.

epiglottis

epigram, **epigraph** The first is a short, witty saying or poem. The second is an inscription, as on a monument or statue, or an introductory quotation at the beginning of a book or substantial block of text.

Epiphany 6 January, or the twelfth day of Christmas, on the Christian calendar; also **epiphany**, a moment of revelation

'Epipsychidion' poem by Shelley (1821)

epistemology the theory of knowledge

epithet, strictly speaking, describes a word or phrase that is used in place of a name. Calling Tarzan 'King of the Jungle' is to employ an epithet. More commonly nowadays, however, *epithet* is used to describe an abusive or contemptuous utterance. A few authorities disdain this looser usage, but it is accepted now by most dictionaries. *Epithet* should not be confused with **epitaph**, which is an inscription on a gravestone or other written memorial to a dead person.

E pluribus unum (Lat.) 'out of many, one'; the motto on the official seal of the United States

eponymous of a tool, for instance, 'named after its inventor'

equable, **equitable** Most dictionaries define *equable* as meaning steady and unvarying, but it should also convey the sense of being remote from extremes. A consistently hot climate is not equable, no matter how unvarying the temperature. Similarly, someone whose outlook is invariably sunny cannot properly be described as having an equable temperament. *Equitable*, with which *equable* is sometimes confused, means fair and impartial. An equitable settlement is a just one.

equally as is always wrong. 'This is equally as good' should be 'This is equally good' or 'This is as good.'

Equatorial Guinea formerly Spanish Guinea; west African country, capital Malabo

equerry royal attendant

equivocator one who uses evasive language

Equuleus constellation near Pegasus

equus (Lat.) horse

Erasmus, Desiderius (1466–1536) Dutch philosopher

Eratosthenes (c. 276–c. 194 BC)   Greek mathematician, astronomer and geographer; calculated Earth's circumference

Erdelyi, Arthur (1908–77)   Hungarian-born British mathematician

Erdoğan, Recep Tayyip (1954–)   Prime Minister of Turkey 2003–

Erewhon (1872) and **Erewhon Revisited** (1901)   satirical novels by Samuel Butler. *Erewhon* is an anagram of *nowhere.*

Erhard, Ludwig (1897–1977)   Chancellor of West Germany 1963–6

Ericson (or **Ericsson** or **Eriksson**), **Leif** (*fl.* 10th c.)   Norse explorer; the Swedish electrical group is **Ericsson**

Erie Lackawanna Railway   The service ran between New Jersey and Chicago.

Eriksson, Sven-Göran (1948–)   Swedish football manager; England national team coach 2002–6

ERNIE   Electronic Random Number Indicator Equipment; the device that selects the winners of British premium bond draws

Ernst & Young   international accountancy firm

escutcheon   a shield bearing a coat of arms

Eskimos is the plural of Eskimo, but the preferred term is **Inuit** (sing. and pl.).

esoteric   obscure; intended for people with specialist knowledge

especially, **specially**   *Specially* means for a specific purpose or occasion, as in 'a specially designed wedding dress'. *Especially* means particularly or exceptionally, as in 'an especially talented singer'. A simple guide is to ask yourself whether you could substitute *particularly*. If so, the word you want is *especially.*

estimated at about, as in 'The crowd was estimated at about 50,000,' is wrong. Because *estimated* contains the idea of an approximation, *about* is superfluous. Delete it.

Eszterhas, Joe (1944–) Hungarian-born American screenwriter

ETA Euzkadi ta Azkatasuna (Basque Nation and Liberty); Basque separatist organization. (*ETA* can also mean 'estimated time of arrival'.)

et al. abbr. of Latin *et alia*, *et alibi* and *et alii*, meaning respectively 'and other things', 'and other places' and 'and other persons'; note full stop after *al* only

et cetera when spelled out, but **etc.** (closed up) when abbreviated

Etherege, Sir George (c. 1635–91) English playwright

Ethernet (cap.) computer networking system

etiolated, aetiology (US **etiology**) *Etiolated* means weak and pale, especially from lack of light; *aetiology* is the investigation of the causes of disease.

Etobicoke Toronto suburb

Étoile, l' area around the Arc de Triomphe in Paris

'Et tu, Brute?' (Lat.) 'You too, Brutus?', Julius Caesar's dying words in Shakespeare's play *Julius Caesar* (III. i. 77); used to signify a feeling of betrayal

etymology the study of the origin and development of words; not to be confused with **entomology**, the study of insects

eucalyptus, pl. **eucalyptuses**

Euclidean

eukaryote a kind of organism

Eumenides in Greek mythology, another name for the Furies

euonymus any tree or shrub of the genus *Euonymus*

euphemism a mild expression substituted for another

more objectionable or indelicate one

euphonious pleasant-sounding

euphuism and **euphuistic** describe a pretentiously elevated style of writing, after John Lyly's *Euphues: the Anatomy of Wit* (1578).

Euratom European Atomic Energy Community

Euripides (c. 484–406 BC) Greek dramatist

euro (lower case) for the unit of currency used by most, but not all, of the nations of the European Union since early 2002

European Court of Human Rights, based in Strasbourg, deals with issues of civil liberties arising out of the European Convention on Human Rights; it has no connection with the European Union or UN. See also INTERNATIONAL COURTS.

European Court of Justice, in Luxembourg, is a European Union institution dealing exclusively with disputes involving member states.

European Organization for Nuclear Research is more commonly called CERN (from Conseil Européen de Recherches Nucléaires)

European Union What is now the European Union was formed in 1967 with a merger between the European Economic Community, the European Coal and Steel Community and the European Atomic Energy Community. As of 2007, it had 27 members: Austria, Belgium, Bulgaria, Cyprus, Czech Republic, Denmark, Estonia, Finland, France, Germany, Greece, Hungary, Ireland, Italy, Latvia, Lithuania, Luxembourg, Malta, Netherlands, Poland, Portugal, Romania, Slovakia, Slovenia, Spain, Sweden, United Kingdom.

Eurydice in Greek mythology, the wife of Orpheus

Eustachian tube (cap.) passage connecting the middle ear to the nasopharynx

euthanasia

evangelical, evangelistic Generally, *evangelical* is better reserved for contexts pertaining to adherence to the Christian gospel. If you need a word to describe militant zeal or the like, *evangelistic* is almost always better (e.g., 'the evangelistic fervour of the Campaign for Nuclear Disarmament').

Evatt, Herbert Vere (1894–1965) Australian statesman

eventuate 'Competition for economic interest, power and social esteem can eventuate in community formation only if . . .' (*British Journal of Sociology*, cited by Hudson). A pompous synonym for *result*.

everyday (adj.), **every day** (noun) 'He was wearing everyday clothes' but 'We come here every day.' Similar care is needed with **everybody** and **everyone**.

exaggerate

exalt praise highly

exasperate

Excalibur, not -*er* King Arthur's sword

ex cathedra (Lat.) with authority

excavator

exception proves the rule, the A widely misunderstood expression. As a moment's thought should confirm, it isn't possible for an exception to confirm a rule – but then that isn't the sense that was originally intended. *Prove* here is a 'fossil' – that is, a word or phrase that is now meaningless except within the confines of certain sayings (*hem and haw, rank and file* and *to and fro* are other fossil expressions). Originally *prove* meant test (it comes from the Latin *probo*, 'I test'), so 'the exception proves the rule' meant – and really still ought to mean – that the exception tests the rule. The original meaning of *prove* is preserved more clearly in two other expressions: *proving ground* and *the proof of the pudding is in the eating.*

exchangeable

excisable

excitable

exhalation

exhaustible

exhilarate

exhort, **exhortation**

exigent, **exiguous** The first means urgent and pressing or exacting and demanding; the second means scanty and slender. But both have a number of synonyms that may spare the reader a trip to the dictionary.

ex officio (Lat.) by virtue of one's office or position

Exon signature of the Bishop of Exeter

exorbitant

exorcise drive out an evil spirit

exotic colourful; from a remote country

expatriate one who lives abroad; in short, **expat**, not *ex-pat*; not to be confused in spelling or meaning with *compatriot*

expectorate, **spit** The distinction between these two is not, it must be conceded, often a matter of great moment, but still it is worth noting that there is a distinction. To *spit* means to expel saliva; to *expectorate* is to dredge up and expel phlegm from the lungs. *Expectorate* therefore is not just an unnecessary euphemism for *spit*; it is usually an incorrect one.

Expedition of Humphry Clinker, The, not *Humphrey*

novel by Tobias Smollett (1771)

ex post facto (Lat.) 'from what is done after'; retrospective

expressible, not -*able*

extempore, impromptu   Although both words describe unrehearsed remarks or performances, their meanings are slightly different in that *impromptu* can apply only to acts that are improvised at the time of performance, whereas *extempore* suggests only that the actions were undertaken without the benefit of notes or other formal props. *Impromptu*, in other words, conveys a greater element of surprise on the part the speaker or performer.

extraneous, not *exter-*

extrovert, not *extra-*

exult rejoice

ExxonMobil Corporation US oil company

eyeing

eyewitness (one word)

Eyre & Spottiswoode British publisher, no longer trading

eyrie (US **aerie**) eagle's nest

Ezeiza Airport, Buenos Aires

E-ZPass trademarked US toll collection system

FAA US Federal Aviation Administration

Faber and Faber British publisher; not *&*

fable, parable, allegory, myth *Fables* and *parables* are both stories intended to have instructional value. They differ in that parables are always concerned with religious or ethical themes, while fables are usually concerned with more practical considerations (and frequently have animals as the characters). An *allegory* is an extended metaphor – that is, a narrative in which the principal characters represent things that are not explicitly stated. Orwell's *Animal Farm* is an allegory. *Myths* originally were stories designed to explain some belief or phenomenon, usually the exploits of superhuman beings. Today the word can signify any popular misconception or invented story.

Facebook social networking internet site

facile is usually defined as easy, smooth, without much effort. But the word should contain at least a suggestion of derision. Facile writing isn't just easily read or written, it is also lacking in substance or import.

facsimile an exact copy

factious, factitious *Factious* applies to factions; something that is factious promotes internal bickering or disharmony. *Factitious* applies to that which is artificial or a sham; applause for a despotic ruler may be factitious. Neither should be confused with *fractious*, a term for something that is unruly or disorderly, as in 'a fractious crowd'.

Faerie Queene, The epic poem by Edmund Spenser (1589–96)

Faeroe (or **Faroe**) **Islands** Danish islands in the North Atlantic between Scotland and Iceland; capital Tórshavn; in Danish, *Faeröerne*

Fahd bin Abdul Aziz (1923–2005) King of Saudi Arabia 1982–2005

Fahrenheit (cap.) temperature scale that sets the freezing point of water at 32 degrees and boiling at 212; named after the German physicist Gabriel Daniel Fahrenheit (1686–1736). To convert Celsius to Fahrenheit, multiply the Celsius temperature by 1.8 and add 32, or use the table in the Appendix.

faience a kind of glazed pottery

faint, **feint** The first means weak or pale or to lose consciousness; the second refers to a misleading movement, and in the UK is also used to describe pale printing, as in feint-ruled paper.

fairway, not *fare-*, in golf

fait accompli (Fr.) an accomplished fact; pl. ***faits accomplis***

Falange, **Phalange** The first is a political party in Spain, the second a political party in Lebanon.

Falkland Islands, in Spanish **Islas Malvinas** British Crown colony in the South Atlantic; capital Port Stanley. The fighting between Britain and Argentina in 1982 is properly called the Falklands conflict (or something similar), since war was never declared.

fallible

Fallujah Sunni Muslim stronghold in central Iraq besieged by American troops in 2004

fandango lively Spanish dance; pl. **fandangoes/fandangos**

Faneuil Hall, Boston, Massachusetts pronounced *fan-yull*

Fannie Mae, Fannie May The first is the nickname for the US Federal National Mortgage Association and the bonds it issues; the second is a long-established confectionery company. See also FREDDIE MAC.

FAO Food and Agriculture (not *Agricultural*) Organization; a UN body

Farabundo Martí National Liberation Front Salvadoran revolutionary movement

Faraday, Michael (1791–1867) British chemist and physicist

FARC Fuerzas Armadas Revolucionarias de Colombia, Revolutionary Armed Forces of Colombia; guerrilla group

Far from the Madding Crowd, not *Maddening* novel by Thomas Hardy (1874)

Farne Islands, Northumberland

Faroe (or **Faeroe**) **Islands** Danish islands in the North Atlantic between Scotland and Iceland; capital Tórshavn; in Danish, *Faeröerne*

Farquhar, George (1678–1707) Irish playwright

farrago a confused mixture; pl. **farragoes**

Farrar, Straus & Giroux US publisher; not *Strauss*

farther, further In so far as the two are distinguished, *farther* usually appears in contexts involving literal distance ('New York is farther from Sydney than from London') and *further* in contexts involving figurative distance ('I can take this plan no further').

farthing old British coin worth one quarter of a penny; withdrawn in 1961

fascia, **facia**   The first is preferable, though both are acceptable.

fascism, **fascist**

Fassbinder, Rainer Werner (1946–82) German film-maker

fatal, **fateful**   The first means causing death, the second describes something with long-term (negative) consequences.

Fates, the   in Greek mythology, the three daughters of Nyx: Clotho, Lachesis and Atropos; they are known as the **Moerae** or **Moirai** in Greek and **Parcae** in Latin

Father's Day (sing.)

fatwa   Islamic decree

Faubourg St-Honoré, Rue du, Paris   Note *du*.

fauna, **flora**   The first means animals, the second plants.

faute de mieux (Fr.)   for lack of anything better

fauvism (no cap.)   short-lived school of expressionist art in France whose proponents, known as Les Fauves, included Matisse, Dufy, Braque and Rouault

faux bonhomme (Fr.)   a person whose superficial good nature disguises a darker side

faux pas (Fr.)   an error or blunder; pl. same

favela (Port.)   a Brazilian shanty town

Fawkes, Guy (1570–1606)   Catholic rebel caught up in England's unsuccessful Gunpowder Plot. Guy Fawkes' Day (note apos.) is 5 November and marks the date of his capture, not his execution.

faze   to disturb or worry; not to be confused with *phase*

FCC   US Federal Communications Commission; authority responsible for regulating television and radio

FDIC   US Federal Deposit Insurance Corporation; authority that steps in when banks fail

feasible, not -*able*   The word does not mean probable or plausible, as is sometimes thought, but simply capable of being done. An action can be feasible without being either desirable or likely.

FedEx Corporation

feet, foot An occasional error is seen here: 'Accompanied by Interior Secretary Gale Norton, the president also stopped at the 275-feet-high General Sherman Tree, a sequoia thought to be one of the largest living things on Earth . . .' When one noun qualifies another, the first is normally singular. That is why we talk about toothbrushes rather than teethbrushes and horse races rather than horses races, and write cow's milk and goat's cheese. Exceptions can be found – *systems analyst*, *singles bar* – but usually these appear only when the normal form would produce ambiguity. When a noun is not being made to function as an adjective, the plural is the usual form. Thus a wall that is six feet high is a six-foot-high wall.

Fehn, Sverre (1924–) Norwegian architect

feijoada Brazilian national dish; bean stew with rice and meat

Feininger, Lyonel (1871–1956) American artist; note unusual spelling of first name

Feinstein, Dianne (1933–) Democratic Senator from California

feisty

feldspar a mineral

Fellini, Federico (1920–93) Italian film director

FEMA US Federal Emergency Management Agency

femto- prefix meaning one quadrillionth

Ferlinghetti, Lawrence (1920–) American poet and writer

Fermanagh Northern Ireland county

Ferrara city in Emilia-Romagna, Italy

Ferrari Italian sports car manufacturer

Ferraro, Geraldine (Anne) (1935–) American Democratic politician, ran as vice-presidential candidate with Walter Mondale in 1984

ferrule, ferule A *ferrule* is a metal cap or band used to strengthen a tool, as with the metal piece that attaches the brush to the handle of a paintbrush. A *ferule* is a ruler or stick used for punishment.

Ferruzzi Italian commodities business

fervent passionate

fervid means intense; not to be confused with **fetid**, meaning foul-smelling.

fettuccine

Feuchtwanger, Lion (1889–1958) German writer; not *Leon*

feu de joie (Fr.) bonfire, ceremonial salute with gunfire; pl. ***feux de joie***

Feuerbach, Ludwig (1804–72) German philosopher

feuilleton serial; second section of French newspaper containing literary reviews, fiction serializations or other pieces of light journalism

fever, temperature You often hear sentences like 'John had a temperature yesterday' when in fact John has a temperature every day. Strictly speaking, what he had yesterday was a fever.

fewer, less Use less with singular nouns (less money, less sugar) and fewer with plural nouns (fewer houses, fewer cars).

Feydeau, Georges (1862–1921) French playwright known for farces

Feynman, Richard (1918–88) American physicist

fiancé (masc.)/**fiancée** (fem.)

Fianna Fáil Irish political party; pronounced *fee-yan´-a foil*
fiasco, pl. **fiascos**
Fiat abbr. of Fabbrica Italiana Automobile Torino; Italian car
    manufacturer
fibre (US **fiber**)
fiddle-de-dee
FIDE Fédération Internationale des Échecs, world governing
    body of chess
fidei defensor (Lat.) defender of the faith
Fiennes, Sir Ranulph (Twisleton-Wykeham-) (1944–) pro-
    nounced *fines*; English explorer, cousin of the actors
    Ralph Fiennes (1962–) and **Joseph Fiennes** (1970–)
FIFA Fédération Internationale de Football Associations,
    world governing body of soccer
fifth column enemy sympathizers working within their own
    country; the term comes from the Spanish Civil War,
    when General Emilio Mola boasted that he had four
    columns of soldiers marching on Madrid and a fifth col-
    umn of sympathizers waiting in the city
Fifth Third Bancorp US banking group
Figheldean, Wiltshire
filament
filet, **fillet** Use the first when the phrase or context is
    distinctly French (*filet mignon*), but otherwise use *fillet*.
filial
filibuster long speech designed to delay progress of
    legislation
filigree
Filipino (masc.)/**Filipina** (fem.) a native of the Philippines
fille de joie (Fr.) a prostitute; pl. *filles de joie*
Fillmore, Millard (1800–74) thirteenth US President, 1850–3
filo pastry used in Eastern Mediterranean cookery

FIMBRA Financial Intermediaries, Managers and Brokers Association, British financial regulatory body

finagle to secure by cajoling; to use trickery

finalize is still objected to by many as an ungainly and unnecessary word, and there is no arguing that several other verbs – *finish, complete, conclude* – do the job as well without raising hackles.

Financial Times **Ordinary Share Index** abbr. FT Index or FT30 Index; measures the performance of 30 leading shares on the London Stock Exchange

Financial Times–**Stock Exchange 100-Share Index** abbr. FT–SE Index, but more commonly called Footsie; measures the performance of 100 leading shares on the London Stock Exchange

fin de siècle (Fr.) 'end of the century'; normally applied to the end of the nineteenth century

Fine Gael Irish political party; pronounced *feen gayle*

finial ornament on the pinnacle of a roof or similar

finical, finicky Both mean fussy, over-precise.

Finisterre, Cape westernmost point of the Spanish mainland

Finnegans Wake (no apos.) novel by James Joyce (1939)

fiord/fjord Either is correct.

Firenze Italian for Florence

first and foremost Choose one.

first come first served (no comma)

first floor Depending on the context, it may be pertinent to remember that in North America the first floor is the ground floor, not the floor above it.

First Man in the Moon, The H. G. Wells novel (1901); note *in*, not *on*

Fischer, Bobby (1943–2008) American chess player; world champion 1972–5

Fischer-Dieskau, Dietrich (1925–) German baritone
Fishburne, Laurence (1961–) American actor
fish/fishes Either is correct as a plural.
Fisherman's Wharf, San Francisco; not -*men's*
fission, **fusion** in physics, ways of producing nuclear
    energy: *fission* by splitting the nucleus of an atom,
    fusion by fusing two light nuclei into a single, heavier
    nucleus
fisticuffs
Fittipaldi, Emerson (1946–) Brazilian racing driver
FitzGerald, Edward (1809–83) English scholar and poet,
    translator of Omar Khayyám's *Rubáiyát*
Fitzwilliam Museum, Cambridge
Fiumicino Airport, Rome Formally it is Aeroporto
    Intercontinentale Leonardo da Vinci, but it is more
    commonly known by the name of its locality.
fjord/fiord Either is correct.
fl. (Lat.) *floruit*, meaning flourished; used to indicate the pro-
    ductive period of a person ('*fl.* 2nd c. BC') for whom
    more specific dates are lacking
flack, **flak** In the US, the first is a slightly pejorative term for
    a publicist. The second, a contraction of the German
    Fliegerabwehrkanone, is anti-aircraft fire and by
    extension criticism or abuse.
flagon a large vessel from which to serve or consume drink
flair, **flare** *Flair* is a knack for doing something well;
    flare describes a burst of flame or other phen-
    omenon involving light. Nostrils and skirts may be
    flared.
flak See FLACK, FLAK.
flaky
flamingoes

flammable, inflammable *Inflammable* means capable of burning, but has so often been taken to mean the opposite that most authorities now suggest it be avoided. It is generally better to use *flammable* for materials that will burn and *non-flammable* for those that will not.

Flamsteed, John (1646–1719) first astronomer royal of England

flannel, flannelled, but **flannelette**

flaunt, flout To *flaunt* means to display ostentatiously, to show off. To *flout* means to treat with contempt, to disregard in a smug manner.

flautist a person who plays the flute

Fledermaus, Die operetta by Johann Strauss the younger (1874)

Fleming a native of Flanders, the Dutch-speaking part of Belgium; the adjective is **Flemish**

Fleming, Sir Alexander (1881–1955) British bacteriologist, discoverer of penicillin; shared Nobel Prize for Physiology or Medicine 1945

fleur-de-lis, pl. **fleurs-de-lis**

flexible

flibbertigibbet a scatterbrain

floccinaucinihilipilification the act of estimating as worthless; sometimes cited as the longest non-technical word in English

Flodden Field, Battle of (1513) battle in which the Scottish forces of James IV were routed by the English

flora, fauna The first means plants, the second animals.

florescent, fluorescent The first means in flower, the second radiating light.

floruit (Lat.) abbr. *fl.*; 'flourished'; used when the exact dates someone lived are not known, e.g., 'Caedmon (*fl.* 7th c.)'

flotsam and jetsam *Jetsam* is that part of a shipwreck that has been thrown overboard (think of *jettison*) and *flotsam* that which has floated off of its own accord. (A third type, wreckage found on the sea floor, is called *lagan.*) There was a time when the distinction was important: flotsam went to the Crown and jetsam to the lord of the manor on whose land it washed up.

flounder, founder *Founder* means to sink, either literally (as with a ship) or figuratively (as with a project). *Flounder* means to flail helplessly. It too can be used literally (as with someone struggling in deep water) or figuratively (as with a nervous person making an extemporaneous speech).

flourish

flout, flaunt The first means to disregard, the second to show off.

flugelhorn brass musical instrument

flummox bewilder

flunkey (or **flunky**) one who performs menial tasks; pl. **flunkeys** (or **flunkies**)

fluorescent light

fluoridate, fluoridation to add fluoride; the act of adding fluoride

fluoroscope

focaccia an Italian bread

fo'c'sle forecastle

foehn/föhn a warm southerly wind on the northern side of the Alps

foetus (US **fetus**) *Fetus* is now commonly used in UK medical writing.

fogey (or **fogy**)   an old-fashioned person; pl. **fogeys** (or **fogies**)

Fogg, Phileas, not *Phogg*, not *Phineas*, for the character in Jules Verne's *Around the World in Eighty Days* (1873)

Fogg Art Museum, Cambridge, Massachusetts

föhn   See FOEHN.

foie gras   fattened goose liver

foley artist (not cap.)   a specialist in dubbing sounds on film; named for Jack Foley (1891–1967), Hollywood sound effects editor

Folger Shakespeare Library, Washington, DC

folie à deux (Fr.)   a delusion shared by two people

Folies-Bergère   Parisian music hall

Folketing   Danish parliament

Fond du Lac, Wisconsin

Fontainebleau   château, town and forest on the Seine near Paris

Fonteyn (de Arias), Dame Margot (1919–91) born Margaret Hookham; English prima ballerina

Foochow   Use **Fuzhou** for the capital of Fujian Province, China. It is pronounced *foo-jo´*.

foot-and-mouth disease (hyphens)

Footsie   *Financial Times*–Stock Exchange 100-Share Index

forbear, forebear   The first is a verb meaning to avoid or refrain from. The second is a noun and means ancestor.

forbid, prohibit   The words have the same meaning, but the construction of sentences often dictates which should be used. *Forbid* may be followed only by *to* ('I forbid you to go'). *Prohibit* may not be followed by *to*, but only by *from* ('He was prohibited from going') or by an object noun ('The law prohibits the construction of houses without planning consent'). Thus the following is wrong: 'They are forbidden from uttering any public comments.' Make it either 'They are prohibited from uttering . . .' or 'They are forbidden to utter . . .' A small additional point is that *forbid*'s past tense form, *forbade*, has the preferred pronunciation *for-bad*, not *for-bade*.

forceful, forcible, forced *Forcible* indicates the use of brute force ('forcible entry'). *Forceful* suggests a potential for force ('forceful argument', 'forceful personality'). *Forced* can be used for *forcible* (as in 'forced entry'), but more often is reserved for actions that are involuntary ('forced march') or occurring under strain ('forced laughter', 'forced landing').

force majeure (Fr.) an uncontrollable event or superior strength

forego, forgo The first means to precede; the second means to do without. One of the most common spelling errors in English is to write *forego* when *forgo* is intended.

Forester, C. S. (for **Cecil Scott**) (1899–1966) English writer, chiefly remembered for naval adventures involving Horatio Hornblower; not to be confused with E. M. Forster

foreword an introduction to a book written by someone other than the book's author. See also PREFACE.

forgather, not *fore-* The need for the word is doubtful since *gather* says as much and says it more quickly.

formaldehyde (not cap.)

Formentera, Balearic Islands, Spain

former, latter *Former*, properly used, should refer only to the first of two things and *latter* to the second of two things. Both words, since they require the reader to hark back to an earlier reference, should be used sparingly and only when what they refer to is immediately evident. Few editing shortcomings are more annoying and less excusable than requiring a reader to re-cover old ground.

Formica is a trademark.

Formosa former name of Taiwan

Fornebu Airport, Oslo

Forster, E. M. (for **Edward Morgan**) (1879–1970) English novelist

forswear

forsythia yellow-flowered shrub

forte in music, loud; abbr. *f.*; also a person's strong point

fortissimo, fortississimo The first (abbr. *ff.*) means very loud; the second (abbr. *fff.*) means as loud as possible.

Fort-Lamy former name of N'djaména, capital of Chad

Fort Sumter, Charleston, South Carolina site of first action in the American Civil War

fortuitous means by chance; it is not a synonym for *fortunate*. A fortuitous event may be fortunate, but equally it may not.

forty-niner (no cap.) participant in the 1849 California gold rush. The San Francisco football team is the **49ers** (no apos.).

For Whom the Bell Tolls, not *Bells Toll* novel by Ernest Hemingway (1940)

Foucault pendulum, pronounced *foo-ko´*, for the device, but *Foucault's Pendulum* for the novel by Umberto Eco (1988)

founder, flounder *Founder* means to sink, break down or fail; *flounder* means only to struggle. A drowning person flounders; ships founder.

foundry, not *-ery*

Four Horsemen of the Apocalypse represent Conquest, Slaughter, Famine and Death.

fourth estate In Britain, the press. The other three estates are the Lords, the Commons and the Church of England.

Fowler's common name for *A Dictionary of Modern English Usage* by H. W. Fowler (1926)

Fox, Charles James (1749–1806) British politician, anti-slavery campaigner

Fox, George (1624–91) English religious reformer, founder of the Society of Friends, or Quakers

Foxe, John (1516–87) English clergyman, most remembered for the book commonly known as *Foxe's Book of Martyrs*; not to be confused with **George Fox**, above

fraction A few authorities continue to maintain that *fraction* in the sense of a small part is ambiguous: $^{99}\!/_{100}$ is also a fraction but hardly a negligible part. The looser usage, however, has been around for at least 300 years. Even so, it would be more precise to say 'a small part' or 'a tiny part'.

fractious disorderly

France is divided into the following 22 regions (English version in parentheses where appropriate): Alsace, Aquitaine, Auvergne, Basse-Normandie, Bretagne (Brittany), Bourgogne (Burgundy), Centre, Champagne-Ardennes, Corse (Corsica), Franche-Comté, Haute-Normandie, Île de France, Languedoc-Roussillon, Limousin, Lorraine, Midi-Pyrénées, Nord-Pas-de-Calais, Pays de la Loire, Picardie (Picardy), Poitou-Charentes, Provence-Alpes-Côte d'Azur, Rhône-Alpes.

Franche-Comté region of France

Francis of Assisi, St (1182–1226) born Giovanni Francesco Bernardone; founder of the Franciscan order of monks

Franck, César Auguste (1822–90) Belgian-born French composer

Franco (y Bahamonde), Francisco (1892–1975) Spanish general and dictator 1937–75; called *Caudillo* (leader) in Spain, General Franco elsewhere

Francome, John (1952–) British jockey, trainer and novelist

Frankenstein The full title of the novel by Mary Wollstonecraft Shelley (1797–1851) is *Frankenstein, or the Modern Prometheus* (1818). Frankenstein is the scientist, not the monster.

Frankfurt am Main, western Germany, not to be confused with **Frankfurt an der Oder**, eastern Germany, on the border with Poland. The towns in Indiana, Kentucky, Michigan, Ohio and several other US states are all **Frankfort**.

Frankfurter, Felix (1882–1965) American jurist

Franz Josef Land archipelago in the Barents Sea

frappé (Fr.) iced, artificially chilled

Fraser, Peter (1884–1950) Scottish-born Prime Minister of New Zealand 1940–9

Frau (Ger.) married woman, pl. *Frauen*

Fräulein (Ger.) unmarried woman, pl. same

Frayn, Michael (1933–) English novelist and playwright

Frazer-Nash British sports car; not *Fraser-*

FRCS Fellow of the Royal College of Surgeons

Freddie Mac nickname of US Federal Home Loan Mortgage Corporation; see also FANNIE MAE, FANNIE MAY

Fredericksburg, Virginia site of a battle in the American Civil War

Frederick II (1712–86) King of Prussia 1740–86; known as Frederick the Great

Fredericton capital of New Brunswick, Canada

Frederiksberg suburb of Copenhagen

Frederikshavn, Denmark

Freefone (cap.) free telephone service of British Telecom

freesia sweet-scented flowering plant

Freeview free-to-air digital terrestrial TV service

Freiburg (im Breisgau) for the ancient university town in Baden, Germany, but **Freiberg** for its near namesake in Saxony

Fremantle, Western Australia

French Guiana an overseas region of France on the South American mainland; capital Cayenne

Frenchman Flat, Nevada site of atomic bomb tests in the 1950s

French Somaliland former name of Djibouti

fresh Usually the word serves as an unobjectionable synonym for *new*, but it has additional connotations that make it inappropriate in some contexts, as the following vividly demonstrates: 'Three weeks after the earthquake, fresh bodies have been found in the wreckage' (cited by Spiegl in *The Joy of Words*).

FRIBA Fellow of the Royal Institute of British Architects

fricassée, fricasséed

fricative a type of consonant

FRICS Fellow of the Royal Institution of Chartered Surveyors

Friedan, Betty (1921–2006) American feminist; born Elizabeth Naomi Goldstein

Friedman, Milton (1912–2006) American economist, awarded Nobel Prize for Economics 1976

Friedrichshafen, Germany

Friesian, Frisian *Friesian* is a breed of cattle; *Frisian* is a north Germanic language and the name of a chain of islands lying off, and politically divided between, the Netherlands, Denmark and Germany. Friesian cattle in the US are normally called *Holsteins*. *Frisian* is also sometimes applied to people from Friesland, the Dutch province that partly encompasses the Frisian islands.

frieze

Friml, Rudolf (1879–1972) Czech-born American pianist and composer of light operas

frisbee (no cap.)

frisson 'A slight frisson went through the nation yesterday' (*The Times*). There is no other kind of frisson than a slight one. The word means shiver or shudder.

Friuli-Venezia Giulia region of Italy

fromage (Fr.) cheese

front bench (noun), **frontbench** (adj.)

frontispiece illustration facing the title page of a book

frowsty, frowzy The first means musty or stale, the second untidy or dingy.

FRS Fellow of the Royal Society

Frühstück (Ger.) breakfast

FTC US Federal Trade Commission

fuchsia flowering plant or shrub

Fuhlsbuttel Airport, Hamburg

Führer (Ger.) leader, term adopted by Adolf Hitler; *Führer* is the preferred spelling but *Fuehrer* is also accepted.

Fujiyama means Mount Fuji, so 'Mount Fujiyama' is tautological. Make it either *Fujiyama* or *Mount Fuji*. The Japanese also call it Fujisan and Fuki-no-Yama.

fulfil, fulfilment, fulfilled, fulfilling (US **fulfill, fulfillment**)

fulsome means odiously insincere. 'Fulsome praise', properly used, isn't a lavish tribute; it is unctuous and insincere toadying.

furore (US **furor**)

further, farther In so far as the two are distinguished, *farther* usually appears in contexts involving literal distance

('New York is farther from Sydney than from London') and *further* in contexts involving figurative distance ('I can take this plan no further').

Fusaichi Pegasus racehorse, winner of 2000 Kentucky Derby

fusion, fission Both describe ways of producing nuclear energy: *fusion* by fusing two light nuclei into a single, heavier nucleus; *fission* by splitting the nucleus of an atom.

future plans and similar locutions are nearly always tautological. If a person makes plans, it would follow that they are for the future.

Fuzhou formerly often written Foochow or Fouchou, capital of Fujian Province, China; pronounced *foo-jo´*

G

gaberdine a type of worsted cloth; also spelled **gabardine**

Gaborone capital of Botswana

Gaddafi (or **Qaddafi**), **Muammar** (1942–) Libyan head of state 1969– . He has no official title or position.

Gadsden Purchase large purchase of territory by the United States from Mexico in 1853

Gaeltacht any region of Ireland where Gaelic is the vernacular

Gagarin, Yuri (1934–68) Soviet cosmonaut, first man in space (1961)

gage, gauge The first is a pledge or a type of plum (as in greengage); the second is to do with scales and measurements.

Gaia (also, but rarely, **Gaea** or **Ge**) in early Greek mythology, the Earth personified; later, goddess of the Earth

Gaia theory ecological hypothesis proposed by James Lovelock (1919–)

gaiety

gaijin (Jap.) 'outsider'; used of foreigners

gaillardia (lower case) type of flower of the genus *Gaillardia* (cap.)

Gainsborough, Thomas (1727–88) English painter

Gaitskell, Hugh (1906–63) British politician

Galahad, Sir the purest and noblest knight in the Arthurian legend

Galápagos Islands Pacific islands belonging to Ecuador; their Spanish name is Archipiélago de Colón

Galeries Lafayette Paris department store

Galeries St-Hubert, Brussels

Galileo (1564–1642) Italian astronomer and mathematician; full name Galileo Galilei

Gallaudet College, Washington, DC

gallimaufry a jumble; pl. **gallimaufries**

Gallipoli Turkish peninsula and site of a First World War campaign; in Turkish, Gelibolu

gallivant to wander in search of pleasure

Galsworthy, John (1867–1933) English novelist, awarded Nobel Prize for Literature 1932

Gama, Vasco da (not *de*) (c. 1469–1524) Portuguese explorer

Gambia (not *the*) west African country, capital Banjul

gambit Properly, a *gambit* is an opening move that involves some strategic sacrifice or concession. All gambits are opening moves, but not all opening moves are gambits.

gamut the whole series or extent of something

gamy, not *-ey*

Gandhi, Mohandas Karamchand (1869–1948) Indian leader; called Mahatma, 'great soul'

ganef (or **ganof** or **gonif**) (Yiddish) a thief or disreputable person

gangrene, not *-green*

gannet seabird; greedy person

Gannett Company newspaper group

Gannett Peak, Wyoming

Ganymede fourth moon of Jupiter; in Greek mythology, the young Trojan who was made cupbearer to the gods

García Lorca, Federico (1899–1936) Spanish poet and playwright

García Márquez, Gabriel (1928–) Colombian novelist; awarded Nobel Prize for Literature 1982

Garda Siochána formal name of the police force in the Republic of Ireland, usually shortened to Garda; a member of the force is called a **garda** (not cap.), pl. **gardai**

Gardner, Erle Stanley (1889–1970) American writer of crime and courtroom fiction; note unusual spelling of first name

Garibaldi, Giuseppe (1807–82) Italian leader; played a central role in national unification

garish gaudy

Garmisch-Partenkirchen Bavarian resort

Garonne French river

garrotte (US **garrote**) to strangle with an object. **Garotte** is also accepted in the UK.

gas, **gases**, **gaseous**, **gasify**, **gasification**, but **gassed** and **gassing**

gasoline (US) petrol

Gasthaus, Gasthof The first is German for an inn or guest-house; the second is German for a hotel. The plurals are *Gasthäuser* and *Gasthöfe*.

gastronome a connoisseur of food

gateau, pl. **gateaux**

GATT General Agreement on Tariffs and Trade; UN agency that attempts to regulate world trade

Gaudier-Brzeska, Henri (1891–1915) French sculptor

gauge, gage The first is to do with scales and measurements; the second is a pledge or a type of plum (as in greengage).

Gauguin, (Eugène Henri) Paul (1848–1903) French painter
Gauloise brand of French cigarettes
gauntlet a glove thrown down in challenge; or (US **gantlet**) in the sense of running between two lines of aggressors (whether literally or metaphorically)
Gauthier-Villars French publisher
gauzy
Gawain, Sir one of the knights of Arthurian legend
Gay-Lussac, Joseph Louis (1778–1850) French chemist and physicist
gazetteer
gazpacho Spanish cold soup
GCE General Certificate of Education (UK); replaced by GCSE (see below)
GCHQ Government Communications Headquarters, base for British intelligence-gathering operations, Cheltenham, Gloucestershire
GCSE General Certificate of Secondary Education (UK)
Gdańsk, Poland formerly Danzig
GDP, GNP *GNP*, gross national product, is the total worth of everything produced by a nation during a given period, including earnings from abroad. *GDP*, gross domestic product, is everything produced by a nation during a given period, except earnings from abroad.
GDR German Democratic Republic; the former East Germany
Gebrselassie, Haile (1973–) Ethiopian long-distance runner, twice Olympic gold medallist and marathon world record holder
Geelong, Victoria, Australia
geezer in the UK a man, informal; in the US, an old man, derogatory
Geffrye Museum, London

gefilte fish (Yiddish) chopped fish dish

Gehrig, Lou (1903–41) baseball player; full name Henry Louis Gehrig. **Lou Gehrig disease** is a progressive neurodegenerative disease; see ALS.

Gehry, Frank (1929–) Canadian-American architect; born Ephraim Owen Goldberg

Geiger counter (cap.) measures radioactivity; devised by the German physicist Hans Geiger (1882–1945)

Geisenheimer wine a white wine from the Rhine

gelatin is the usual spelling, but **gelatine** is also accepted.

Gell-Mann, Murray (1929–) American physicist, awarded Nobel Prize for Physics 1969

gemütlich (Ger.) agreeable, comfortable, good-natured

Gemütlichkeit (Ger.) congeniality, friendliness

gendarmes are not policemen; they are soldiers employed in police duties, principally in the countryside. Police officers in French cities and towns, *agents de police*, are just that – police officers.

genealogy

General Agreement on Tariffs and Trade abbr. GATT; UN body set up to regulate world trade

generalissimo, pl. **generalissimos**; but note in Spanish it is *generalisimo* (one *s*)

General Strike (caps) national strike in Britain, 4–12 May 1926

Genet, Jean (1910–86) French novelist and playwright

Geneva, Switzerland; **Genève** in French, **Genf** in German, **Ginevra** in Italian; **Lake Geneva** is **Lac Léman** in French and **Genfer See** in German

Geneva Convention (1864, revised 1950, 1978) international agreement on the conduct of war and treatment of wounded and captured soldiers

Geneviève, St (c. 422–c. 512) patron saint of Paris

Genghis Khan (1162–1227) Mongol conqueror

genie, pl. **genies** or **genii**

Genova Italian for Genoa

gentilhomme (Fr.) gentleman or nobleman; pl. *gentilshommes*

Gentleman's Magazine, The UK periodical 1731–1914

Gentlemen's Quarterly, not -*man's* US magazine, now called *GQ*

gentoo a type of penguin

genus, **species** The second is a subgroup of the first. The convention is to capitalize the genus but not the species, as in *Homo sapiens*. The plurals are *genera* and *species*. The traditional order of divisions in taxonomy is phylum, class, order, family, genus, species.

Geographic Names, US Board on, not *Geographical*, not *of*

George Town, **Georgetown** *George Town* is the spelling for the capital of the Cayman Islands and the principal city of the island and state of Penang in Malaysia. Almost all others, including the capital of the South American country Guyana and the district and university in Washington, DC, use the spelling *Georgetown*.

Gephardt, Richard Andrew ('Dick') (1941–) Democratic politician, US Representative from Missouri 1977–2005

gerbil, not *jer-*

Géricault, Jean Louis André Théodore (1791–1824) French painter

germane, **relevant**, **material** *Germane* and *relevant* are synonymous. Both indicate a pertinence to the matter under discussion. *Material* has the additional connotation of being necessary. A material point is one without which an argument would be incomplete. A germane or relevant point will be worth noting but may not be essential to the argument.

Germany was partitioned into East Germany (Deutsche Demokratische Republik), with its capital in East Berlin, and West Germany (Bundesrepublik Deutschland), with its capital at Bonn, in 1949. The two Germanys (not -*ies*) were reunited on 3 October 1990. The 16 states, or Länder, are Baden Wurttemberg, Bavaria, Berlin, Brandenburg, Bremen, Hamburg, Hesse, Lower Saxony, Mecklenburg-West Pomerania, North Rhine-Westphalia, Rhineland Palatinate, Saarland, Saxony, Saxony-Anhalt, Schleswig-Holstein and Thuringia.

gerrymander is to distort or redraw to one's advantage, especially a political boundary. Not to be confused with *jerry-built*, meaning badly built.

gerunds are verbs made to function as nouns, as with the italicized words in 'I don't like *dancing*' and '*Cooking* is an art.' Two problems commonly arise with gerunds:

1. Sometimes the gerund is unnecessarily set off by an article and preposition, as here: 'They said that *the* valuing *of* the paintings could take several weeks.' Deleting the italicized words would make the sentence shorter and more forceful.

2. Problems also occur when a possessive noun or pronoun (called a *genitive*) qualifies a gerund. A common type of construction is seen here: 'They objected to him coming.' Properly it should be: 'They objected to his coming.' Similarly, 'There is little hope of Smith gaining admittance to the club' should be 'There is little hope of Smith's gaining admittance . . .'

Gestapo short for Geheime Staatspolizei, German secret police during the Third Reich

Gesundheit! 'Health!'; an interjection made in response to a
   sneeze

Gethsemane olive grove at Jerusalem where Jesus was betrayed

gettable

Getty, J. (for **Jean**) **Paul** (1892–1976), not *John* US oil man
   and benefactor; his son Jean Paul Getty II (1932–) is
   also often given wrongly as John.

Gettysburg, Pennsylvania site of the decisive (but not final)
   battle of the American Civil War (July 1863)

gewgaw worthless bauble

Ghanaian for a person or thing from Ghana

ghettos, not -*oes*

ghillie (or **gillie**) Scottish hunting or fishing assistant; also a
   type of shoe

Ghirardelli Square, San Francisco

ghiribizzoso musical term for whimsical playing

Ghirlandaio, Domenico (1449–94) Florentine painter; real
   name Domenico di Tommaso Bigordi

Giacometti, Alberto (1901–66) Swiss sculptor and painter

Giannini, A. P. (1870–1949) American banker, founded Bank
   of America; full name Amadeo Peter Giannini

Giant's Causeway, Northern Ireland; not *Giants'*

Gibbon, Edward (1737–94) English historian; not *Gibbons*

Gibbons, Grinling (1648–1721) Dutch-born English
   sculptor and woodcarver

Gielgud, Sir John (1904–2000) English actor

giga- prefix meaning one billion

gigolo, pl. **gigolos**

Gilbert and Ellice Islands equatorial islands in Pacific
   Ocean; the Gilbert Islands are part of the Republic of
   Kiribati; the Ellice Islands seceded in 1978 to form the
   independent state of Tuvalu

gild the lily The passage from Shakespeare's *King John* is: 'To gild refined gold, to paint the lily . . ./Is wasteful and ridiculous excess.' Thus it is both wrong and hackneyed to speak of 'gilding the lily' in the sense of overdoing something.

Gilgamesh, Epic of Babylonian epic poem

Gillette razor manufacturer

Gillray, James (1757–1815) British caricaturist

Gimbel Brothers former New York department store; commonly referred to as Gimbels (no apos.)

Gimpel Fils London art dealers

gingivitis, not -*us* inflammation of the gums

ginkgo, not *gingko* Asian tree; pl. **ginkgoes**

Ginsberg, Allen (1926–97) American beat poet

Gioconda, La alternative name for the *Mona Lisa*

Giorgione (1478–1510) Italian painter; full name Giorgio Barbarelli da Castelfranco

Giotto (c. 1266–1337) Italian painter and architect; full name Giotto di Bondone

girlfriend, boyfriend (one word)

giro, not *gyro* Post Office system for transferring money; colloquially, the name for dole money, or unemployment benefit

Giuliani, Rudolph ('Rudy') W. (1944–) Republican Mayor of New York City 1994–2001

giveable

gizmo, pl. **gizmos**

gladiolus, pl. **gladioli**

Gladstone, William Ewart (1809–98) British Liberal politician and four times Prime Minister

Glamis, Tayside pronounced *glahmz*

glamour, but **glamorous, glamorize**

glandular fever (US **mononucleosis**)

glasnost (Russian)   literally 'publicity'; the effort to make Soviet government and life more open

glassful, pl. **glassfuls**

Glaswegian a person from Glasgow

GlaxoSmithKline (all one word) Anglo-US pharmaceuticals company

GLC Greater London Council

Glencoe mountain pass in the Highland region of Scotland, site of the 1692 massacre of the MacDonalds by the Campbells

Glendower, Owen (in Welsh, **Owain Glyndwr**) (c. 1354–1416) Welsh chieftain

Glenlivet Scotch whisky

Glens Falls, New York

Gloria in excelsis Deo (Lat.) 'Glory be to God on high'

Glorious Revolution (1688–9) the removal of James II as king and his replacement by William of Orange and James's daughter Mary, who ruled as William III and Mary II

Glorious Twelfth 12 August, first day of the grouse-shooting season

Gloucestershire English county, abbr. Glos

Glyndebourne, East Sussex

Glyndwr, Owain See GLENDOWER, OWEN.

GMB formally the General, Municipal, Boilermakers and Allied Trades Union

GmbH, *Gesellschaft mit beschränkter Haftung* (Ger.) limited liability company

GMT Greenwich Mean Time

gneiss a kind of rock, similar to granite; pronounced *nice*

gnocchi, for a type of small Italian dumpling, is plural; a single dumpling is a **gnocco** (no *h*).

GNP, GDP *GNP*, gross national product, is the total worth of everything produced by a nation during a given period, including earnings from abroad. GDP, gross domestic product, is everything produced by a nation during a given period, except earnings from abroad.

gobbledygook

Gobelin tapestry named for a textile works in Paris

Gobi Desert

Godard, Jean-Luc (1930–) French film director

Goddard, Robert Hutchings (1882–1945) American rocket scientist

Goderich, Frederick John Robinson, Viscount (1782–1859) British statesman, Prime Minister 1827–8; later became first Earl of Ripon

godsend, godforsaken, godhead (no caps), but **God-awful, God-fearing** and **Godspeed** (caps)

Godthaab former name of the capital of Greenland; now called Nuuk

Godwin Austen (not *Austin*; no hyphen) more commonly called K2, the highest mountain in the Karakoram Range of the Himalayas

Goebbels, Joseph (1897–1945) Nazi propaganda chief

Goering/Göring, Hermann (1893–1946) leading Nazi, second in command to Hitler

Goethe, Johann Wolfgang von (1749–1832) German poet and dramatist

Gogol, Nikolai (1809–52) Russian novelist and playwright

Golders Green, London (no apos.)

Golgi body structure found within cells

Gollancz, Sir Victor (1893–1967) British author, philanthropist and publisher after whom the publishing firm was named

Gomorrah ancient city in Palestine

Goneril one of Lear's daughters in Shakespeare's *King Lear* (1608)

gonif (or **ganef** or **ganof**) (Yiddish) a thief or disreputable person

gonorrhea

Gonville and Caius College, Cambridge University; normally referred to as just Caius; pronounced *keys*

goodbye (one word)

Good-natur'd Man, The comedy by Oliver Goldsmith (1768)

good will is the usual spelling, though **goodwill** is acceptable, particularly when referring to the reputation and trading value of a business.

Good Woman of Setzuan, The play by Bertolt Brecht (1941)

Google for the search engine, but **googol** for the very large number: a 1 followed by 100 zeroes

googly a cricketing term

GOP abbr. of Grand Old Party, nickname of the US Republican Party

Gorbachev, Mikhail (Sergeyevich) (1931–) General Secretary of the Communist Party of the Soviet Union 1985–91, President of the Supreme Soviet 1988–91, President of the USSR 1990–1

Gordian knot a complex problem; according to legend, King Gordius of Phrygia tied the knot and it was said that anyone who could undo it would rule Asia; Alexander the Great cut it with his sword. 'To cut the Gordian knot' is to solve a difficult problem by a decisive action.

Gordonstoun School, private school in the Grampian region of Scotland, but **Gordonstown**, Grampian

gorgheggio musical term for a trill

Gorgons in Greek mythology, three creatures (Medusa,

Stheno and Euryale) so ugly that anyone gazing at them turned to stone; thus **gorgon**, a terrifying woman

Gorgonzola (cap.) for the cheese and the village in Italy in which it originated

gorilla

Göring, Hermann Use Goering.

Gorky, Maxim pseudonym of Aleksei Maksimovich Peshkov (1868–1936), Russian writer. The Russian city named for him has reverted to its original name of Nizhny Novgorod.

GOSH abbr. for Great Ormond Street Hospital for Children

Gothenburg, Sweden in Swedish, **Göteborg**

Götterdämmerung (Ger.) *Twilight of the Gods*, the last part of Wagner's *Ring* cycle; figuratively, a complete downfall

gouache a kind of opaque watercolour paint mixed with a gluelike preparation; a picture painted in this way or with such a pigment

Gould, Bryan (1939–) British politician

Gould, Elliott (1938–) American film actor; note unusual spelling of first name; born Elliot Goldstein

gourmand is a word to be used carefully. Some dictionaries now define it only as a person who likes to eat well, but others equate it with gluttony. Unless you mean to convey a pejorative sense, it would be better to use *gourmet*, *gastronome*, *epicure* or some other more flattering term.

goy (Yiddish) a gentile; pl. *goyim*

gracias (Sp.) thank you

Gradgrind (cap.) a cold, emotionless person, after a character in Charles Dickens's *Hard Times*

Graeae in Greek mythology, three sisters who guard the Gorgons

Graf, Steffi (1969–) German tennis player

graffiti is, strictly speaking, a plural. If all you mean is a single embellishment, the proper term is *graffito*. However, it must also be noted that fewer and fewer authorities insist on the distinction.

graham cracker (not cap.)

Grahame, Kenneth (1858–1932) British writer, author of *The Wind in the Willows* (1908)

Graian Alps stretch of the Alps along the French–Italian border

Gramm-Rudman Act law intended to reduce and eliminate US federal deficit; formally, it is the Gramm-Rudman-Hollings Act

Grammy, pl. **Grammys** musical awards formally known as the National Academy of Recording Arts and Sciences Awards

gramophone, not *grama-*

Granada, Grenada The first is the historic city in Spain, the second the Caribbean island state, capital St George's. They are pronounced respectively *gra-nah-da* and *gra-nay-da*.

grandad or **granddad**, **granddaughter**

Grand Coulee Dam, Columbia River, Washington

Grand Guignol high drama constructed around a sensational theme. The term comes from the Théâtre de Grand Guignol in Paris, where such plays were in vogue in the last years of the 19th century.

grandiloquence, not *-eloquence* inflated speech

grand jury in US law, a jury of up to twenty-three people empowered to decide whether enough evidence exists for a case to proceed against an accused person

Grand Ole Opry, Nashville, Tennessee

Grasmere, Cumbria site of Dove Cottage, home of the poet William Wordsworth

gratia Dei (Lat.) by God's grace

Gray, Thomas (1716–71) English poet

Gray's Inn and **Gray's Inn Road**, London (apos.)

grazie (It.) thank you

Great Hautbois, Norfolk pronounced *hob´-iss*

Greater London, **Greater Paris**, etc. Capitalize *Greater*.

Great Ormond Street Hospital for Children, London abbr. GOSH

Great Smoky Mountains National Park, North Carolina and Tennessee

Greco, El (1541–1614) Cretan-born Spanish painter; real name Domenikos Theotokopoulos

Greeley, Horace (1811–72) American politician and journalist, founder of the *New York Tribune* (1841). The expression 'Go west, young man' is frequently attributed to him, probably wrongly.

Greene, Graham (1904–91) British writer

Greene, Nathanael (1742–86) American Revolutionary War general

Green Paper, **White Paper** A *Green Paper* is a consultative document, outlining UK government proposals for discussion. A *White Paper* outlines the government's planned legislation.

Greenstreet, Sydney (1879–1954) British character actor

Gregorian calendar is the type now in use in most of the world; named for Pope Gregory XII.

Grenada small island state in the Caribbean, capital St George's; not to be confused with the Spanish city of **Granada**

grenadier

grenadine (lower case) for the fabric and flavouring, but **Grenadines** (cap.) for the Caribbean island chain

Grendel monster in *Beowulf*

Gresham's Law is that 'bad money drives out good'; attributed to Sir Thomas Gresham (1519–79), British financier.

Greuze, Jean Baptiste (1725–1805) French painter

grey (US **gray**)

Grey, Lady Jane (1537–54) Queen of England for 10 days in 1553

Grey, Zane (1875–1939) American author

Grey Friars for the Franciscan monks, but **Greyfriars College**, University of Oxford

greyhound

Greylock, Mount, Massachusetts

Grieg, Edvard (1843–1907) Norwegian composer

grievous, not -*ious*

griffin is the usual spelling for a creature with an eagle's head and wings and a lion's body, but many dictionaries also accept **gryphon**.

Griffith-Joyner, Florence (1959–1998) American sprinter

grille is the usual spelling for the front part of a car or other metal grating, though **grill** is also acceptable.

Grimethorpe, South Yorkshire pronounced *grim´-thorp*

Grimm, Brothers Jacob Ludwig Carl Grimm (1785–1863) and Wilhelm Carl Grimm (1786–1859), German writers and philologists, authors of *Grimm's Fairy Tales*

Grimond, Jo (for **Joseph**), **Lord** (1913–93) British politician, leader of Liberal Party 1956–67 and May–July 1976

grisly, gristly, grizzly Occasionally and variously confused. The first means horrifying or gruesome. The second applies to meat that is full of gristle. The third means grey, especially grey-haired, and in the US is a cliché when applied to old men. The bear is a *grizzly*.

Grisons/Graubünden are respectively the French and German names for a single Swiss canton.

Grobbelaar, Bruce (1957–) South African-born British soccer player

grosbeak species of finch

groschen former Austrian coin

gros rouge (Fr.) ordinary red table wine

gross domestic product, **gross national product** *Gross domestic product* is everything produced by a nation during a given period except earnings from overseas. *Gross national product* is everything produced by a nation during a given period including earnings from overseas. In most contexts, the reader is entitled to an explanation of the difference.

Grosse Pointe, Michigan

Grossmith, George (1847–1912) British comedian and entertainer, and with his brother, **Weedon Grossmith** (1852–1919), co-author of *The Diary of a Nobody* (1892)

Grosz, George (1893–1959) German-born American artist

Grósz, Karoly (1930–96) Prime Minister of Hungary 1987–8

grotto, pl. **grottoes**

Group of Eight, or **G8** leading industrial nations that meet regularly to discuss economic and trading issues. They are Canada, France, Germany, Italy, Japan, Russia, the United Kingdom and the United States.

grovelling

gruelling

gruesome

Gruinard Bay, Highland Region, Scotland pronounced *grin´-yard*

Grunewald, Mathias (c. 1480–1528) German Gothic artist and architect

Gruner + Jahr German magazine publisher, part of Bertelsmann. Note the use of a plus sign instead of an ampersand.

gruyère cheese, but the Swiss town from which it takes its name is **Gruyères**

gryphon Use **griffin**.

GT, Gran Turismo series of racing video games produced for Sony PlayStations

Guadalajara cities in Spain and Mexico

Guadalcanal, Solomon Islands site of ferocious fighting in the Second World War

Guadalupe, Guadeloupe The cluster of islands in the Caribbean, which together form an overseas *département* of France, is *Guadeloupe*. Most other geographical features bearing the name, including a river and range of mountains in the south-western United States, and towns or cities in California, Spain, Peru and the Azores, spell it *Guadalupe*.

Guadalupe Hidalgo, Treaty of 1848 treaty in which Mexico ceded to the United States what would become the states of Arizona, California, Colorado, Nevada, Texas and Utah

Guangdong, Guangzhou *Guangdong* is the Chinese province formerly known as Kwantung. Its capital is *Guangzhou*, formerly Canton.

Guantánamo Bay, Cuba site of US naval base and prison

Guaragigna African language

guarantee, guaranty *Guarantee* is the usual spelling for both the verb ('I guarantee a positive result') and the noun ('The TV is still under guarantee'), although *guaranty* also exists as a verb and a noun with a specific legal meaning to do with assuming responsibility for someone's debts.

Guatemala   Central American country, capital Guatemala City

Guayaquil, Santiago de   largest city in Ecuador

Guernica   Spanish town near Bilbao, ancient capital of the Basques; its bombing by German aircraft in April 1937 during the Spanish Civil War was the subject of a celebrated painting by Picasso. The town's full, formal name is Guernica y Luno, but this is seldom used and not necessary in most contexts.

guerrilla, also **guerilla**   a fighter in an irregular force

guesstimate   is much overused and generally unnecessary in serious writing; all estimates are fundamentally guesses.

gueuze   type of Belgian beer

Guggenheim   The New York museum is formally the Solomon R. Guggenheim Museum. Guggenheim Fellowships are awarded by the John S. Guggenheim Memorial Foundation.

Guiana, **Guyana**   Some scope for confusion here, particularly if using old references. The name Guiana has at various times been attached to three contiguous territories on the Atlantic coast of northern South America. The westernmost, British Guiana, is now called Guyana. The central territory, Dutch Guiana, is now Suriname. The easternmost, an overseas *département* of France, remains French Guiana.

Guildford, Surrey, but the **Earl of Guilford** (no middle *d*)

Guildhall, London, not *the* Guildhall

guillemet, guillemot   The first is the word for the chevron-like quotation marks [« »] used primarily in French and

Spanish; pronounced *gee-yuh-meh*. Not to be confused with the type of sea bird known as a guillemot, pronounced *gill'-a-mot*.

guillotine

GUM Gosudarstvennyi Universal'nyi Magazin (Russian, Government Universal Store), Moscow department store; pronounced *gay-oo-em*

guinea (not cap.) in Britain, a sum equivalent to one pound and one shilling or a coin of that value; no longer used

Guinea, **Guinea-Bissau**, **Equatorial Guinea** These are separate countries, all in west Africa. Guinea was formerly French Guinea. Guinea-Bissau was formerly Portuguese Guinea. Equatorial Guinea was formerly Spanish Guinea.

Guinevere wife of King Arthur

Guinness stout, **Sir Alec Guinness** (1914–2000), *Guinness Book of World Records*, etc.

Guizhou Chinese province, formerly spelled **Kweichow**

Gujarat Indian state; capital Gandhinagar

gunny sack a coarse sack made of jute fibre

Gunpowder Plot conspiracy among a group of English Catholics to blow up the Houses of Parliament in 1605

gunwale, not -*whale* the topmost edge of the side of a ship; pronounced *gunnel* and sometimes so spelled

Guomindang (formerly spelled **Kuomintang**) Chinese Nationalist Party, founded by Sun Yat-sen. The syllable *dang* contains the notion of party, so refer only to the Guomindang, not the Guomindang Party.

Gurdjieff, Georgei Ivanovitch (c. 1874–1949) Russian mystic

Gurkha (cap.) Nepalese soldier in the British army

guten Abend, but ***gute Nacht*** German for 'good evening' and 'good night'. The daytime salutations are **guten Morgen** for 'good morning' and **guten Tag** for 'good day'.

Gutenberg, Johann (c. 1400–68) born Johannes Gensfleisch; German credited with the invention of movable type

gutta-percha hard, rubbery substance produced from the latex of various tropical trees

guttural, not -*er*-

Guyana formerly British Guiana; South American country, capital Georgetown

Guy's Hospital, London named after Thomas Guy (c. 1645–1724), its founder; now part of Guy's and St Thomas' NHS Foundation Trust

Gwent county of Wales, formerly Monmouthshire, county town Cwmbran

Gwynedd county of Wales; pronounced *gwin´-neth*

Gwynn, Nell (1605–87) born Eleanor Gwynne; actress and mistress of Charles II

Gyllenhaal, Maggie (1977–) American actress, sister of actor **Jake Gyllenhaal** (1980–)

gymkhana

gynaecology (US **gynecology**)

gypsy, pl. **gypsies**

ha abbr. of hectare

Häagen-Dazs ice cream

Haakon VII (1872–1957) King of Norway 1905–57

Haarlem, Netherlands, but **Harlem**, New York

Haas, Ernst (1921–86) Austrian-born photographer

Haas-Lilienthal House, San Francisco

habeas corpus (Lat.) 'deliver the body'; writ requiring that a person be brought before a court. Its purpose is to ensure that prisoners are not unlawfully detained.

Habgood, Most Revd Dr John (Stapylton) (1927–) Bishop of Durham 1973–83, Archbishop of York 1983–95; later Lord Habgood

habits Take care not to write of someone's 'customary habits' or 'usual habits' and the like. Habits are always customary and always usual. That is, of course, what makes them habitual.

habitué (masc.)/**habituée** (fem.)

Habsburg Use **Hapsburg**.

Hadid, Zaha (1950–) Iraqi-born British architect

Haeckel, Ernst (1834–1919) German naturalist

haematology, haematoma, haematemesis (US **hematology, hematoma, hematemesis**)

haemoglobin, haemophilia (US **hemoglobin, hemophilia**)

haemorrhage (US **hemorrhage**)

haemorrhoids (US **hemorrhoids**)

Hågatña (formerly **Agana**) capital of Guam

Haggai (*fl.* 6th c. BC) Hebrew prophet; also the book of his prophecies in the Old Testament

Haggard, Sir H(enry) Rider (1856–1925) British author of adventure stories

haggis Scottish dish of offal mixed with suet and oatmeal, boiled in a bag traditionally made from an animal's stomach

Hague, The (cap. T) in Dutch Den Haag or 's-Gravenhage; seat of government of the Netherlands (though Amsterdam is the capital)

Hahnenkamm mountain above Kitzbühel in Austria, famous for its downhill ski race

hail, hale *Hale* means robust and vigorous, or to drag or forcibly draw (as in 'haled into court'), in which sense it is related to *haul*. *Hail* describes a greeting, a salute or a downpour (as in 'hailstorm' or 'hail of bullets'). The expressions are *hale and hearty* and *hail-fellow-well-met*.

Haile Selassie (1892–1975) Emperor of Ethiopia 1930–6, 1941–74

Hainault district of London

hairbrained is wrong; it's **hare-brained**.

hair's breadth (US **hairbreadth** or **hairsbreath**)

Haiti republic in the West Indies on the island of Hispaniola, which it shares with the Dominican Republic; capital Port-au-Prince

Haitink, Bernard (1929–) Dutch conductor

hajj, also **haj** a pilgrimage to Mecca; one who has made the pilgrimage is a **hajji** or **haji**

haka Maori war dance widely associated with New Zealand rugby appearances

Hakluyt, Richard (c. 1553–1616) English geographer; pronounced *hak´-loot*

halberd a combined spear and battleaxe, carried by a **halberdier**

Halberstam, David (1934–2007) American author and journalist

hale See HAIL, HALE.

Haleakala National Park, Maui, Hawaii

half a crown former coin worth two shillings and sixpence, equivalent to 12½ p in UK decimal currency

halfpenny/ha'penny pronounced *hape´-nee*

halfpennyworth/ha'p'orth pronounced *hay-puth*

halibut

halitosis

hallelujah

Hallé Orchestra, Manchester

Halley, Edmond (1655–1742) not *Edmund*; English astronomer. He did not discover the comet named after him, but rather predicted its return.

Halloween, in preference to *Hallowe'en*, 31 October

halo, pl. **haloes** or **halos**

Hamelin (Ger., Hameln) city in Germany, source of the legend of the Pied Piper of Hamelin

Hamlisch, Marvin (1944–) American composer

Hammarskjöld, Dag (1905–61) Swedish statesman, Secretary-General of the United Nations 1953–61, awarded Nobel Peace Prize posthumously 1961

Hammerstein II, Oscar (1895–1960) American dramatist and lyric writer, known for his collaborations with Jerome Kern and Richard Rodgers

Hammett, (Samuel) Dashiell (1894–1961) American writer of detective fiction

Hammonasset River, Connecticut

Hammurabi (*fl.* 18th c. BC) Babylonian king, codifier of laws

Hampton Court Palace, not just *Hampton Court*, is the title of the former royal residence in outer London.

Hamtramck suburb of Detroit; pronounced *ham-tram-ick*

Handel, George Frideric (1685–1759) German-born composer; originally Georg Friederich Händel

handicraft, **handiwork**, not *handy-*

Handschrift (Ger.) manuscript

Haneda Airport, Tokyo

hangar, not *-er* the place where aircraft are stored

hanged, **hung** People are hanged; objects are hung.

Hangzhou (formerly **Hangchow**) Chinese city, capital of Zhejiang province

Hannover German spelling of Hanover

Hansard, not *Hansard's*, is the unofficial name of the record of proceedings in Britain's Parliament, equivalent to America's *Congressional Record*. Formally, it is *The Official Report of Parliamentary Debates*, but that title is almost never used even on first reference.

Hansen's disease alt. name for leprosy

hansom cab

Hants (no full point) abbr. of Hampshire

Hantuchova, Daniela (1983–) Czech tennis player

Hanukkah is the most widely used spelling for the Jewish festival of lights.

haole Hawaiian term for a non-Polynesian person

Happisburgh, Norfolk pronounced *hayz´-burr-a*

Hapsburg Austrian imperial family; in German, **Habsburg**

hara-kiri is the correct spelling for the ritual form of suicide involving disembowelment. In Japan, it is normally known as *seppuku*.

Harald V (1937–) King of Norway 1991–

harangue, tirade Each is sometimes used when the other is intended. A *tirade* is always abusive and can be directed at one person or at several. A *harangue*, however, need not be vituperative, but may merely be prolonged and tedious. It does, however, require at least two listeners. One person cannot, properly speaking, harangue another.

Harare capital of Zimbabwe, formerly called Salisbury

harass, harassment Note one *r*, two *s*'s.

Hardie, Keir (1856–1915) British socialist politician, one of the founders of the Labour Party

hardiness

Harding, Warren G(amaliel) (1865–1923) twenty-ninth US President, 1921–3

Hardwicke, Sir Cedric (1893–1964) British actor

hare-brained, harelipped, not *hair-*

Hare Krishna a member of a religious sect

Haresceugh, Cumbria pronounced *hare´-skewf*

Harewood House, West Yorkshire, and the **Earl of Harewood** are both pronounced *har´-wood*, but the nearby village is *hair´-wood*.

Hargreaves, James (c. 1720–78) English inventor of the spinning jenny

Haringey London borough; see also HARRINGAY.

hark, but **hearken**

Harland and Wolff Northern Irish shipbuilding company

HarperCollins Publishers formerly Harper & Row in the US, William Collins in the UK

Harper's Bazaar US fashion magazine

Harpers Ferry, West Virginia (no apos.)

Harper's Magazine US magazine

Harpers & Queen UK fashion magazine, now published as *Harper's Bazaar UK* (note apos. now)

Harraden, Beatrice (1864–1936) English novelist and suffragist

harridan bad-tempered old woman

Harriman, Averell (1891–1986) US politician and diplomat; full name William Averell Harriman

Harringay a district of the London borough of Haringey, and a British Rail station

Harrington, Padraig (1971–) Irish golfer; Open champion in 2007

Harrisons & Crosfield, not *Cross-* British trading company

Harrods (no apos.) London department store

Harte, Bret (1836–1902) American writer and editor; born Francis Bret Harte

hartebeest for the African antelope; not -*beast*

Hartsfield-Jackson Atlanta International Airport, Atlanta

harum-scarum impetuous

Harvard Business School is formally the Harvard Graduate School of Business Administration, though in most contexts the formal title is unnecessary.

Harvard University but **Harvard College Observatory**

Harvey Nichols London department store

Harz Mountains, Germany; not *Hartz*

Hasid, pl. **Hasidim**, **Hasidic** (adj.) Jewish sect

Hasselblad Swedish cameras

Haulgh, Greater Manchester pronounced *hoff*

Hauptmann, Gerhart (1862–1946) German novelist, poet and playwright; awarded Nobel Prize for Literature 1912

Hausfrau (Ger.) housewife; pl. *Hausfrauen*

Haussmann, Boulevard, Paris named after Baron Georges

Eugène Haussmann (1809–91), who led the rebuilding of the city

haute couture (Fr.) high fashion

Havel, Václav (1936–) Czech playwright and reformist politician

Havering-atte-Bower, Essex   pronounced *hay-vring att-ee bau-er*

Havre de Grace, Maryland

Hawaiian Islands   The eight principal islands are Hawaii, Kaho'olawe, Kauai, Lanai, Maui, Molokai, Niihau and Oahu.

Haw-Haw, Lord   nickname of William Joyce (1906–46), American who made propaganda broadcasts for Germany in the Second World War

Hawker Siddeley (no hyphen) British aviation company

Hawksmoor, Nicholas (1661–1736) English architect

Hawthorne, Nathaniel (1804–64)   American writer. (But **hawthorn** for the tree or shrub)

Haydn, Franz Joseph (1732–1809) Austrian composer

Hazlitt, William (1778–1830) English essayist and critic

headmaster, **headmistress**, but **head teacher**

healthy, **healthful**, **salutary**   Some authorities maintain that *healthy* should apply only to those things that possess health and *healthful* to those that promote it. Thus we would have 'healthy children', but 'healthful food' and 'healthful exercise'. There is no harm in observing the distinction, but also little to be gained from insisting on it. *Salutary* has a wider meaning than the other two words. It too means conducive to health, but can also apply to anything that is demonstrably beneficial ('a salutary lesson in etiquette').

'Hear, hear!' is the exclamation of British parliamentarians, not *'Here, here!'*

Hebrew, Yiddish The two languages have almost nothing in common except that they are spoken primarily by Jewish people. Yiddish (from the German *jüdisch*, 'Jewish') is a modified German dialect and thus a part of the Indo-European family of languages. Hebrew is a Semitic tongue and therefore is more closely related to Arabic. Yiddish writers sometimes use the Hebrew alphabet, but the two languages are no more closely related than, say, English and Swahili.

Hebrides pronounced *heb'-rid-eez*; group of islands off the west coast of Scotland, divided between the Inner Hebrides and Outer Hebrides; also called the Western Isles

hectare abbr. **ha**, 10,000 square metres; equivalent to 2.47 acres

hecto- prefix meaning 100

Hecuba in Greek mythology, the wife of Priam, King of Troy, and mother of Hector, Paris and Cassandra

Hedda Gabler, not *-bb-* play by Henrik Ibsen (1890)

Heeger, Alan J. (1936–) American scientist, awarded Nobel Prize for Chemistry 2000

Heep, Uriah character in Dickens's *David Copperfield* (1849–50)

Hegel, Georg Wilhelm Friedrich (1770–1831) German philosopher

Hegira (Arabic *hijrah*) the flight of Muhammad from Mecca to Medina on 16 July 622, used as the starting point for the Muslim era

Heian former name of Kyoto, Japan

Heidegger, Martin (1889–1976) German philosopher

Heidelberg German university city

Heidsieck champagne

heifer, not *-ff-* a young cow

Heifetz, Jascha (1901–87) Russian-born American violinist

Heilbroner, Robert L. (1920–2005) American economist

Heineken Dutch beer

Heinemann, William British publisher, now an imprint of Harcourt Education

heinous wicked

heir apparent, heir presumptive The first inherits no matter what; the second inherits only if a nearer relation is not born first.

Heisenberg, Werner (1901–76) German physicist, formulator of the Uncertainty Principle; awarded the Nobel Prize for Physics 1932

Heisman Trophy annual award to an outstanding US college football player; named for John W. Heisman (1869–1936), director of athletics at the New York Downtown Athletics Club

Hekmatyar See HIKMATYAR.

Helens, Mount St (no apos.) volcanic mountain in Washington state

Hellespont former name of the Dardanelles, the strait connecting the Sea of Marmara to the Aegean

Hellman, Lillian (1905–84) American playwright

Hello! magazine Note exclamation mark.

Héloïse (1101–64) lover of Pierre Abelard; but the poem of Alexander Pope is 'Eloisa to Abelard'

Helsingør Danish name for the Danish port known in English as Elsinore, setting of Shakespeare's *Hamlet*

hem and haw be indecisive; in the UK, usually **hum and haw**

Hendrix, Jimi (1942–70) born Johnny Allen Hendrix; American rock musician

Hennes & Mauritz clothing retailer

Hennessy cognac

hepatitis

Hephaestus Greek god of fire and metalworking; analogous to the Roman god Vulcan

Hephaisteion Temple of Hephaestus, Athens

Hepplewhite 18th-century style of furniture, named after English cabinetmaker George Hepplewhite (d. 1786)

Hera Greek goddess and wife of Zeus; identified with the Roman goddess Juno

Heracles/Hercules The first was a Greek demi-god; the second was a Roman god derived from Heracles.

herbaceous

Herculaneum Roman city destroyed with Pompeii in AD 79

herculean

Heriot-Watt University, Edinburgh

hermaphrodite plant or animal having male and female characteristics; from the Greek god Hermaphroditus

hermeneutics (sing.) the science of interpretation, especially of biblical texts

Hermes in Greek mythology, the messenger to the gods and guide to the souls of the dead, as well as god of science, commerce, oratory and travel; identified with the Roman god Mercury

Hero and Leander tragic lovers in Greek legend; Hero drowned herself in despair after Leander perished while swimming the Hellespont to see her

heroin, heroine The first is a dangerous drug; the second is a female hero.

herpetology the study of reptiles

Herschbach, Dudley R. (1932–) American scientist, awarded Nobel Prize for Chemistry 1986

Herschel, Sir William (1738–1822) German-born English astronomer, discoverer of Uranus

Hershko, Avram (1932–) Hungarian-born Israeli scientist, awarded Nobel Prize for Chemistry 2004

Herstmonceux, East Sussex The preferred pronunciation is *hurst´-mon-so*, though *hurst´-mon-soo* is also acceptable; site of Royal Observatory 1948–90.

Herzog & de Meuron Swiss architectural firm named for Jacques Herzog (1950–) and Pierre de Meuron (1950–)

Herzegovina region of Bosnia-Herzegovina, a former republic of Yugoslavia

Heseltine, Michael (1933–) British politician; now Lord Heseltine

Hess, Rudolf (1894–1987) German politician, Hitler's Deputy as Nazi party leader

Hesse, Hermann (1877–1972) German writer

heterogeneous made of unrelated parts

heureusement (Fr.) happily

heuristics the solving of problems through trial and error; the word is singular

Hewitt, Lleyton (1981–) Australian tennis player; note unusual spelling of first name

Hewlett-Packard Company (hyphen)

Heyerdahl, Thor (1914–2002) Norwegian anthropologist

Hezbollah (or **Hizbollah**) militant Lebanese Shiite Muslim group

HI postal abbreviation of Hawaii. The traditional abbreviation is **Ha.**

Hiawatha, The Song of epic poem by Henry Wadsworth Longfellow (1855)

hiccup, **hiccough** The first is now generally the preferred spelling.

hic et nunc (Lat.) here and now

Hicpochee, Lake, Florida

hierarchy, **hierarchies**, **hierarchical**

hieroglyphics

higgledy-piggledy at random, in confusion

high dudgeon, in feeling offended

highfalutin (no apos.) is the standard spelling, though many dictionaries also accept *highfaluting*, *highfaluten* and *hifalutin*. It is still considered informal by most sources. It means pompous and its origin is uncertain.

high-flier

high jinks (two words) is the usual spelling, though some dictionaries also accept *hijinks*. The derivation is unknown but the term is not related to (or to be confused with) *jinx* as in bad luck. The words can be used as either a singular or a plural.

Highlands, Scottish The general area is called the Highlands, but the specific governmental region is Highland (sing.).

high street Unless you are talking about a specific high street, there is no reason to capitalize it.

hijab scarf or head cover for Muslim women and, by extension, the system of modesty that goes with it

hijack, not *highjack*

Hikmatyar (or **Hekmatyar**), **Gulbuddin** (1947–) Afghan warlord, leader of Hizb-e-Islami faction; Prime Minister of Afghanistan 1993–4

Hilary an academic term at Oxford and some other universities, and a session of the High Court of Justice, beginning in January

Hillary, Sir Edmund (1919–2008)   New Zealand explorer and mountaineer; with Tensing, first person to scale Everest (1953)

Hilliard, Nicholas (c. 1547–1619)   English court goldsmith and painter of miniatures

Himmler, Heinrich (1900–45)   Nazi politician

Hinckley, Leicestershire, but **Hinkley Point Power Station**, Somerset

Hindenburg   airship that exploded at Lakehurst, New Jersey, in 1937

Hindi, Hindu, Hinduism, Hindustani   *Hindi* is the main language of India and *Hindustani* is its main dialect. *Hinduism* is the main religious and social system of India. *Hindu* describes a follower of Hinduism.

hindrance, not *-erance*

Hindu Kush   mountain range in Afghanistan

hippie, not *-ppy*

Hippocrates (c. 460–377 BC)   Greek physician, considered the father of medicine

hippopotamus, pl. **hippopotamuses**

hireable

Hirschfield, Abe (1920–2005)   American caricaturist

Hirshhorn Museum, Washington, DC   Note *-hh-*.

HIS, HJS *hic iacet sepultus/sepulta, hic jacet sepultus/sepulta* (Lat.) 'here lies buried'; often seen on gravestones

Hispaniola   Caribbean island shared by Haiti and the Dominican Republic

historic, historical   Something that makes history or is part of history is *historic*. Something that is based on history or describes history is *historical* ('a historical novel'). A historic judicial ruling is one that makes history; a historical ruling is based on precedent. There are, however, at least two exceptions to the rule – in account-ancy ('historic costs') and, curiously, in grammar ('historic tenses').

histrionics is plural

hitchhike, hitchhiker Note -*hh*-

hitherto 'In 1962, the regime took the hitherto unthinkable step of appropriating land' (*Daily Telegraph*). *Hitherto* means 'until now', so in the example cited it is out of step with the sentence's tense. The writer meant *thitherto* ('until then'), but *theretofore* would have been better and *previously* better still.

Hitler, Adolf (not *Adolph*) for the German Nazi leader (1889–1945)

Hittites ancient people of Asia Minor

HIV Human Immunodeficiency Virus; virus associated with AIDS. 'HIV virus' is redundant.

Hizbollah alt. spelling of **Hezbollah**

hoagie a type of sandwich

hoard, horde An accumulation of valuables, often hidden, is a *hoard*. *Horde* applies to any crowd, but particularly to a thronging and disorganized one ('hordes of Christmas shoppers').

hoary, not -*ey* grey or aged

Hobbema, Meindert (1638–1709) Dutch artist

Hobbes, Thomas (1588–1679) English philosopher

hobnob mix socially. The British biscuit is a **HobNob**.

hobo in the US, a tramp; pl. **hoboes**

Hoboken, New Jersey

Hobson's choice is sometimes taken to signify a dilemma or difficult decision, but in fact means having no choice at all. It is said to derive from a 16th-century stable-keeper in Cambridge named Thomas Hobson, who hired out horses in strict rotation. The customer was allowed to take the one nearest the stable door or none at all.

Hochhuth, Rolf (1931–) German playwright

Ho Chi Minh City, Vietnam formerly Saigon

Hodder & Stoughton British publisher, now an imprint of Hodder Headline; pronounced *stoe´-tun*

Hodgkin, Howard (1932–) English artist

Hodgkin's (or **Hodgkin**) **disease** a cancer of the lymphatic system first described by the British physician Thomas Hodgkin (1798–1866)

Hoek van Holland Dutch spelling of Hook of Holland

Hoffman, Dustin (1937–) American actor

Hoffmann, The Tales of opera by Jacques Offenbach (1881). Note *-ff-*, *-nn-*.

Hoffmann-La Roche Swiss pharmaceuticals company

Hofheinz Pavilion, Houston, Texas

Hofstadter, Richard (1916–70) American historian

Hogmanay Scottish name for New Year's Eve

Hohenzollern German royal family and a former province of Prussia

hoi polloi means 'the masses', 'the common populace', and not 'the elite' as is often thought. A second problem is that in Greek *hoi* means *the*, so to speak of 'the hoi polloi' is repetitious.

Hokkaido Japanese island; capital Sapporo

Hokusai, Katsushika (1760–1849) Japanese artist and wood engraver

Holbein, Hans, the Elder (c. 1460–1524) German painter and father of **Hans Holbein the Younger** (1497–1543), court painter to Henry VIII of England

Holiday, Billie (1915–59) American singer; born Eleanor Fagan Holiday

Holinshed, Raphael (d. c. 1580)   English historian, known for *The Chronicles of England, Scotland and Ireland* (1577), popularly known as *Holinshed's Chronicles*

hollandaise sauce (not cap.)

Holland America Line (no hyphen)   cruise ship company

Holmegaard   Danish crystal

Holmes, Oliver Wendell (1809–94), physician, professor at Harvard, poet, essayist and novelist, father of **Oliver Wendell Holmes Jr** (1841–1935), Associate Justice of the US Supreme Court 1902–32

holocaust   In Greek the word means 'burnt whole' and, generally speaking, it is better reserved for disasters involving fiery destruction. You should not, for instance, use the word to describe the devastation wrought by a hurricane or a mudslide. However, a clear exception is in references to the slaughter of Jews by Germany during the Second World War, when it describes the entire extermination process. In such contexts, the word is normally capitalized.

Holyoake, Sir Keith Jacka (1904–83)   Prime Minister of New Zealand 1957, 1960–72

Holyroodhouse, Palace of, Edinburgh, Scotland   pronounced *holly-*

Home Counties   in British usage, the counties immediately around London

Home of the Hirsel, Lord   title of Alec Douglas-Home (1903–95), British Prime Minister 1963–4; Home is pronounced *hume*

homely   If writing for an international audience, you should be aware (or beware) that the word has strikingly different connotations in different countries. In Britain and most of its former dominions *homely* means comfortable and appealing, having the warm and familiar qualities associated with a home. In America, for obscure reasons, it has long signified something that is unattractive, particularly in respect to the human face. If the audience is international and confusion likely to follow, clearly a more neutral term is advised. In any case, to describe someone as homely, in the American sense, is inescapably subjective, generally uncharitable and may cause needless hurt.

homogeneous, homogenous *Homogeneous* means consistent and uniform; *homogenous* is almost always restricted to biological contexts, where it describes organisms having common ancestry.

homonym, homophone Both describe words that have strong similarities of sound or spelling, but different meanings. A *homophone* is a word that sounds like another but has a different meaning or spelling, or both. A *homonym* is a word that also has a different meaning, but the same spelling or sound. Thus *blue* and *blew* are both homonyms and homophones. However, *bow* as in a ship and *bow* as in a tie are homonyms (because they are spelled the same) but not homophones (because they have different pronunciations). In short, unless the intention is to emphasize the equivalence of pronunciations, *homonym* is generally the better word.

Honecker, Erich (1912–94) chairman of the East German Communist Party (i.e., head of state) 1977–89

Honegger, Arthur (1892–1955) Swiss-French composer

Hong Kong/Hongkong *Hong Kong* is the more common spelling, but either is correct.

Honiara capital of the Solomon Islands

Honi soit qui mal y pense (Fr.) usually translated as 'Evil to him who evil thinks'; motto of the royal Order of the Garter in Britain

honnête homme (Fr.) an honest man

honorificabilitudinitatibus nonce word – a term created for a specific occasion – in Shakespeare's *Love's Labour's Lost*

honour, but **honorable, honorarium, honorary**

Honshu main island of Japan, site of Tokyo and Yokohama

Hooch/Hoogh, Pieter de (c. 1629–c. 1684) Dutch painter; pronounced *hoke* for either spelling

hoodie a young man in a hooded sweatshirt

Hoofddorp, Netherlands Note -*dd*-.

Hook of Holland in Dutch, Hoek van Holland

Hoosick Falls, New York

hopefully Much ink has been expended arguing whether the word is acceptable when used in an absolute sense, as in 'Hopefully the sun will shine tomorrow.' Many usage authorities argue that that sentence should be recast as 'It is to be hoped that the sun will shine tomorrow' or something similar. However, other authorities say that such a stand is pedantic and inconsistent, since no one objects to other -*ly* words, such as *apparently, sadly, thankfully* and *mercifully*, being used absolutely. I side with the second group, but you should be aware that the use of *hopefully* in an absolute sense is still widely, and often hotly, objected to.

Hopkins, Gerard Manley (1844–89) British poet and Jesuit priest. His poetry was published posthumously.

Hopkins, Johns (1795–1873), not *John* American financier who endowed the now-famous hospital and university, both in Baltimore

Horae Greek goddesses who presided over the weather and
seasons

horde, **hoard** The first is a swarm of people, the second a
cache.

Horowitz, Vladimir (1904–89) Russian-born American
concert pianist

hors de combat (Fr.) out of action

hors-d'oeuvre an appetizer; pl. **hors-d'oeuvres**

'*Horst Wessel Lied*' Nazi song

hosanna a shout of praise

Hosokawa, Morihiro (1938–) Japanese Prime Minister 1993–4

hotchpotch (US **hodgepodge**)

hot dog (two words) for the food, but (US) **hotdog** as a verb
meaning to show off and for associated words such as
hotdogging and **hotdogger**

Hôtel des Invalides, Paris site of Napoleon's tomb

hôtel de ville (Fr.) town hall

Houellebecq, Michel (1958–) French novelist, pronounced
well-beck

Housman, A. E. (for **Alfred Edward**) (1859–1936), not
House-; English poet, and brother of **Laurence
Housman** (1865–1959), a noted artist, novelist and
playwright

Houston, Whitney (1963–) American singer. (But note it is
Anjelica Huston.)

Houyhnhnms pronounced *win-ums*; in *Gulliver's Travels*, a
race of horses with the finer qualities of humans

Hovenweep National Monument, Utah

hovercraft (no cap.) The name is no longer a trademark.

Howards End (no apos.) novel by E. M. Forster (1910)

Howells, William Dean (1837–1920) American critic, editor
and writer

Howerd, Frankie (1921–92) born Francis Alex Howard; British comic actor

howitzer a cannon

Hoxha, Enver (1908–85) pronounced *hod'-juh*; head of state of Albania 1944–85

Hrvastska Croatian name for Croatia

HTML short for Hypertext Markup Language; language used for communicating on World Wide Web

HTTP short for Hypertext Transfer Protocol; governing standard for World Wide Web information transfers

Hua Guofeng (formerly **Hua Kuo-feng**) (1920–) Chinese Communist leader, Premier 1976–80

Huanghe Pinyin name for the Hwang-Ho or Yellow River, China; in most contexts a reference to one or both of the older names would be helpful.

hudibrastic in a mock-heroic manner, from the epic satirical poem *Hudibras* by Samuel Butler (1663–78)

Hudson Bay, **Hudson Strait**, **Hudson River**, but **Hudson's Bay Company**

hue and cry, not *hew* an uproar

Huguenots 16th–17th-century French Protestants

Hu Jintao (1942–) President of China 2003–

hullabaloo a commotion

hum and haw (US **hem and haw**) be indecisive

Human Immunodeficiency Virus HIV, virus associated with AIDS

humerus bone in the arm between the elbow and the shoulder; pl. **humeri**

humour, but **humorous**, **humorist**, **humoresque**

Humperdinck, Engelbert (1854–1921) German composer; also the stage name of a British popular singer, born Arnold Dorsey (1935–)

Humphry Clinker, The Expedition of, not *Humphrey* novel by Tobias Smollett (1771)

humus, hummus The first is broken-down plant material in soil, the second a dish made from mashed chickpeas.

Humvee name derived from the initials HMMWV (high mobility multipurpose wheeled vehicle)

Hundred Years' War (1337–1453) series of wars in which France wrested back from England all its territory except Calais

Hunt, (William) Holman (1827–1910) English painter

hurdy-gurdy musical instrument activated by a crank

hurly-burly lively activity

Hurston, Zora Neale (1891–1960) American writer, associated with the movement known as the Harlem Renaissance

Husbands Bosworth, Leicestershire

Hussein, Saddam (1937–2006) President of Iraq 1979–2003. His name in full was Saddam Hussein Abd al-Majid al-Tikrit.

Huston, Anjelica (1951–), American actress, daughter of film director **John Huston** (1906–87) and granddaughter of actor **Walter Huston** (1884–1950)

Huxley, Aldous (1894–1963), English novelist and brother of **Sir Julian Huxley** (1887–1975), biologist and writer; their grandfather was **T. H. Huxley** (1825–95), scientist and champion of Charles Darwin

Huygens, Christiaan (1629–95) Dutch mathematician and scientist; note -*aa*- in first name

Huysmans, Joris Karl (1848–1907) French novelist

Huyton, Merseyside pronounced *hie´-tun*

Hwang-Ho Chinese river now more commonly known as **Huanghe**

hyacinth flower

Hyannis Port, but **West Hyannisport**, Cape Cod, Massachusetts

Hyderabad capital of Andhra Pradesh, India. There is also a city in Pakistan of the same name, which is sometimes spelled Haidarabad.

Hydra in Greek mythology, a many-headed monster

hydrangea flowering shrub

hydrography the study and mapping of oceans, rivers and lakes

hyena

Hygeia Greek goddess of health

hygiene, hygienic

hymen, not -*man* vaginal membrane, named after Hymen, Greek god of marriage

Hynes Convention Center, Boston, Massachusetts formally it is the John B. Hynes Veterans Memorial Convention Center

hyperbole exaggeration

hypertension high blood pressure

hypochondria

hypocrite, hypocrisy

hypotenuse on a right-angled triangle, the side opposite the right angle

hypothermia lack of body warmth

hypothesis, pl. **hypotheses**

hysterectomy

hysterics is plural.

Hywel pronounced *howl*; Welsh forename

I

Iacocca, Lee (1924–) American businessman

IAEA International Atomic Energy Agency, UN nuclear watchdog

IATA International Air Transport Association

Iberia Airlines, not *Iberian*

ibex a mountain goat; pl. **ibexes**

ibid. abbr. of *ibidem* (Lat.), 'in the same place'; used in reference notes to indicate that a source is the same as the one in the previous note; see also OP. CIT.

ibis wading bird

-ible/-able No reliable rules exist for when a word ends in *-ible* and when in *-able*; see Appendix for a list of some of the more frequently confused spellings.

Ibsen, Henrik (1828–1906) Norwegian playwright

Ibstock Johnsen, not *Johnson* British company

ICBM intercontinental ballistic missile

iceberg

iced tea, not *ice*

Icelandair Icelandic airline

Iceni British tribe that revolted against Rome under the leadership of Boudicca in the 1st century AD

Ich dien (Ger.) 'I serve'; motto of the Prince of Wales

ichthyology the study of fishes

ichthyosaur/ichthyosaurus prehistoric marine reptile

ici on parle français (Fr.) 'French spoken here'; note lower case *f* for *français*

Icknield Way prehistoric track running from Salisbury Plain to the Wash

I, Claudius note comma; novel by Robert Graves (1934)

Ictinus (*fl.* 5th c. BC) Greek architect, co-designer with Callicrates of the Parthenon

idée fixe (Fr.) an obsession or fixation. The plural is *idées fixes.*

Identikit (cap.)

ideology, ideological, ideologue

ides of March 15 March, the day on which Julius Caesar was assassinated. In the Roman calendar, the ides fell on the 15th of March, May, July and October, and the 13th of the other months.

idiosyncrasy One of the most commonly misspelled of all words. Note that the ending is *-sy*, not *-cy*.

idyll a peaceful interlude; poem or prose depicting rural bliss

i.e., *id est* (Lat.) 'that is to say'; used to introduce an elaboration, as in 'He is pusillanimous, i.e., lacking in courage.'

if Problems often arise in deciding whether *if* is introducing a subjunctive clause ('If I were . . .') or an indicative one ('If I was . . .'). The distinction is straightforward. When *if* introduces a notion that is hypothetical or improbable or clearly untrue, the verb should be in the subjunctive: 'If I were king . . .'; 'If he were in your shoes . . .' But when the *if* is introducing a thought that is true or could well be true, the mood should be indicative: 'If I was happy then, I certainly am not now.' One small hint: if the sentence contains *would* or *wouldn't*, the mood is subjunctive, as in 'If I were you, I wouldn't take the job.'

if and when   almost always unnecessary. Choose one or the other.

igneous rock

ignominy, ignominious

ignotum per ignotius (Lat.) 'the unknown by the even less known'; used of an explanation that is more confusing than what it is meant to explain

Iguassu (or **Iguaçu**) **Falls** waterfall on the Argentina–Brazil border; in Portuguese **Saltos do Iğuaçu**; in Spanish **Cantaratas del Iguazú**

iguana large lizard

iguanodon dinosaur

IJsselmeer, the Netherlands note double caps; freshwater lake created by damming part of the Zuider Zee

ILEA Inner London Education Authority, abolished 1990

Île de France region of France that includes Paris

ileum, ilium The *ileum* is part of the small intestine; the *ilium* is part of the pelvis and, when capitalized, is also the Latin name for Troy.

Iliad epic poem attributed to Homer (*fl.* 8th c. BC)

illegitimate, illegitimize

illicit forbidden

Illinoian, not *Illinoisian* someone or something from Illinois

illuminati (always pl.) enlightened people

illustrator

imbroglio   a predicament, a complicated situation; pl. **imbroglios**

immanent, imminent The first means inherent, the second impending; neither should be confused with *eminent*, which means outstanding.

immaterial

immeasurable

immoral, amoral *Immoral* applies to things that are evil; *amoral* describes matters in which questions of morality do not arise or are disregarded.

Immortels, Les nickname of members of the Académie française

immovable, immovability

immutable unchanging, incapable of change

impala, not -*ll*- antelope

impassable, impassible The first means impossible to negotiate; the second means impervious to pain.

impazientemente (It.) in music, to perform in an impatient manner

imperative

imperceptible

impermeable

impertinent

implacable

imply, infer *Imply* means to suggest: 'He implied that I was a fool.' *Infer* means to deduce: 'After three hours of waiting, we inferred that they weren't coming.'

imports, exports It is implicit in *imports* that their source is foreign, so it is tautological to write 'imports from abroad'. Similar phrases involving *exports*, such as 'exports overseas fell slightly last month' equally cry out for pruning.

impostor, not -*er*

impractical, impracticable, unpractical If a thing could be done but isn't worth doing, it is impractical or unpractical (the words mean the same). If it can't be done at all, it's impracticable (the word means 'incapable of being put into practice').

impresario

impressible

imprimatur official authorization

improvable

improvvisata (It.) in music, improvised. Note -*vv*-.

impugn, **impunity** The first is to criticize or attack; the second means the condition of enjoying freedom from punishment.

in, **into**, **in to** Generally, *in* indicates a fixed position ('he was in the house') while *into* indicates movement towards a fixed position ('he went into the house'). There are, however, many exceptions (e.g., 'he put the money in his pocket'). As so often with idiom, there is no describable pattern to these exceptions; it is just the way it is.

Whether to write *into* as one word or two also sometimes causes problems. The simple rule is that *in to* is correct when *in* is an adverb, but the distinction can perhaps best be seen in paired examples: 'He turned himself into [one word] an accomplished artist' but 'The criminal turned himself in to [two words] the police.'

in absentia (Lat.) while absent

inadmissible, not -*able*

inadvertent

inadvisable

inamorata (fem.), **inamorato** (masc.) lover; pl. **inamorati**

inasmuch as

in camera behind closed doors, not in open court

incessant

inchoate undeveloped, just starting out

incidentally

incisor

include indicates that what is to follow is only part of a greater whole. To use it when you are describing a totality (as in 'The 630 job losses include 300 in Redcar and 330 in Port Talbot') is careless and possibly misleading.

incognito

incombustible cannot be burned

incommodious causing inconvenience

incommunicado unable or unwilling to communicate

incomparable

incompatible

incomprehensible, not -*able*

incongruous, **incongruity**

incorrigible

incubus an evil spirit that has intercourse with sleeping women; a nightmare or something that oppresses like a nightmare. See also SUCCUBUS.

inculcate means to persistently impress a habit upon or belief into another person. You inculcate an idea, not a person. 'My father inculcated me with a belief in democracy' should be 'My father inculcated in me a belief in democracy.'

incunabulum a book printed at an early date, especially before 1501; the early stages of development of something; pl. **incunabula**

in curia (Lat.) in open court

indefatigable tireless

indefeasible permanent, cannot be made void

indefensible

indefinitely means only 'without prescribed limits', not 'lasting for ever'. To say that a process will last indefinitely doesn't necessarily mean that it will last for a very long time, but simply that its duration is unknown.

indelible

Independence Day (US), 4 July, marks the signing of the Declaration of Independence (1776).

indescribable

indestructible

indexes/indices Either is acceptable, though some dictionaries favour *indices* for technical applications.

Index Librorum Prohibitorum catalogue of books forbidden to Roman Catholics by their Church. Not to be confused with **Index Expurgatorius**, a catalogue of books in which only certain passages are forbidden.

india ink (not cap.)

indict, indite The first means to accuse formally of a crime; the second means to set down in writing, but in fact is rare almost to the point of obsolescence.

indigenous occurring naturally in a particular place

indigent needy

indigestible

indiscreet, indiscrete The first means lacking discretion; the second means not composed of separate parts.

indispensable, not -*ible*

individual is unexceptionable when you are contrasting one person with an organization or body of people ('How can one individual hope to rectify the evils of society?'). But as a simple synonym for *person* ('Do you see that individual standing over there?') it is still frowned upon by many authorities as casual and inelegant.

indivisible

indomitable

indubitable, indubitably

Induráin, Miguel (1964–) Spanish cyclist

Industrial Workers of the World abbr. IWW, a radical

international trade union movement at its height from 1905 to 1925, often called the Wobblies, particularly by detractors

inebriate, inebriety

inedible

ineffaceable indelible (which in most cases is to be preferred)

inefficacious a longer way of saying ineffective

ineligible

ineluctable inevitable, unavoidable

inequable, inequitable The first means not even or uniform; the second means unfair.

ineradicable

inevitable

in excelsis (Lat.) to the highest degree

inexcusable

inexplicable

inexpressible

in extenso (Lat.) at full length

inextinguishable

in extremis (Lat.) in dire circumstances; at the point of death

infallible

infamous famous in a negative way; notorious

infer, imply *Imply* means to suggest: 'He implied that I was a fool.' *Infer* means to deduce: 'After three hours of waiting, we inferred that they weren't coming.' The condition of being able to be inferred is **inferable**.

infinitesimal

infinitude

in flagrante delicto (Lat.) in the act of committing an offence

inflammable, flammable, non-flammable Although *inflammable* means 'capable of being burned', it has so often been taken to mean the opposite that most authorities now suggest that it be avoided. It is deemed generally better to use *flammable* for materials that will burn and *non-flammable* for those that will not.

inflammation, **inflammatory**, not *im-*

inflation has become so agreeably quiescent in recent years that the word and its several variant forms are much less troublesome than they were when this book first appeared. However (and just in case), it is worth noting a few definitions. *Inflation* itself means that the money supply and prices are rising. *Hyperinflation* means that they are rising rapidly (at an annual rate of at least 20 per cent). *Deflation* means that they are falling, and *reflation* that they are being pushed up again after a period of deflation. *Stagflation* means that prices are rising while output is stagnant. *Disinflation*, a word so vague in sense to most readers that it is almost always better avoided, means that prices are rising but at a rate slower than before. Finally, bear in mind that if the rate of inflation was 4.5 per cent last month and 3.5 per cent this month, it does not mean that prices are falling; they are still rising, but at a slower rate.

inflexible

infra dig. abbr. of *infra dignitatem*, 'without (or beneath) dignity'

ingenious, ingenuous The first means to be clever or inventive; the second means innocent, unsophisticated, guileless. *Disingenuous* means pretending to be ingenuous.

ingénue innocent young woman

Ingushetia (or **Ingushetiya**) Russian republic

inimical harmful, antagonistic

iniquitous wicked

Inkatha Freedom Party South Africa

in loco parentis (Lat.) in place of the parent
in media res (Lat.) in the middle of things
in memoriam, not -*um*
Innes, George (1825–94) American landscape painter of the
     Hudson River school
innocent It is pedantic to insist on it too rigorously on all
     occasions, but it is worth noting that people do not
     actually plead innocent (since one of the hallmarks of
     our legal system is that innocence is presumed). Strictly,
     they plead guilty or not guilty.
innocuous harmless
Inns of Court, London There are four: Gray's Inn, Lincoln's
     Inn, Inner Temple and Middle Temple.
innuendo, pl. **innuendoes**
inoculate
in order to A wordy locution. In nearly every instance,
     removing *in order* tightens the sentence without altering
     the sense. See also IN, INTO, IN TO.
inquiry See QUERY.
inscrutable
insects It is always worth remembering that the term does
     not apply to spiders, mites and ticks, which are
     arachnids, a different class of creature altogether.
     Although some dictionaries (*American Heritage*, for
     one) allow the looser usage in informal or in non-
     technical writing, it is unquestionably incorrect and
     thus better avoided almost always. If you need a term to
     describe insects and spiders together, the word is
     arthropods.
inshallah (Arabic) if Allah wills it
insidious, **invidious** *Insidious* indicates the stealthy or tardily
     detected spread of something undesirable ('an insidious

leak from the pipe'). *Invidious* means offensive or inviting animosity ('I was angered by his invidious remarks').

insignia (sing. and pl.) Historically, *insigne* is the correct singular, but almost no authority insists on it now.

in situ (Lat.) in place

in so far or **insofar**

insouciance, insouciant lack of concern, carefree

install, installation, but **instalment**

instantaneous

instil, but **instilling, instilled**

Institut de France, not -*tute* umbrella organization for the five French academies: Académie des Beaux-Arts, Académie française, Académie des Inscriptions et Belles-Lettres, Académie des Sciences, and the Académie des Sciences Morales et Politiques

Institute for Fiscal Studies, not *of*

Institution of Professionals, Managers and Specialists formerly the Institution of Professional Civil Servants

insuperable

insuppressible

insurer, not -*or*

intelligentsia the intellectual élite of a society

intelligible

in tenebris (Lat.) in the dark, in doubt

intense, intensive *Intense* should describe things that are heavy or extreme or occur to a high degree ('intense sunlight', 'intense downpour'). *Intensive* implies a concentrated focus ('intensive care', 'an intensive search'). Although the two words often come to the same thing, they needn't. An intense bombardment, as Fowler pointed out, is a severe one. An intensive bombardment is one directed at a small (or relatively small) area.

inter alia (Lat.) among other things

interface point where two things meet and interact

intermezzo in music, a short piece between longer ones; pl. **intermezzi/intermezzos**

interminable

International Atomic Energy Agency, not *Authority*

international courts Understandably, these sometimes cause confusion. The International Court of Justice, or World Court, in The Hague, Netherlands, is an offspring of the United Nations and deals with disputes between or among UN member states. The European Court of Justice, in Luxembourg, is a European Union institution dealing exclusively with disputes involving EU member states. The European Court of Human Rights, in Strasbourg, France, addresses issues of civil liberties arising from the European Convention on Human Rights. It has no connection with the United Nations or European Union.

International Olympic Committee, not *Olympics*

internecine For more than 200 years writers have used *internecine* in the sense of a costly or self-destructive conflict even though etymologically the word signifies only a slaughter or massacre without any explicit sense of cost to the victor. It has been misused for so long that it would be pedantic and wildly optimistic to try to enforce its original meaning, but it should at least be reserved for bloody and violent disputes and not mere squabbles.

interpolate to insert

interregnum period between reigns; pl. **interregnums**

interrelated Note -*rr*-.

in toto (Lat.) in total

intransitive verbs are those that cannot take a direct object, as with *sleep* in the sentence 'He sleeps all night.' See also TRANSITIVE VERB.

intrauterine device

intra vires (Lat.) within one's powers

intrigue Originally *intrigue* signified underhanded plotting and nothing else. The looser meaning of arousing or fascinating ('We found the lecture intriguing') is now established. It is, however, greatly overworked and almost always better replaced by a more telling word.

Inuit indigenous people of northern Canada and parts of Alaska and Greenland, and their language. The term is preferable to *Eskimo*.

in utero (Lat.) in the uterus

in vacuo (Lat.) in a vacuum

invariably does not mean *frequently* or *usually*. It means constantly, not subject to change – in short, without variance.

inveigh, inveigle Occasionally confused. The first means to speak strongly against ('He inveighed against the rise in taxes'). The second means to entice or cajole ('They inveigled an invitation to the party').

Inveraray, Strathclyde

Inverness-shire former Scottish county, now part of Highland region

Investors in Industry UK investment group, familiarly known as 3i

invidious, insidious *Invidious* means unfair or likely to cause offence; *insidious* describes the stealthy spread of something undesirable.

in vino veritas (Lat.) in wine there is truth

in vitro (Lat.) literally 'in glass', i.e., in a test tube, as with *in vitro* fertilization

in vivo (Lat.) in a living organism

IPO Initial Public Offering, the term for stock issued on a company's market début

iPod portable media player

ipsissima verba (Lat.) the very words

ipso facto (Lat.) by the very fact

IQ intelligence quotient

Iraqi, pl. **Iraqis**

Ireland, Republic of (in Gaelic **Eire**) consists of the following provinces (and their counties): Connacht (Galway, Leitrim, Mayo, Roscommon, Sligo), Leinster (Carlow, Dublin, Kildare, Kilkenny, Laois, Longford, Louth, Meath, Offaly, Westmeath, Wexford, Wicklow), Munster (Clare, Cork, Kerry, Limerick, Tipperary, Waterford), Ulster (Cavan, Donegal, Monaghan).

Irgun Zvai Leumi Jewish guerrilla organization (1931–48) whose aim was to establish an Israeli state

iridescence, iridescent

irony, sarcasm *Irony* is the use of words to convey a contradiction between the literal and intended meanings. *Sarcasm* is very like irony except that it is more stinging. Where the primary intent behind irony is to amuse, with sarcasm it is to wound or score points.

Iroquois native American group consisting of Cayuge, Mohawk, Oneida, Onondaga, Seneca and Tuscaroras peoples; pl. **Iroquois**

Irrawaddy principal river of Burma/Myanmar

irreconcilable

irrefragable, irrefrangible. The first means indisputable, the second indestructible, but both are inescapably pretentious when such useful synonyms are available.

irregardless is not a real word; make it *regardless.*

irrelevance, **irrelevant**

irreparable

irreplaceable

irrepressible

irresistible

irreversible

IRS Internal Revenue Service, US federal tax authority

Isaiah book of the Old Testament

ISBN International Standard Book Number; identifying number on books

Ischia volcanic island in the Bay of Naples

-ise/-ize Since about the time of Noah Webster (1758–1843), American users have been strongly inclined to use *-ize* terminations on verbs such as *recognize* and *conceptualize*, while in Britain *-ise* endings remain more common. However, it is worth noting that even under the *-ize* system, certain words continue always to end in *-ise*, of which the following are the main ones: *advertise, advise, apprise, chastise, circumcise, comprise, compromise, demise, despise, devise, disguise, excise, exercise, franchise, improvise, incise, merchandise, reprise, supervise, surmise, surprise, televise.*

Iseult/Isolde/Isolt/Ysolt In Arthurian legend, an Irish princess who falls tragically in love with Tristan, the nephew of a Cornish king. Wagner's opera is *Tristan und Isolde* (1857–9).

Ishiguro, Kazuo (1954–) British novelist

isosceles triangle one with two equal sides

Isozaki, Arata (1931–) Japanese architect

Issigonis, Sir Alec (1906–88)   Turkish-born British car designer

Italy is divided into 20 regions: Abruzzi, Basilicata, Calabria, Campania, Emilia-Romagna, Friuli-Venezia Giulia, Lazio, Liguria, Lombardia (Lombardy), Marche (Marches), Molise, Piemonte (Piedmont), Puglia (Apulia), Sardegna (Sardinia), Sicilia (Sicily), Trentino-Alto Adige, Toscana (Tuscany), Umbria, Valle d'Aosta, Veneto.

ITAR-TASS Russian news agency, formerly just called TASS

its, it's *Its* is the possessive form of *it*: 'Put each book in its place.' *It's* is the contraction of *it is*: 'The beauty of solar power is that it's environmentally friendly.'

ITV Independent Television

Ivy League   group of eight universities in the eastern US noted for high academic standards: Brown, Columbia, Cornell, Dartmouth, Harvard, Princeton, University of Pennsylvania and Yale

Iwerne Courtney, Dorset   pronounced *ewe´-urn*

IWW Industrial Workers of the World, a radical international trade union movement at its height from 1905 to 1925; often called the Wobblies

Izmir, Turkey   formerly Smyrna

Izvestia (or *Izvestiya*)   Russian newspaper

J

ja, jawohl (Ger.) yes

'Jabberwocky' poem by Lewis Carroll in *Through the Looking Glass* (1872) and (no cap.) any kind of nonsense writing

jacana tropical bird

jacaranda tropical tree

jackal

jackanapes a cocky person

Jacobean, Jacobin, Jacobite *Jacobean* describes the period of the reign of James I of England (1603–25). *Jacobins* were radical republicans during the French Revolution. *Jacobites* were supporters of James II of England and his heirs following the Glorious Revolution of 1688.

Jacobi, Derek (1938–) English actor

Jacobs Suchard Swiss chocolate company

jactitation Note -*ctit*-; restless twitching of the body

jactitation of marriage falsely claiming to be someone's wife or husband

Jacuzzi (cap.) whirlpool bath

Jaeger clothing company

jai alai also called pelota, a fast-paced ball game popular in Spain and Latin America

Jakarta, not *Djakarta* capital of Indonesia; formerly Batavia

jalopy an old car

jalousie type of slatted shutter

jamb, not *jam* a doorpost or similar

James's, St, for the palace, park and square in London, not *James'*

Janáček, Leoš (1854–1928) Czech composer

Jane Eyre novel by Charlotte Brontë (1847)

Jankovic, Jelena (1985–) Serbian tennis player

Janus   Roman god of the gate of heaven, depicted as having two faces – one at the front of his head and one at the back – because every door or gate looks two ways; also god of beginnings and of the first month, January

Japan Air Lines, not *Airlines*

Jaques, not *Jacques* character in William Shakespeare's *As You Like It*

jardinière ornamental pot or stand for plants; a garnish of mixed vegetables

Jaruzelski, General Wojciech (1923–) Polish general, Prime Minister 1981–5, head of state 1985–9, President 1989–90

Jarvik-7 artificial heart, invented by Robert Jarvik (1946–)

javelin

JCPenney (one word) US department store company

Jeanne d'Arc French for Joan of Arc

Jedda/Jidda, Saudi Arabia

jeep, Jeep Use *jeep* generally for Army vehicles, but *Jeep* specifically for the brand name of cars produced by Chrysler Holding.

Jeffreys, George, Lord (1648–89) British 'hanging' judge, infamous for the severity of his punishments handed down after Monmouth's rebellion (1685)

Jehovah's Witness

jejune insubstantial, naive

Jekyll and Hyde The full title of the book by Robert Louis Stevenson is *The Strange Case of Dr Jekyll and Mr Hyde* (1886)

Jelinek, Elfriede (1946–) Austrian writer, awarded Nobel Prize for Literature 2004

Jellicoe, John Rushworth, Earl (1859–1935) British admiral

Jell-O American jelly dessert

Jemaah Islamiah Islamist group responsible for several bombings in Indonesia

je ne sais pas (Fr.) I don't know

je ne sais quoi (Fr.) 'I don't know what'; applied to the indescribable

Jenkins' Ear, War of (1739–48) war between Britain and Spain over trade with South America, ostensibly provoked by an incident in which Spanish sailors boarded a British vessel in the Caribbean and cut off the ear of the captain, Robert Jenkins, but this was seven years before the hostilities began

jeopardy, jeopardize

jeremiad elaborate lamentation

jeroboam wine bottle containing the equivalent of four ordinary wine bottles

jerry-built, jury-rigged Occasionally confused. The first applies to things that are built cheaply and sloppily without regard to quality. The second describes things made in haste, with whatever materials are at hand, as a temporary or emergency measure.

Jervaulx Abbey, North Yorkshire pronounced *jer-vó*

jetsam, flotsam *Jetsam* applies to goods that have been thrown overboard (jettisoned) at sea; *flotsam* describes goods that have floated free from wreckage. Historically, flotsam went to the Crown and jetsam to the lord of the manor on whose land it washed up.

Jeu de Paume, Musée du, Paris

jeune fille (Fr.) a girl

jew's harp (no caps)

Jhabvala, Ruth Prawer (1927–) German-born British novelist and screenwriter

jib be reluctant to do something; also a kind of sail

jibe means to be in agreement and is also a nautical term for the act of changing tack.

jihad a Muslim holy war

Jinnah, Mohammed Ali (1876–1948) founder of Pakistan, Governor-General 1947–8

Jobs, Steven (1955–), not *-ph-* computer entrepreneur, co-founder of Apple Computer Inc.

jodhpurs riding breeches, named after the Indian city of Jodhpur

Jodrell Bank observatory The formal name (seldom used) is Nuffield Radio-Astronomy Laboratories of the University of Manchester.

Johannesburg, South Africa, but the German wine is **Johannisberger**.

John Newbery Medal US award for outstanding children's literature

John o' Groats house and ferry site in Scotland traditionally (but incorrectly) given as the northernmost point on the British mainland

Johns Hopkins (note *s* on both) is the name of the university and medical centre in Baltimore.

Johnson, Nunnally (1897–1977) American screenwriter, film director and producer

joie de vivre (Fr.) 'joy of living'; exuberance

Joiners' and Ceilers' Company London livery company. *Ceiler* is an old term for a woodcarver.

Joliet, Illinois

Joliet (or **Jolliet**), **Louis** (1645–1700) French-Canadian explorer

Joliette County, Quebec

Jones, Inigo (1573–1652) English architect and designer

Joneses, keeping up with the, not *Jones'* or *Jones's* or other common variants

Jones Lang Wootton UK property group

jonquil species of narcissus

Jonson, Ben (1572–1637), not *John-* English dramatist and poet

Jordaens, Jakob (1593–1678) Flemish painter

Joslyn Art Museum, Omaha

joss stick fragrant stick, burnt as incense

Jove alt. name for the Roman god Jupiter

JPMorgan Chase & Co. financial services company

Juan de Fuca Strait passage between Washington State and Vancouver Island, British Columbia

Juárez, Mexico formally it is **Ciudad de Juárez**

Judas Iscariot apostle who betrayed Jesus for 30 pieces of silver

jugular vein

Juilliard School of Music, New York City Note *Jui-*.

jujitsu Japanese form of unarmed combat

julienne vegetables cut into strips; a soup containing such vegetables

Juno and the Paycock play by Sean O'Casey (1924)

junta properly pronounced *hoon´-ta*, commonly pronounced *jun´-ta*; government run by a political or military clique after a coup d'état

Jupiter supreme Roman god, also called Jove; also fifth planet from the Sun

just deserts, not *desserts* The expression has nothing to do with the sweet course after dinner. It comes from the French for *deserve*, which may help you to remember that it has just one middle *s*.

Juvenal (c. 60–c. 140) Roman poet; full name Decimus Junius Juvenalis

j'y suis, j'y reste (Fr.) here I am, here I stay

K

Kaaba sacred shrine at Mecca
Kabardino-Balkariya Russian republic
kabuki Japanese theatre
Kaczyński, Lech, and **Kaczyński, Jaroslaw** (1949–) identical twin brothers, respectively President (2005–) and Prime Minister (2006–7) of Poland
Kádár, János (1912–89) Hungarian politician
Kaddish (cap.) type of Jewish prayer
kaffeeklatsch (Ger.) a gathering for coffee and conversation
Kahlúa coffee liqueur
Kahneman, Daniel (1934–) Israeli-American academic; awarded Nobel Prize for Economics 2002
Kaho'olawe (or **Kahoolawe**) smallest of the main Hawaiian islands
Kakadu National Park, Northern Territory, Australia
kakapo endangered flightless bird from New Zealand
Kalamazoo, Michigan
Kalashnikov rifle
kaleidoscope
Kalgoorlie mining town in Western Australia
Kali Hindu goddess
Kamchatka Peninsula, Russia
kamikaze reckless, self-destructive

Kampuchea official name for Cambodia, 1975–89

Kandinsky, Wassily (or **Vasily**) (1866–1944) Russian-born French artist

Kaneohe city and bay on Oahu, Hawaii

Kansas City Its name notwithstanding, Kansas City is mostly in Missouri, not Kansas.

Kant, Immanuel (1724–1804) German philosopher

Kaohsiung second largest city in Taiwan

Kapuściński, Ryszard (1932–2007) Polish writer

Karachayevo-Cherkesiya Russian republic

Karadžić, Radovan (1945–) Bosnian Serb politician accused of genocide and war crimes

Karajan, Herbert von (1908–89) Austrian conductor

Karamanlis, Kostas (or **Costas**) (1956–) Prime Minister of Greece 2004–; formally Konstantinos Karamanlis

Karl-Marx-Stadt (hyphens) name of Chemnitz, Germany, during Communist era

Karlovy Vary Czech spa formerly known as Carlsbad

Kármán, Theodor von (1881–1963) Hungarian-born American physicist

Karolinska Institute, Stockholm

Kaskaskia River, Illinois

Kasparov, Garry (1963–) Note -*rr*-; born Harry Weinstein; Russian chess player

Kassel, Germany

Katherina character in *The Taming of the Shrew* by William Shakespeare

Katharine's Docks, St, London Note the unusual spelling of *Katharine*.

Kathasaritsagara Sanskrit epic

Katmandu (or **Kathmandu**) capital of Nepal

Katrine, Loch, Central Region, Scotland pronounced *kat´-trin*

Kattegatt the strait between Denmark and Sweden; in Danish, Kattegat

Kauai Hawaiian island

Kaufingerstrasse, Munich

Kaufman, George S. (for **Simon**) (1889–1961) American dramatist

Kaufman, Gerald (1930–) British politician

Kazakhstan Central Asian republic, formerly part of the Soviet Union; capital Alma Ata

Kazantzakis, Nikos (1883–1957) Greek poet and novelist

KCB Knight Commander of the Order of the Bath; note second *the*

KCMG Knight Commander of the Order of St Michael and St George

Kean, Edmund (c. 1787–1833) English actor

Kearsley, Greater Manchester pronounced *kurz´-lee*

Keble College, Oxford named after John Keble (1792–1866)

kedgeree

keelhaul drag someone under the keel from one side of a boat to the other as a punishment

keenness, but **keenest**

keeshond breed of dog; pl. **keeshonden**

Kefauver, (Carey) Estes (1909–63) American politician

Keino, Kip (1940–) Kenyan runner; full name Kipchoge Keino

Keneally, Thomas (1935–) Australian writer

Kenyatta, Jomo (c. 1897–1978) born Kamau Ngengi; President of Kenya 1964–78

kerb (US **curb**) the raised edging along a street

Kerensky, Alexander (Feodorovich) (1881–1970) Russian revolutionary, briefly Prime Minister 1917

kerfuffle disorder, commotion

Kerguelen Islands group of islands in the southern Indian Ocean

Kerkyra Greek for Corfu

Kern, Jerome (1885–1945) American composer

kerosene

Kerouac, Jack (1922–69) born Jean Louis Kerouac; American novelist, a spokesman for the 'beat generation'

Kerrey, Bob (1943–) US politician and academic; president of the New School

Kerry, John (1943–) US Democratic Senator from Massachusetts; ran for President in 2004

Kertész, Imre (1929–) Hungarian writer; awarded Nobel Prize for Literature 2002

kewpie doll

Key, Francis Scott (1780–1843) author of 'The Star-Spangled Banner'

Keynes, John Maynard, Lord (1883–1946) pronounced *kainz*; British economist

KGB Komitet Gosudarstvennoi Bezopasnosti, Commission of State Security the secret service of the former Soviet Union. The name ceased to be used after 1991.

khaki, pl. **khakis**

Khalilzad, Zalmay (1951–) Afghan-born American academic and diplomat; US ambassador to United Nations 2007–

Khamenei, Ayatollah Sayyid Ali (1939–) Supreme Leader of Iran 1989–; note that Sayyid has many variant spellings, among them Seyyed, Seyed and Said. See also KHOMEINI.

Khartoum capital of Sudan

Khayyám, Omar Omar was not his first name, so alphabetically this Persian poet and mathematician (c. 1050–c. 1125) should be listed under O.

Khomeini, Ayatollah Ruhollah (1908–89) Iranian religious and political leader, head of state 1979–89. See also KHAMENEI.

Khrushchev, Nikita Few errors make a publication look more careless than misspelling the name of a world leader, and few leaders' names have been misspelled more frequently or variously than that of the Soviet leader Nikita Khrushchev. Note that the surname has three *h*s.

Kibaki, Mwai (1931–) President of Kenya 2002–

kibbutz, kibitz The first refers to Israeli communal settlements (pl. **kibbutzim**). The second is to watch others playing at cards or some other such activity, often in an interfering manner.

kibosh on, put the put a stop to

kidnapped, kidnapper, kidnapping (US **kidnaped, kidnaper, kidnaping**)

Kidston, Cath British fabric designer

kielbasa Polish sausage

Kierkegaard, Søren (Aabye) (1813–55) Danish philosopher

Kigali capital of Rwanda

Kilimanjaro mountain in Tanzania, the highest point in Africa (19,340 feet/5,895 metres); at the end of a line it should be divided Kilima-njaro.

Killauea active volcano on Mauna Loa, Hawaii

Kill Van Kull strait between Staten Island, New York, and New Jersey

kiloton abbr. **kT**; an explosive force equal to 1,000 tons of TNT

kilowatt abbr. **kW**; 1,000 watts

Kimberley, South Africa and Australia

Kimberly-Clark US paper and forest products group

Kim Il Sung (1912–94), North Korean Prime Minister 1948–72 and President 1972–94; succeeded by his son, **Kim Jong Il** (1942–)

kimono, pl. **kimonos**

kind, **kinds** There should always be agreement between *kind* or *kinds* and its antecedents. 'These kind of mistakes' should be either 'This kind of mistake' or 'These kinds of mistakes'.

kindergarten, but **kindergartner**

kinesiology the study of body movement

kinetics, a branch of physics, is singular.

King, (William Lyon) Mackenzie (1874–1950) Prime Minister of Canada 1921–6, 1926–30, 1935–48

King's Bromley, Staffordshire

Kings Canyon National Park, California (no apos.)

King's Cross, London

Kingsford-Smith (hyphen) for the airport in Sydney, Australia, but **Sir Charles Kingsford Smith** (1897–1935) (no hyphen) for the aviator after whom it was named

King's Langley, Hertfordshire

King's Lynn, Norfolk

King's Norton, Leicestershire

King's Road, London

Kingston upon Hull (no hyphens) formal name of Hull

Kingston upon Thames (no hyphens)

King's Walden, Hertfordshire

Kinshasa formerly Léopoldville; capital of the Democratic Republic of the Congo

Kirghizia now called **Kyrgyzstan**

Kirgizstan Use **Kyrgyzstan**.

Kiribati remote coral-islands state in the Pacific Ocean; capital Tarawa

Kirin/Jilin (Pinyin) Chinese province

Kirkcudbright, Dumfries and Galloway   pronounced *kur-koo´-bree*

Kirkpatrick, Jeane (1926–2006) American diplomat and academic. Note irregular spelling of first name.

Kissimmee, Florida

Kitakyushu, Japan

kitemark (one word, no cap.) logo of the British Standards Institution indicating that a product has been approved as safe

kith and kin Your kin are your relatives. Your kith are your relatives, friends and acquaintances.

kittiwake type of gull

Kitty Litter is a trademark.

Kitzbühel, Austrian resort

Klein, Calvin (Richard) (1942–) American fashion designer

klieg light powerful light used in filming

KLM abbr. of Koninklijke Luchtvaart Maatschappij, national airline of the Netherlands; merged with Air France in 2004 to form **Air France-KLM**

Klinefelter syndrome, not *-felter's* genetic disease that causes language difficulties

Klitschko, Vitali (1971–) and **Klitschko, Wladimir** (1976–) Ukrainian boxing brothers, both world heavyweight champions

Klöckner-Werke German steel manufacturer

Kmart for the stores group. The formal name is Kmart Corporation.

knackwurst (or **knockwurst**) spicy German sausage

knead to manipulate, as with bread dough

Knesset Israeli parliament

knick-knack

Knight Commander of the Order of the Bath for the British honorary title. Note the second *the*.

Knossos ancient capital of Crete

knot a speed of one nautical mile an hour. A ship does eight knots or it does eight nautical miles an hour, but not eight knots an hour. A nautical mile equals 1.15 land miles, and in most contexts the reader will appreciate having that difference elucidated.

koala bears is wrong. Koalas are marsupials and have no relation to bears. Just call them koalas.

København Danish spelling of Copenhagen

Koblenz, Germany

Kohinoor/Koh-i-noor famous Indian diamond, now part of the crown jewels

Köhler, Horst (1943–) President of Germany 2004–

Kohlberg Kravis Roberts (no commas) American investment firm

kohlrabi, pl. **kohlrabies** a cabbage with an edible stem

Kohn Pedersen Fox (no commas) US architectural firm

Kokoschka, Oskar (1886–1980) Austrian-born British artist and writer

Kolkata is the new official name for the Indian city traditionally known as Calcutta; until the new name is fully established, both should be used on first reference.

Köln German spelling of Cologne

Komunyakaa, Yusef (1947–) American poet

Konditorei (Ger.) bakery

kookaburra Australian kingfisher

Koolhaas, Rem (1944–) Dutch architect; full name Remment Koolhaas

kopek (or **kopeck**) small Russian coin

Koppel, Ted (1940–) American television journalist

Koran (or **Qur'an**) Muslim holy book

Korea was partitioned in 1948 into **South Korea** (officially **Republic of Korea**), capital Seoul; and **North Korea** (officially **People's Democratic Republic of Korea**), capital Pyongyang.

Korean names are similar to Chinese in that the family name comes first; thus after the first reference Park Chung Hee becomes Mr Park. Koreans tend not to hyphenate their given names, nor as a rule do they write the second given name without caps as in the old Chinese system.

Korematsu v. United States 1944 Supreme Court case that upheld the internment of Japanese-American citizens on grounds of national security

Korsakoff's syndrome dementia associated with chronic alcoholism or vitamin deficiency

koruna basic unit of currency in the Czech Republic and Slovakia

Kosciusko, Thaddeus (1746–1817) in Polish, Tadeusz Kościuzko; Polish general; fought on the American side in the Revolutionary War. But note that it is the **Kosciuszko Bridge** in New York.

Kosinski, Jerzy (1933–91) Polish-born American novelist

Kosovar of or from Kosovo (e.g., 'Kosovar Albanians')

Kosygin, Alexei (Nikolayevich) (1904–80) Prime Minister of Soviet Union 1964–80

Kournikova, Anna (1981–) Russian tennis player

Krafft-Ebing, Richard, Baron von (1840–1902) German psychiatrist

Kraków, Poland in English, Cracow

Krapp's Last Tape one-act play by Samuel Beckett (1958)

Kreuger, Ivar (1880–1932), not *Ivan* Swedish financier who perpetrated a $500-million fraud on investors

Kriss Kringle alt. US name for Santa Claus

Kristallnacht (Ger.) 'crystal night'; so called because of all the glass broken during the looting and destruction of Jewish businesses and synagogues in Germany and Austria on 9–10 November 1938

krona, krone, kronor, etc. The currencies of Scandinavia are easily confused. In Sweden, the basic unit of currency is a *krona*, pl. *kronor*; in Denmark and Norway it is a *krone*, pl. *kroner*; in Iceland it is a *króna*, pl. *krónur.*

Krugerrand South African gold coin (used as an investment vehicle and not as a currency). Note -*rr*-.

Krung Thep Thai name for Bangkok

Krusenstern, Cape, Alaska

Kuala Lumpur capital of Malaysia

Kublai Khan (1216–94) Mongol emperor of China 1279–94

'Kubla Khan' unfinished poem by Samuel Taylor Coleridge (1797)

kudos is a Greek word meaning fame or glory. Though often treated as a plural, it is in fact singular. Thus it should be 'the kudos that was his due'.

Kuiper belt band of comets in the outer solar system, named for Gerard Kuiper (1905–73), Dutch-born American astronomer who posited their existence

Ku Klux Klan (no hyphens) US white supremacist secret society

kulak Russian peasant

Kumagai Gumi Company Limited Japanese construction company

kumquat citrus-like fruit

Kuomintang/Guomindang The first is the former spelling, the second the preferred current spelling for the Chinese Nationalist Party, founded by Sun Yat-sen. The syllable *tang/dang* contains the notion of party, so refer only to the Kuomintang, not Kuomintang Party.

Kurile Islands island chain between Russia and Japan

Kurosawa, Akira (1910–98) Japanese film director

Kuwaiti, pl. **Kuwaitis**

Kuybyshev formerly Samara; Russian city

Kuznetsov, Anatoly (1930–79) Russian novelist

Kuznetsova, Svetlana (1985–) Russian tennis player

kW kilowatt; 1,000 watts

KwaNdebele former South African homeland, now part of Mpumalanga province

kwashiorkor nutritional disorder in young children

KwaZulu-Natal province of South Africa

Kyd, Thomas (1558–94) English playwright

Kydland, Finn E. (1943–) Norwegian-American academic, awarded Nobel Prize for Economics 2004

Kyrgyzstan, or **Kyrgyz Republic** formerly Kirghizia; central Asian republic, formerly part of Soviet Union; capital Bishkek

Kyzyl-Kum desert in Kazakhstan and Uzbekistan

L

labyrinth
lackadaisical casual, without enthusiasm; not *lacks-*
Lackawanna, New York
Lackawaxen River, Pennsylvania
lacquer
La Crosse, Wisconsin, but **lacrosse** for the sport
lacuna a missing part; pl. **lacunas/lacunae**
lacy, not *-ey*
laddie, not *-dy*
Ladies' Home Journal US magazine
Ladies Professional Golf Association (no apos.)
Lady Chatterley's Lover novel by D. H. Lawrence (1928)
Lafayette, Marie Joseph Paul Yves Roch Gilbert du Motier, Marquis de (1757–1834) French general who played a leading role in both the American and the French revolution
Laffitte, Jacques (1767–1844) French statesman
Lafite, Château celebrated wine from Bordeaux
Lafitte/Laffite, Jean (c. 1780–c. 1826) French pirate
La Follette, Robert M. (for **Marion**) (1855–1925) American politician; ran for President as a Progressive in 1924
Lag b'Omer Jewish holiday
lagniappe (US) a small, unexpected gift; pronounced *lan-yap*

La Guardia Airport, New York Some users make the name one word, as in Fiorello H. LaGuardia Community College in Queens, but the two-word form is more general for both the man and any entities named after him, particularly the airport. For the record, Fiorello Henry La Guardia (1882–1947) was a New York Congressman 1917–21 and 1923–33 and mayor of New York City 1934–45.

laissez-faire (hyphen) policy of non-interference by government in trade and industry

Laius in Greek mythology, the King of Thebes and father of Oedipus

La Jolla, California pronounced *la hoya*

Lake Wobegon fictional town in stories by Garrison Keillor

lama, Lammas, llama *Lama* describes a Buddhist monk from Tibet or Mongolia (his dwelling place is a lamasery). *Lammas* is a type of harvest festival. The *llama* is a wool-bearing animal from South America.

lambaste, not -*bast*; to criticize sharply

Lamborghini Italian sports car

lamb's wool, not *lambswool*

LAN Airlines formerly LanChile, principal airline of Chile

Lancelot/Launcelot Both spellings have been used for the Arthurian knight, the first notably by Tennyson, the second notably by Malory.

Lancing College, West Sussex, but **Lansing**, Michigan

Land Rover, Range Rover (two words, no hyphen) British cars

Land's End, Cornwall, but **Lands' End** for the clothing company

Langtry, Lillie (1853–1929) British actress; but her nickname was 'the Jersey Lily'

Languedoc-Roussillon region of France, capital Montpellier

languid, limpid Not to be confused. *Limpid* means clear, calm, untroubled ('a limpid stream'). It has nothing to do with being limp or listless – meanings that are covered by *languid*.

languor, languorous

lanyard, not -*iard* short rope or cord

Lanzhou capital of Gansu Province, China; formerly known in English as **Lanchow**

Laois (pronounced *lay-ish*) Irish county; in Gaelic, **Laoighis**; formerly called **Leix** (pronounced *laix*) or **Queen's**

Laomedon in Greek mythology, the founder of Troy

Lao-tze (or **Lao-tzu**) (c. 600–530 BC) in Pinyin **Lao Zi**; Chinese philosopher, reputed founder of Taoism. On first reference it is probably best to give both the traditional and the Pinyin spellings of the name.

laparotomy surgical incision into the abdominal wall

La Paz administrative capital and main city of Bolivia; the official capital is Sucre

Laphroaig whisky pronounced *la-froyg*

lapis lazuli type of gemstone

La Plata, Argentina, but **Rio de la Plata**

Lapp, Lappish, but **Lapland, Laplander** Although *Lapp* is often used, the correct name for the people is Sami.

lapsus memoriae (Lat.) a lapse of memory

largesse (or **largess**) generosity

La Rochefoucauld, François, Duc de (1613–80) French writer known for his maxims

Larousse French publisher of reference books

larrikin Australian term for an uncultured or ill-behaved person

larynx, pl. **larynges/larynxes** *Larynges* should be the preferred term for medical or academic writings, but *larynxes* is probably better, and certainly more immediately understood, in more general contexts.

lasagne (or **lasagna**)

La Scala celebrated opera house in Milan; its formal name is Teatro alla Scala

Laski, Harold (1893–1950) British political theorist

LaSorda, Tom (1954–) CEO of Chrysler Group, but **Tommy Lasorda** (1927–), baseball player and manager

Lassen Peak volcanic mountain in northern California

lasso, pl. **lassos**

last, **latest** Various authorities have issued strictures against using *last* when you mean *latest*. Clearly, *last* should not be used when it might be misinterpreted, as in 'the last episode of the television series' when you mean the most recent but not the final one. However, it should also be noted that *last* in the sense of latest has a certain force of idiom behind it, and when ambiguity is unlikely (as in 'He spoke about it often during the last presidential election campaign') a reasonable measure of latitude should be granted.

Lateran Treaty (1929) treaty between Italy and the Vatican by which the papacy recognized Italy as a state and Italy recognized the Vatican City as a sovereign papal state

latitude location of a place north or south of the equator. See also LONGITUDE.

Latour, Château a wine from Bordeaux

La Tour, Georges de (1593–1652) French artist

Latter-day Saints the Mormons' name for themselves

Lauda, Niki (1949–) Austrian motor-racing driver and businessman, three times Formula 1 champion

laudable, laudatory Occasionally confused. *Laudable* means deserving praise. *Laudatory* means expressing praise.

Laugharne, Dyfed pronounced *larn*

Launcelot/Lancelot Both spellings are used for the Arthurian knight, the first by Malory, the second by Tennyson.

law and order is singular.

lawful, legal In many contexts the words can be used interchangeably, but not always. *Lawful* means 'permissible under the law' (*lawful behaviour*, *lawful protest*). *Legal* has that meaning plus the additional sense of 'relating to the law', as in *legal system* or *legal profession*.

lay, lie *Lay* and *lie*, in all their manifestations, are a constant source of errors. There are no simple rules for dealing with them. You must either commit their various forms to memory or avoid them altogether. The forms are:

	lay	**lie**
present:	I lay the book on the table.	I lie down; I am lying down.
past:	Yesterday I laid the book on the table.	Last night I lay down to sleep.
present perfect:	I have already laid the book on the table.	I have lain in bed all day.

The most common type of error is to say: 'If you're not feeling well, go upstairs and lay down.' It should be 'lie down'.

Lazarus, Emma (1849–87) American poet, remembered chiefly for 'The New Colossus', the poem inscribed on the Statue of Liberty

L-dopa drug used for treatment of Parkinson disease

leach, leech The first describes the seepage of fluids, the second a bloodsucking invertebrate.

Leacock, Stephen (1869–1944)   Canadian economist and humorist

Leadbelly (or **Lead Belly**) (1888–1949)   American folk and blues musician; born Huddie William Ledbetter

lead, led   The past tense of the verb to lead is *led*. When *lead* is pronounced *led* it applies only to the metallic element.

Leavis, F. R. (for **Frank Raymond**) (1895–1978)   English critic and essayist

Leavitt, Henrietta Swan (1868–1921)   American astronomer

Leazes Park, Castle Leazes, Newcastle upon Tyne

Lebensborn (Ger.)   Nazi human breeding programme

Lebensraum (Ger.)   'living space'; imperialist notion pursued by Hitler that Germans were entitled to occupy neighbouring lands

le Carré, John (1931–)   pen name of David Cornwell, British novelist

Le Corbusier (1887–1965)   pseudonym of Charles Édouard Jeanneret, Swiss architect and town planner

Lederberg, Joshua (1925–)   American biologist, awarded Nobel Prize for Physiology or Medicine 1958

lederhosen   leather shorts

Lee Kuan Yew (1923–)   Prime Minister of Singapore 1959–90

Leeuwarden, Netherlands   capital of Friesland province

Leeuwenhoek, Anton van (1632–1723)   Dutch naturalist and microscopist

Leeuwin, Cape, Western Australia

Leeward Islands   former British colony in the Caribbean comprising Anguilla, Antigua, the British Virgin Islands, Montserrat, Nevis and St Kitts. The name now applies to all those plus Guadeloupe, the US Virgin Islands, and other smaller islands in the Lesser Antilles north of the Windward Islands.

Le Fanu, J. (for **Joseph**) **Sheridan** (1814–73) Irish writer
Lefschetz, Solomon (1884–1972) Russian-born American mathematician
Léger, Fernand (1881–1955) French painter
legerdemain, not -*der*- dexterity, trickery
Leghorn English name, now seldom used, for Livorno, Italy
legible, legibility
Légion d'honneur supreme French order of merit
Legionnaire's disease
legitimize, not *legitimatize*
Lehman Brothers US financial services firm; formally Lehman Brothers Holdings Inc.
Lehman College, City University of New York
Lehmann, Rosamond (1901–90) English novelist
Leibniz, (Gottfried Wilhelm) Baron von (1646–1716) German philosopher and mathematician
Leibovitz, Annie (1949–) American portrait photographer
Leicestershire abbr. Leics
Leiden, Leyden The first is the usual spelling for the Dutch town, the second for the scientific instrument known as a Leyden jar.
Leinster province of the Republic of Ireland comprising the counties of Carlow, Dublin, Kildare, Kilkenny, Laois, Longford, Louth, Meath, Offaly, Westmeath, Wexford and Wicklow
Leipzig, Germany
leitmotif (or **leitmotiv**) a recurring idea, or a dominant theme associated with a particular character or idea in a musical or literary work
Leitrim Irish county; pronounced *lee'-trim*
Lely, Sir Peter (1618–80) Dutch-born British painter
Léman, Lac French name for Lake Geneva

Le Mesurier, John (1912–83) British actor

Lemmon, Jack (1925–2001) American actor

LeMond, Greg (1961–) American cyclist

lend, loan *Loan* as a verb ('He loaned me some money') is now more or less standard, though one or two authorities continue to disdain it, favouring *lend* on grounds of tradition.

Lendl, Ivan (1960–) Czech tennis player

Leningrad name of Russian city 1924–91; see PETROGRAD

lens, pl. **lenses**

Leonardo da Vinci (1452–1519) Renaissance genius. *The Da Vinci Code* notwithstanding, a work or object associated with him should be called a Leonardo, not a Da Vinci.

Léopoldville former name of Kinshasa, Democratic Republic of the Congo.

Le Pen, Jean-Marie (1928–) French politician, founder of the Front National

leprechaun, not *lepra-* Irish sprite

lèse-majesté (Fr.) 'wounded majesty': treason or a similar offence or insolence towards anyone to whom deference is due. The spelling is sometimes anglicized to **lese-majesty**.

Lesotho small landlocked African kingdom, capital Maseru; formerly called Basutoland. The people of Lesotho are known as Basotho (sing. and pl.).

less, fewer The simplest rule is to use *less* with singular nouns (less money, less sugar) and *fewer* with plural ones (fewer houses, fewer cars).

Lesseps, Ferdinand Marie, Vicomte de (1805–94) French engineer closely associated with the Suez Canal. On second reference, **de Lesseps**.

l'Étoile area around the Arc de Triomphe, Paris

Letzeburgesch German dialect spoken in Luxembourg
leukaemia (US **leukemia**)
level, **mark** are often pointlessly employed. 'Stock prices once
again fell below the 12,000 level' says no more than 'fell
below 12,000'.
Leverrier, Urbain Jean Joseph (1811–77) French astronomer
Lévesque, René (1922–88) Canadian politician, leader of
Parti Québécois
Levi's jeans produced by Levi Strauss
Lévi-Strauss, Claude (1908–) French anthropologist
Leviticus book of the Old Testament
Levy, Andrea (1956–) British novelist, Orange prizewinner
2004
Lévy, Bernard-Henri (1948–) French philosopher
Lewis, Meriwether (1774–1809), not -*whether* co-leader
(with William Clark) of the Lewis and Clark expedition
of 1804–6, overland to the US Pacific Coast and back
Lewis, Wyndham (1884–1957) English writer and artist
Lewycka, Marina (1946–) British novelist of Ukrainian origin
Leyden jar, but the Dutch town is now usually spelled Leiden
Lhasa capital of Tibet
Lhasa apso breed of dog
liable, **likely**, **apt**, **prone** All four indicate probability, but
they carry distinctions worth noting. *Apt* is better
reserved for general probabilities ('It is apt to snow in
January') and *likely* for specific ones ('It is likely to snow
today'). *Liable* and *prone* are better used to indicate a
probability arising as a regrettable consequence: 'People
who drink too much are prone to heart disease'; 'If you
don't pay your taxes, you are liable to get caught.'
A separate but common problem with *likely* is seen in
this sentence: 'Cable experts say the agreement will likely

strengthen the company's position.' Used as an adverb, *likely* needs to be accompanied by one of four helping words: *very*, *quite*, *more* or *most*. Thus the sentence should say 'will very likely strengthen'.

liaison

libel, **slander**   Although nearly all dictionaries define *libel* merely as a statement that defames or damages a person's reputation, it is worth remembering that it must do so unreasonably or inaccurately. It is the wrongness of a contention that makes it libellous, not the harshness or hostility of it. Although a libel usually takes the form of a written utterance, drawings and other visual depictions may also be libellous. In all cases, a libel must be published (the word comes from the Latin *libellus*, meaning 'little book'). When defamatory remarks are merely spoken, the term to describe the act is *slander*.

liberté, égalité, fraternité (Fr.) 'liberty, equality, fraternity'; slogan of the French Revolution

Liberty, Statue of was set in place in New York Harbour in 1886. It is officially known as *Liberty Enlightening the World*. Its designer was Frédéric August Bartholdi. Liberty Island was formerly called Bedloes Island.

Libeskind, Daniel (1946–) Polish-born American architect

LIBOR   London interbank offered rate; benchmark interest rate for international loans

licence, **license**   The first is a noun (fishing licence, licence to sell alcohol), the second a verb (licensed premises, licensed driver). In the US, *license* is used for all forms.

Lichfield, for the town and cathedral in Staffordshire, and for the photographer **Patrick Lichfield** (1939–2005), who was formally the Earl of Lichfield, Viscount Anson and Baron Soberton

Lichtenstein, Roy (1923–97) American artist

lickerish greedy, lascivious

licorice US spelling of **liquorice**

Liebfraumilch white Rhine wine; in German it is Liebfrauenmilch

Liechtenstein diminutive Alpine principality; capital Vaduz

lifelong Though the term needn't be taken absolutely literally in most contexts, it should have some sense of at least approximately covering the whole of the subject's existence, so that one might be called a lifelong Yankees fan, but not, say, a lifelong drug addict.

lighted, lit Either is correct. *Lighted*, however, is more usual when the word is being used as an adjective ('a lighted torch').

lightning, lightening The first is the flash of light, the second means growing lighter.

light year the distance that light travels through empty space in one year (about 5,878 billion miles/9,460 billion kilometres)

like, as Problems often arise in choosing between *like* and *as*. On the face of it, the rule is simple: *as* and *as if* are always followed by a verb; *like* never is. Therefore you would say, 'He plays tennis like an expert' (no verb after *like*), but 'He plays tennis as if his life depended on it' (verb *depended*). Except in the most formal writing, however, only a stickler would object to such formations as 'She looks just like her mother used to' and 'He can't dance like he used to.' There is also one apparent inconsistency in the rule in that *like* may be used when it comes between 'feel' and an '-ing' verb: 'He felt like walking'; 'I feel like going abroad this year.'

likeable (US **likable**)

likelihood

Lilienthal, Otto (1849–96) German inventor

Lilliput (cap.) for the fictional place, but **lilliputian** (no cap.) for something small

Lilly, Eli, not -*ey* US pharmaceuticals company

Lilongwe capital of Malawi

lily, pl. **lilies**

Limassol, Cyprus

Limbourg, Limburg The first is a province of Belgium, the second a province of the Netherlands. The cheese is Limburg or Limburger.

limited means constrained, set within bounds. Unless there is the idea of a limit being imposed, the word is better avoided. It is reasonable enough to say that a special offer is available for a limited time, but to write that 'there was a limited demand for tickets' is absurd when what is meant is that fewer customers than had been hoped showed up.

linage, lineage The first refers to lines of text, the second to ancestry.

linchpin, but **lynch law, lynch gang**

Linnaean for the system of naming plants and animals by genus and species names (e.g., *Homo sapiens*). Some dictionaries also accept *Linnean* as an alternative spelling. The term comes from the Swedish botanist Carl Linné (1707–78), who chose to Latinize his name as Carolus Linnaeus. For the rules of application concerning the Linnaean system, see GENUS, SPECIES.

lion's share is a cliché. Why not say 'most' or 'the larger part' or whatever is appropriate?

Lipari Islands group of islands off Sicily, also known as the Aeolian Islands

Lipchitz, Jacques (1891–1973) French sculptor

Lippmann, Walter (1889–1974) American journalist

liquefy, **liquefaction**

liqueur a flavoured alcoholic spirit

liquorice (US **licorice**)

lira currency of Turkey; pl. **liras**. It has not been the currency of Italy since 2002, but for historical purposes it may be worth noting that the Italian plural was *lire*.

lissom or **lissome** slim, supple

literally means actually, not figuratively. If you don't wish to be taken literally, don't use *literally*.

literati literary élite; learned people. But *littérateur* for a person of letters.

liveable (US **livable**)

Livingston, West Lothian

Livingstone, David (1813–73) Scottish explorer and missionary

Livni, Tzipora (1958–) Deputy Prime Minister of Israel 2006–

Ljubicic, Ivan (1979–) Croatian tennis player

Ljubljana capital of Slovenia; pronounced *loob-lee-yah´-na*

Llanfairpwllgwyngyllgogerychwyrndrobwllllantysilio-gogogoch village in Wales, on Anglesey, famous for having the longest name in Britain

Lloyd George, David (no hyphen) (1863–1945), British Prime Minister 1916–22; but **Earl Lloyd-George of Dwyfor** (hyphen) for his title as a peer

Lloyd's of London (apos.) for the venerable insurance exchange, but **Lloyds TSB** (no apos.) for the British bank

Lloyd Webber, Andrew (1948–), now **Lord Lloyd-Webber** (hyphen), British composer of musicals; brother of **Julian Lloyd Webber** (1951–), cellist

Llullaillaco mountain on border of Argentina and Chile

LME London Metal Exchange

loath, loathe The first is an adjective meaning reluctant, the second a verb meaning to detest.

loathsome

loc. cit., *loco citato* (Lat.) in the place cited

local residents Residents generally are local, so in most contexts the first word can be deleted.

Locke, John (1632–1704) English philosopher

locum tenens, pl. **locum tenentes** colloquially **locum, locums**; a temporary replacement

lodestar, lodestone are the preferred spellings, but **loadstar** and **loadstone** are also accepted.

Łódź, Poland pronounced *woodj*

logarithm mathematical term

Lomé capital of Togo

London interbank offered rate See LIBOR.

Longchamp, not *-champs* French racecourse

Longfellow, Henry Wadsworth (1807–82) American poet

Longleat House, Wiltshire

longueur note *-ueu-*; boring interval or section of a work meant for entertainment

Look Homeward, Angel novel by Thomas Wolfe (1929); note comma

Lord's Cricket Ground, London

Lorenz, Konrad (1903–89) Austrian zoologist

losable

Los Alamitos Race Course, Los Angeles

Louis Roederer champagne

Louis Vuitton French luxury goods company

Lourenço Marques former name of Maputo, capital of Mozambique

Louvain French and English spelling of the Belgian

university town known as Leuven in Flemish

louvre (US **louver**) a type of slatted cover

Love's Labour's Lost comedy by Shakespeare. There may also have been a companion play, now lost, called *Love's Labour's Won.*

LPG liquefied petroleum gas

luau Hawaiian feast

Lubitsch, Ernst (1892–1947) German-born film director

lubricious is generally the preferred spelling for the word meaning slippery or lewd, but most dictionaries also accept **lubricous.**

Lubyanka infamous Moscow prison

Luddite a worker opposed to new technology

Ludwigshafen, Germany

Lufthansa German national airline

Luftwaffe German air force

luge type of sled

luminesce, luminescence

lumpenproletariat bottom of the working class

Lusitania Cunard liner sunk off Ireland by the Germans, 7 May 1915

Luxembourg, Grand Duchy of in French, Grand-Duché de Luxembourg; the capital is also Luxembourg (or Luxembourg City for clarity)

Luxemburg, Rosa (1871–1919) political activist

lux mundi (Lat.) light of the world

luxuriant, luxurious The words are not interchangeable, though the meanings sometimes overlap. *Luxuriant* indicates profusion ('luxuriant hair'). *Luxurious* means sumptuous and expensive ('a luxurious house'). A luxuriant carpet is a shaggy one; a luxurious carpet is an expensive one.

lychee (or **litchi**) Chinese tree and its fruit
lychgate roofed gateway to a churchyard
Lyly, John (c. 1555–1606) English playwright
Lympne, Kent pronounced *limm*
Lyonnaise, **lyonnaise** The first is an area of France, the
     second a style of cooking.
Lysistrata comedy by Aristophanes
Lytham St Annes (no punc.), Lancashire

M

Maas Dutch name for the European river known in English as the **Meuse**

Ma'at Egyptian goddess of truth

Mac, Mc, M' In British usage all such words are treated as if they were spelled *Mac* when determining alphabetical order. Thus *McGuire* would precede *Mason*. In the US the alphabetical order of the letters is followed literally, and *Mason* would precede *McGuire*.

macadam a type of road surface, named after John McAdam (1756–1836), a Scottish engineer

McAfee Coliseum, Oakland, California

macaque monkey of the genus Macaca

macaronic verse a type of poetry in which two or more languages are mingled

MacArthur, Douglas (1880–1964) American general

MacArthur Foundation, John D. and Catherine T. US charity famous for generous awards

Macaulay, Thomas Babington, Lord (1800–59) British historian

MacBook a notebook computer made by Apple Inc.

Maccabees Jewish dynasty of 2nd and 1st centuries BC

McCarran International Airport, Las Vegas

McCarthy, Cormac (1933–) American novelist

McCarthy, Eugene (Joseph) (1916–2005) American Democratic politician

McCarthy, Joseph (Raymond) (1900–57) US senator notorious for a prolonged campaign against Communists during Congressional hearings, known as the Army-McCarthy hearings, in the 1950s

MacCorkindale, Simon (1952–) British actor

MacCormac, Richard (1938–) British architect

McCormick Place convention centre in Chicago

McCowen, Alec (1925–) British actor

McCrea, Joel (1905–90) American film actor

McCullers, Carson (1917–67) American novelist and playwright

MacDonald, Ramsay (1866–1938) British Prime Minister 1924, 1929–35

Macdonald, Ross pen name of Kenneth Millar (1915–83), Canadian-American author of detective fiction

McDonald's (note apos.) fast food chain. The company is the McDonald's Corporation.

McDonnell Douglas Corporation (now part of Boeing)

Macdonnell Ranges, Northern Territory, Australia

McDowall, Roddy (1928–98) British-born American actor

McEnroe, John (1959–) American tennis player turned commentator

McEwan, Geraldine (1932–) British actress

McEwan, Ian (1948–) British novelist, Booker winner 1998

Macgillicuddy's Reeks mountain range in County Kerry, Ireland

McGillis, Kelly (1958–) American actress

McGill University, Montreal

McGonagall, William (1830–1902) Scottish poet famed for his bad verse

McGoohan, Patrick (1928–) American actor

McGovern, George (1922–) American Democratic politician

MacGraw, Ali (1938–) American actress

McGraw-Hill Companies, The US media and financial services company

MacGregor Scottish clan

McGregor, Ewan (1971–) Scottish actor

McGuffey (not *-'s*) *Eclectic Reader* is the formal name for the American schoolbook popularly known as *McGuffey's Reader*; named for the educator W. H. McGuffey (1800–73).

Machiavelli, Niccolò di Bernardo dei (1469–1527) Florentine statesman and political theorist, best known for *Il Principe* (*The Prince*), 1513

machicolation gallery at the top of a castle tower

Mach number (cap. M) the ratio of the speed of an object to the speed of sound in the medium (usually air) through which the object is travelling: e.g., an aircraft travelling at twice the speed of sound is said to be going at Mach 2; named after Ernst Mach (1836–1916), an Austrian physicist

Macintosh for the computer made by Apple, but **McIntosh** for the apple (after the Canadian John McIntosh). See also MACKINTOSH.

McJob (cap. M, cap. J) slang term for a low-wage job, usually in the service sector

Mackenzie river and mountains in western Canada, but **McKenzie** for the lake and bay in Ontario and **McKenzie Pass**, Oregon

Mackenzie, Sir Compton (1883–1972) British writer

MacKenzie, Kelvin (1946–) British newspaper executive

McKern, Leo (1920–2002) British actor

Mackinac Island and **Straits of Mackinac**, in Lake Huron, but **Mackinaw City**, Michigan. The type of woollen coat is called a **mackinaw**, but **Mackinaw blanket** and **Mackinaw boat** are both capitalized. For all spellings the pronunciation is *mack-in-aw*.

McKinley, Mount, Alaska   The highest peak in North America (20,320 feet/6,194 metres) has the alternative name **Denali**. It stands within Denali National Park and Preserve. Mount McKinley was named for William McKinley (1843–1901), US President 1897–1901

Mackintosh, Charles Rennie (1868–1928) British architect, artist and designer

MacLaine, Shirley (1934–)   American actress; born Shirley MacLean Beaty

McLean, Virginia   suburb of Washington, DC; pronounced *muk-lane´*

MacLean, Alistair (1922–87) British writer of adventure novels

Maclean's Canadian weekly news magazine

MacLehose & Sons Scottish printers

MacLeish, Archibald (1892–1982) American poet

Macleod, Lake, Western Australia

Macmillan, Sir (Maurice) Harold, Earl of Stockton (1894–1986) British Prime Minister 1957–63

MacMurray, Fred (1907–91) American actor

MacNee, Patrick (1922–) British actor

MacNeice, Louis (1907–63) Irish-born British poet

MacNelly, Jeff (1947–2000) American cartoonist

Macon, Georgia, but **Mâcon** for the French city and wine

McShane, Ian (1942–) British actor

Macy's department stores (US)   formally R. H. Macy & Co.; now a subsidiary of Federated Department Stores

Madagascar island republic off south-east Africa, formerly Malagasy Republic; capital Antananarivo

mademoiselle (Fr.) an unmarried female; not -*dam*-; pl. *mesdemoiselles*

Madhya Pradesh Indian state

Madison, Dolley (not *Dolly*) (1768–1849) US First Lady, wife of James Madison. But note that some commercial products spell the name *Dolly Madison*.

Madison Avenue generic term for the US advertising industry

Madras, India now called **Chennai**; on first reference, it is probably best to use both names

Madrileño/Madrileña citizen of Madrid

maelstrom

Maeterlinck, Count Maurice (1862–1949) Belgian poet and dramatist; awarded Nobel Prize for Literature 1911

Mafeking/Mafikeng The first is the historical spelling for the site of a famous siege during the Boer War; the second is the current spelling of the South African town.

mafioso a member of the Mafia; pl. **mafiosi**

Magdalen College, Oxford, but **Magdalene College**, Cambridge. Both are pronounced *maudlin*. The New Testament figure is **Mary Magdalene**.

Magellan, Ferdinand (1480–1521) Portuguese explorer; led first expedition that circumnavigated the globe, though he himself was killed en route; in Portuguese, Fernão de Maghalães. The **Magellan Straits** are named after him.

Maggiore, Lake, Italy

Maghreb, the collective name for Algeria, Morocco and Tunisia

Maginot Line line of defensive fortifications across north-eastern France, breached by Germany in 1940

Magna Carta (or **Charta**) charter of rights signed by King John at Runnymede in 1215

magnum opus, opus magnum The first is an author's principal work; the second is a great work.

Magritte, René (1898–1967) Belgian surrealist painter

Mahabharata Indian epic

maharaja, maharanee Indian prince and princess

Mahatir bin Mohamad, Dr (1925–) Prime Minister of Malaysia 1981–2003

Mahfouz, Naguib (1912–2006) Egyptian novelist; awarded Nobel Prize for Literature 1988

mahjong Chinese game played with tiles

mahogany

Maillol, Aristide (1861–1944) French sculptor

maître d'hôtel (Fr.) hotel manager or head waiter; abbr. **maître d'**; pl. ***maîtres d'hôtel***

Majlis Parliament of Iran

major, as in 'a major initiative', 'major embarrassment', 'major undertaking' and so on, remains a severely overworked word, and thus brings a kind of tofu quality to much writing, giving it bulk but little additional flavour. Nearly always it is worth the effort of trying to think of a more precise or expressive term.

majority should be reserved for describing the larger of two clearly divisible things, as in 'A majority of the members voted for the resolution.' But even then a more specific description is usually better: '52 per cent', 'almost two thirds', 'more than 70 per cent', etc. When there is no sense of a clear contrast with a minority (as in 'The majority of his spare time was spent reading'), *majority* is always better avoided.

Makassar Strait between Borneo and Sulawesi, Indonesia

Makhachkala formerly Petrovskoye, capital of Dagestan, Russia

Maki, Fumihiko (1928–) Japanese architect

Malabo formerly Santa Isabel, capital of Equatorial Guinea

Malagasy Republic former name of Madagascar; **Malagasy** (sing. and pl.) remains the term for a person or persons from the island, and for the language spoken there.

malarkey nonsense

Malawi formerly Nyasaland; African republic; capital Lilongwe

mal de mer (Fr.) seasickness

Maldives island republic in the Indian Ocean, capital Malé

maleficence, **malfeasance** The first means a propensity to cause hurt or harm. The second is a legal term describing wrongdoing.

Mali formerly French Sudan; African republic, capital Bamako

Maliki, Nouri (1950–) Prime Minister of Iraq 2006– ; sometimes also known as Jawad Maliki

Mallarmé, Stéphane (1842–98) French poet

malleable easily shaped or influenced

Mallorca Spanish spelling of Majorca

malmsey a sweet wine; pl. **malmseys**

malodorous

Malory, Sir Thomas (d. 1471), for the 15th-century English author and compiler of Arthurian legends (notably *Le Morte d'Arthur*), but **George Mallory** (two *l*s) for the Everest explorer (1886–1924)

Malvinas, Islas Argentinian name for the Falkland Islands

Mamaroneck, New York

Mammon (cap.) wealth regarded as an object of worship

manacle, not -*icle* shackle

manageable, **manageability**

Managua capital of Nicaragua

Manassas Virginia town near the site of two battles in the American Civil War, usually called the Battles of Bull Run in the North and the Battles of Manassas in the South

manatee sea cow

Man Booker Prize UK literary prize formerly known as the Booker Prize

Mancunian of or from Manchester

mandamus writ commanding that a particular thing be done or public duty be performed

mandatory, **mandatary** The first means compulsory; the second is a much rarer word, which applies to holding a mandate.

Mandlikova, Hana (1962–) Czech tennis player

Manet, Édouard (1832–83) French artist

maneuver US spelling of **manoeuvre**

mangoes or **mangos** Either is correct.

Manhattan, not -*en* island borough at the heart of New York City; the cocktail is a **manhattan** (lower case)

manifesto, pl. **manifestos**

Manila capital of the Philippines. The paper and envelopes, etc., are usually spelled lower case: **manila**.

Manitoulin Island, Lake Huron, Canada

mannequin, **manikin** The words are broadly interchangeable, but the first is usually preserved for the types of dummies found in store windows and the second for anatomical models used for teaching. An alternative spelling of *manikin* is *mannikin*.

manner born, to the Not *manor*. The line is from *Hamlet*.

Mannesmann Kienzle GmbH German manufacturing company

mano a mano (Sp.) hand to hand

manoeuvre, manoeuvrable, manoeuvrability (US **maneuver, maneuverable, maneuverability**)

manqué (Fr.) unsuccessful, would-be; always follows the noun it modifies

Mantegna, Andrea (1431–1506) Italian painter

mantel, mantle The first is the usual spelling for the frame around a fireplace, the second for all other senses. Note also the spellings of the associated words *mantelshelf* and *mantelpiece*.

Mantova Italian name for Mantua

Mao Zedong (formerly **Mao Tse-tung**) (1893–1976) founder and Chairman of the People's Republic of China 1949–59, and Chairman of the Chinese Communist Party 1935–76

Mapplethorpe, Robert (1947–89) American photographer

Maputo formerly Lourenço Marques; capital of Mozambique

Maquis French resistance during the Second World War

Maracaibo city and lake in Venezuela

Maracanã football stadium in Rio de Janeiro, official name Estádio Jornalista Mário Filho

maraschino cherry

Marazion, Cornwall

March, Fredric (1897–1975) not *Frederick*; born Frederick McIntyre Bickel; American actor

marchioness wife or widow of a marquis, or a woman holding the title of marquess

Marciano, Rocky (1923–69) born Rocco Marchegiano; American boxer, world heavyweight champion 1952–6

Marconi, Guglielmo (1874–1937) Italian inventor of wireless telegraphy; awarded Nobel Prize for Physics 1909

margarine, not *-ger-*

margarita a cocktail

Margaux, Château French wine

marginal is unobjectionable when used to describe something falling near a lower limit ('a marginal profit'). But it is a lame choice when all you mean is small or slight.

Margrethe II (1940–) Queen of Denmark 1972–

Mariana Trench site of greatest depth (36,220 feet/11,040 metres) of the Pacific Ocean. The nearby island chain is called the Mariana (not *-s*) Islands or the Marianas.

Mariánské Lázně Czech spa more widely known by its German name of **Marienbad**

Marie Antoinette (1755–93) Austrian-born Queen of France (1774–93), wife of King Louis XVI

Marie Claire magazine

marionette

markka former unit of Finnish currency

Marlboro cigarettes

Marmara, Sea of inland sea separating the European and Asiatic parts of Turkey

marmoset monkey

Maroochydore, Queensland, Australia

marquee large tent used for entertaining; in the US it signifies a projection over an entrance, especially at the front of a theatre

Marquesas Islands archipelago in the South Pacific

Marrakesh, Morocco

Marriage A-la-Mode engravings (1743–5) by William Hogarth

Marriage-à-la-Mode play by John Dryden (1672)

Marriott hotels group

Marsalis, Wynton (1961–) US musician

Marseille, France   The French national anthem is '**La Marseillaise**'.

marshal, not -*all*   The noun describes a senior officer; the verb means to assemble or gather together.

Marshall Islands   island nation in the Pacific Ocean; capital Majuro

Marshall Plan   officially the European Recovery Program, an assistance programme to help European nations rebuild after the Second World War. It was named for George C. Marshall (1880–1959), Secretary of State.

Marshalsea Prison, London

Martel, Yann   Booker prizewinner 2002

Martin Luther King Day   (US) is observed on the third Monday of January.

Marunouchi   financial district of Tokyo

Mary, Queen of Scots   (1542–87)   Scottish queen, executed for treason. Some sources write her name without the comma.

Marylebone   roads, district and church in London

Masaccio   (1401–28)   Italian painter

Masefield, John   (1878–1967)   English poet and novelist

Maserati   Italian sports car

Mason-Dixon line   boundary line between Maryland and Pennsylvania surveyed by Charles Mason and Jeremiah Dixon in 1763–7, traditionally regarded as the dividing line between North and South in the United States

Massachusetts   US state, abbr. **MA**, formerly **Mass.**

Massapequa, **Massapequa Park**, **East Massapequa**, etc., New York state

masseur (masc.), **masseuse** (fem.)

MasterCard

masterful, **masterly**   Most authorities continue to insist that we observe a distinction between these two – namely that *masterly* should apply to that which is adroit and expert and *masterful* to that which is imperious and domineering. Useful as the distinction might be, it has to be noted that no leading dictionary insists on it and most don't even indicate that such a distinction exists.

Matabeleland region of Zimbabwe

Matagordo Bay, Texas

Matamoros, Mexico, but **Matamoras**, Pennsylvania

materialize is usually no more than a somewhat pompous synonym for *occur*, *develop* or *happen*.

materiel military equipment

Mato Grosso, Brazil

Matthau, Walter (1920–2000) American actor

matzo Jewish unleavened bread; pl. **matzos** (or **matzoth** or **matzot**)

Maudsley Hospital, London, not *Maude-*

Maundy Thursday, not *Maunday* the day before Good Friday

Maupassant, (Henri René Albert) Guy de (1850–93) French author

Mauretania, **Mauritania** The first is the spelling for the ancient African country and two famous Cunard ships. The second is the spelling of the modern-day African country formally known as the Islamic Republic of Mauritania.

mausoleum

mauvaise honte (Fr.) dishonest or needless embarrassment or shame

mauvais quart d'heure (Fr.) 'bad quarter-hour'; figuratively, a painful or dreaded experience of short duration

Maxwell Davies, Sir Peter (1934–) English composer

Mayall, Rik (1958–) British comedian
May Fair Hotel, London, but the district of London is **Mayfair**
Mayne, Thom (1944–) American architect
mayonnaise
Mazatlán, Mexico
mazel tov (Yiddish) good luck
mazurka Polish dance
Mazzini, Giuseppe (1805–72) Italian republican and revolutionary
Mbabane capital of Swaziland
Mbeki, Thabo (Mvuytlwa) (1942–) South African President 1999–
ME short for myalgic encephalomyelitis, also known as Chronic Fatigue/Post Viral Fatigue Syndrome, a type of chronic malaise; also, postal abbreviation of Maine, US
mea culpa (Lat.) my fault
mealy-mouthed not straightforward in speech
mean, median Two points to note here. First, each of these terms has a very specific definition, but those definitions don't necessarily translate abroad. *The American Heritage Dictionary*, for instance, defines *mean* as the middle point in a series of numbers, but most British dictionaries define *mean* as the sum of all numbers in a series divided by the number of numbers – in other words, it is the same as average – and that is not the same thing at all. *Median* in both countries signifies the middle number of a series of numbers arranged in order of magnitude. The second problem, which is not unrelated to the first, is that both terms are at best vaguely understood by the general reader, and thus your

most prudent course of action is to use them extremely sparingly in anything other than technical writing.

measurable

Meccano (cap.) brand of bolt-together toy

Mecklenburg former state in Germany, but **Mecklenburgh Square**, London

Medellín, Colombia

media is a plural. The singular is *medium*. Television is a medium; newspapers and television are media. However, *mediums* is the correct plural for describing spiritualists.

Medicaid, Medicare Both are US federal health-care programmes, the first for the poor, the second for the elderly.

Medici leading family of Renaissance Florence, whose more noted members were Cosimo de' Medici (1389–1464), called Cosimo the Elder; Lorenzo de' Medici (1449–92), called Lorenzo the Magnificent; Giovanni de' Medici (1475–1521), later Pope Leo X; Giulio de' Medici (1478–1534), later Pope Clement VII. The French spelling is normally used for Catherine de Médicis (1519–89), wife of Henry II of France, and Marie de Médicis (1573–1642), wife of Henry IV of France.

Médecins Sans Frontières medical aid charity; known in the United States as Doctors Without Borders

medieval

mediocre

Meekatharra, Western Australia

meerschaum white clay-like mineral, traditionally used to make pipe bowls

meet, mete In the sense of justice or punishment, the first means suitable, the second means to allot. Thus one metes out punishment, but a fitting punishment is a meet one.

mega- prefix meaning one million. A megabyte in computing is a million bytes (or a thousand kilobytes).

megahertz (one word, no cap.), but the abbreviation is **MHz**

megalomania

Meigs Field Chicago airport; formally Merril (not -*ll*) C. Meigs Field; closed in 2003

Meiji period reign of the Emperor Mutsuhito (1867–1912), marking Japan's emergence as a modern industrialstate

mein Herr/meine Dame (Ger.) sir/madam; pl. *meine Herren/meine Damen*

Meir, Golda (1898–1978) Israeli Prime Minister 1969–74

Meissen porcelain, named for the German city in which it originated

meitnerium chemical element

melamine a type of plastic. It is not capitalized.

Melanchthon, Philipp (or **Philip**) (1497–1560) German academic, colleague of Martin Luther and a leader of the Reformation

melee in French, *mêlée*

mellifluous sounding sweet

memento, pl. **mementoes**

memorabilia objects collected because of their significance; note that the word is a plural

memorandums

Memorial Day US holiday commemorating the war dead, held the last Monday in May; originally called Decoration Day

ménage à trois (Fr.) sexual relationship among three people living together; pl. *ménages à trois*

menagerie

MENCAP formally the Royal Society for Mentally Handicapped Adults and Children

Mencken, H. L. (for **Henry Louis**) (1880–1956) American writer, critic and editor

Mendel, Gregor Johann (1822–84) Austrian botanist whose work became the basis of modern genetics

Mendelssohn, Felix (1809–47) German composer; full name Jakob Ludwig Felix Mendelssohn-Bartholdy

Mendes da Rocha, Paulo (1928–) Brazilian architect

Mendès-France, Pierre (1907–82) French Prime Minister 1954–5

meningitis inflammation of the **meninges**, or cranial membranes. Note that *meninges* is plural; a single membrane is a **meninx**.

Menninger Clinic, the psychiatric hospital founded in 1925; moved to Houston, Texas, in 2003. The **Menninger Foundation** remains in Topeka.

menorah seven-branched candelabrum used in Jewish worship

Menorca Spanish name for Minorca

Menotti, Gian-Carlo (1911–2007) Italian-born American composer

men's, **women's** However eagerly department stores and the like may strive to dispense with punctuation in their signs (writing 'Mens Clothing' or 'Womens Department') the practice is subliterate and to be avoided in any serious writing. Equally incorrect, if slightly less common, is placing the apostrophe after the *s* (e.g., 'mens' hats', 'womens' facials'). However, note that the apostrophe *is* discarded in such compounds as *menswear* and *womenswear*. See also CHILDREN'S.

Menuhin, Yehudi (1916–99) American-born British violinist

meow US spelling of the sound that cats make

Mephistophelean (or **Mephistophelian**) evil; after Mephistopheles, the devil to whom Faust sold his soul

Mercalli scale a measure of earthquake intensity; named for the Italian vulcanologist Giuseppe Mercalli (1850–1914)

Mercedes-Benz (hyphen) The plural is *Mercedeses*, but is best avoided.

Mercia Anglo-Saxon kingdom roughly corresponding in area to the modern Midlands

meretricious vulgar, insincere

meringue confection made from egg whites and sugar

merino type of sheep; pl. **merinos**

meritocracy system of government in which people are selected on merit

Merkel, Angela (1954–) German Chancellor 2005–

Merrion Square, Dublin

Merthyr Tydfil, Mid Glamorgan

mesmerize grip the attention

Messaggero, Il Italian newspaper

Messerschmitt, not *-schmidt* type of aircraft

metal, mettle *Metal* denotes chemical elements such as gold and copper; *mettle* is for contexts describing courage or spirit.

metamorphose (verb), **metamorphosis** (noun), pl. **metamorphoses**

metaphor, simile Both are figures of speech in which two things are compared. A *simile* likens one thing to another, dissimilar one: 'He ran like the wind'; 'She took to racing as a duck takes to water.' A *metaphor*, on the other hand, acts as if the two compared things are identical and substitutes one for the other. Comparing the beginning of time to the beginning of a day, for instance, produces the metaphor 'the dawn of time'.

metathesis the transposition of sounds or letters in a word or between words; in speech, such slips of the tongue are commonly called **spoonerisms**.

mete, meet The first means to allot; the second means suitable. One metes out punishment, but a fitting punishment is meet.

meteor, meteorite, meteoroid *Meteoroids* are pieces of galactic debris floating through space. If they enter Earth's atmosphere as shooting stars, they are *meteors*. If they survive the fall to Earth, they are *meteorites*.

meter a measuring instrument

meticulous Several usage books, though fewer and fewer dictionaries, insist that the word does not mean merely very careful, but rather excessively so. Unless you mean to convey a negative quality, it is usually better to use *scrupulous, careful, painstaking* or some other synonym.

metonymy figure of speech in which a thing is described in terms of one of its attributes, as in calling the monarch 'the crown'

metre (US **meter**), **metric, metrical** One metre equals 39.37 inches. **Metre** is also the spelling for rhythm in poetry and music.

Metro-Goldwyn-Mayer Hollywood film studio, abbr. MGM

metronome instrument for marking time

mettle courage or spirit

Meuse river in northern Europe; in Dutch, **Maas**

Mezzogiorno the southern, poorer half of Italy

mezzotint method of engraving, and the engraving so produced

MGM Metro-Goldwyn-Mayer

miaow sound a cat makes; the US spelling is **meow**

Michaelmas feast of St Michael and All Angels, 29 September

Michelangelo (1475–1564)   Italian artist, architect and engineer; full name Michelangelo di Lodovico Buonarroti

micro- prefix meaning one-millionth, or very small

Micronesia, Federated States of comprises Korsae, Ponape, Truk and Yap; capital Kolonia

Middlesbrough city in northern England; not -*borough*

Mid Glamorgan (two words, no hyphen) county in Wales

Midi, le southern France

Midi-Pyrénées region of France

Midlothian former Scottish county

Midsomer Norton, Somerset

Midwest (one word), **Middle West** (two words) hazily defined area of the US generally taken to include Ohio, Indiana, Illinois, Iowa, Wisconsin, Missouri, Minnesota and Michigan, and sometimes also Kansas and Nebraska

Mies van der Rohe, Ludwig (1886–1969) German-born US architect

mijnheer The Dutch term for 'sir', which should be capitalized when placed before a name. The Dutch vowel *y* is written with two dots and has therefore been mistaken by English readers for *i* and *j* combined. *Meneer*, less formal, is similar to 'mister'.

Milanković, Milutin (1879–1958) Serbian engineer and geophysicist best known for his theories concerning climate change. **Milankovitch cycles** are named after him.

mileage

miles gloriosus (Lat.) 'glorious soldier', a braggart, particularly a braggart soldier; pronounced *meel-ays glor-ee-oh-sus*

milieu environment

militate, mitigate Often confused. To *militate* is to operate against or, much more rarely, to dispute or debate an issue. To *mitigate* means to assuage, soften, make more endurable: 'His apology mitigated the insult.' *Mitigate against* often appears and is always wrong.

Milius, John (1944–) American film writer and director

Millais, Sir John Everett (1829–96) British painter

Millay, Edna St Vincent (1892–1950) American poet

millennium Note *-nn-*; the preferred plural is **millennia**, but **millenniums** is also accepted.

milli- prefix meaning one-thousandth

milliard British term now almost never used here or anywhere else, meaning 1,000 million

millipede

Milošević, Slobodan (1941–2006) President of Serbia 1989–97. He died while on trial in The Hague on charges of genocide and crimes against humanity.

milquetoast, not *milk-* a timid person. The name comes from an old newspaper cartoon called *The Timid Soul* featuring a character named Caspar (not *-er*) Milquetoast.

Milton Keynes, Buckinghamshire pronounced *keenz*

Mindanao island in the Philippines

Mindszenty, József, Cardinal (1892–1975) Roman Catholic primate of Hungary, long opposed to the Communist regime

minimize, strictly speaking, does not mean merely to play down or soften. It means to reduce to an absolute minimum.

Minneapolis largest city in Minnesota; with St Paul, the state capital, it forms the Twin Cities

Minorca, Balearic Islands, Spain in Spanish, **Menorca**

Minos in Greek mythology, a son of Zeus and Europa, and king of Crete

Minotaur in Greek mythology, a figure that is half-man and half-bull

Minsk capital of Belarus

minuscule frequently misspelled; think of *minus*, not *mini*

minute detail The two words are not only tautological, but also have a kind of deadening effect on any passage in which they appear, as here: 'Samples of the shards were brought back to the college, where they were studied in minute detail.' Why not just say: 'Samples of the shards were brought back to the college for study'? One can normally assume that any objects being subjected to study will be examined closely.

minutia a detail; pl. **minutiae**. Note that the latter is pronounced *min-oo-she*, not *min-oo-she-ay*.

mirabile dictu (Lat.) wonderful to relate

MIRAS abbr. of mortgage interest relief at source

Miricioiu, Nelly (1952–) Romanian opera singer

MIRV multiple independently targeted re-entry vehicle; a type of ballistic missile

misanthrope (or **misanthropist**) someone who dislikes human beings

miscellaneous

mischievous

mise-en-scène stage or film scenery, or the general setting of an event

mishandle

mishit

misogamist, misogynist The first hates marriage, the second hates women. See also MISANTHROPE.

misshapen

Mississauga suburb of Toronto

Mississippi US state and river
Missolonghi, Greece
misspell If there is one word that you don't wish in print to misspell, it is this one. Note -*ss*-.
misspend
misstate
misstep
mistime
mistle thrush (or **missel thrush**)
mistletoe
mistral cold, unpleasant wind in France
MIT Massachusetts Institute of Technology
mitigate, **militate** The first means to soften or make more endurable; the second to act against.
mitochondrion type of cell organelle; pl. **mitochondria**
Mitsukoshi Japanese department store chain
Mitterrand, François (Maurice Marie) (1916–96) President of France 1981–95
Mitzi E. Newhouse Theater, Lincoln Center, New York
Miyazawa, Kiichi (1919–2007) Prime Minister of Japan 1991–3
mizzen, **mizzenmast**
MMR combined vaccine for children against measles, mumps and rubella
Mnemosyne Greek goddess of memory and mother, by Zeus, of the nine Muses; hence **mnemonics**
MO postal abbr. of Missouri (not Montana, whose abbr. is MT). The traditional abbr. is **Mo.**
Möbius strip (or **band**) a piece of paper or other material twisted in such a way as to form a continuous surface; named after its discoverer, German mathematician August Möbius (1790–1868)

Mobutu Sese Seko (1930–97) born Joseph-Desiré Mobuto; President of Zaire, 1965–97

Moby-Dick (note hyphen) novel by Herman Melville (1851). The full title on publication was *Moby-Dick; or, the Whale.*

moccasin

modem, short for modulator/demodulator, is a device that encodes digital signals into analogue signals and vice versa.

Modigliani, Amedeo (1884–1920) Italian artist

modus operandi (Lat.) the way of doing something

modus vivendi (Lat.) way of life, or a kind of truce pending the settlement of a dispute

Mogadishu capital of Somalia

Mohammed (c. 570–632) founder of Islam; now usually spelled **Muhammad**

Mohave, Mojave The first is the spelling for the Native American tribe and mountains in Arizona; the second is the spelling of the desert.

Mohorovičić discontinuity boundary between Earth's crust and mantle, named for the Croatian geophysicist Andrija Mohorovičić (1857–1936)

Mojave Desert, but **Mohave** for the Native American tribe and mountains in Arizona

Moldova (not *Moldavia*) eastern European republic, formerly called Bessarabia, formerly part of Soviet Union; capital Chişinău. The people and language are **Moldovan**.

Molière (1622–73) born Jean-Baptiste Poquelin; French playwright

mollycoddle to overprotect

Molly Maguires secret society active in Pennsylvania in the 19th century

molybdenum chemical element, symbol Mo

Mombasa seaport and resort in Kenya

Mona Lisa painting by Leonardo da Vinci, also called *La Gioconda*

Mönchen-Gladbach, Germany

Mondrian, Piet (1872–1944)   born Pieter Cornelis Mondriaan; Dutch abstract painter

Monégasque for a person or thing from Monaco. Not *Mona-*

moneyed, not *monied*, for someone with wealth

mongooses is the plural of *mongoose*. The word is of Indian origin and has no relation to the English *goose*.

moniker (not *monicker*) for a name or nickname

Monnet, Jean (1888–1979) French statesman; but **Claude Monet** (1840–1926) for the artist

Monongahela river in West Virginia and Pennsylvania

mononucleosis is the American term for the illness known in Britain and elsewhere as glandular fever.

Monserrat, Spain, but **Montserrat**, Leeward Islands

monsieur (Fr.), pl. **messieurs**

Montagnard (Fr.) 'mountain dweller', name given to radical faction during the French Revolution because of the elevated position of their seats in the National Convention. The term is also applied to some south-east Asian hill tribes.

Montaigne, Michel (Eyquem) de (1533–92)   French philosopher and essayist

Mont Blanc, Alpine mountain, but **Montblanc** for the pen

Montenegro, Republic of formerly part of Yugoslavia; capital Podgorica

Monterey for the city and bay in California and towns in Indiana, Massachusetts, Tennessee and Virginia, but **Monterrey** for the city in Mexico and town in Colorado

Montesquieu, Charles Louis de Secondat, Baron de la Brède et de (1689–1755) French philosopher and jurist

Montessori system of teaching developed by Maria Montessori (1870–1952), Italian doctor and educator

Monteverdi, Claudio Giovanni Antonio (1567–1643) Italian composer

Montevideo capital of Uruguay

Montparnasse, Paris

Montpelier, capital of Vermont, but **Montpellier**, France

Mont-Saint-Michel, France (hyphens)

Montserrat, Leeward Islands, but **Monserrat**, Spain

moose, pl. same

moot A *moot point* is a point that is subject to discussion.

More, Sir Thomas (also St Thomas) (1478–1535) English statesman and author

morganatic marriage one between a noble and a commoner in which the commoner and his or her descendants enjoy no privileges of inheritance

Morgan le Fay sister of King Arthur

Morganthau, Jr, Henry (1891–1967) American statesman, Secretary of the Treasury 1934–45

moribund does not mean sluggish or declining; it means dying, on the point of death. To be moribund is to be critically, indeed irreversibly, ill.

Morison, Samuel Eliot (1887–1976) American historian

Mormon Church officially the Church of Jesus Christ of Latter-Day Saints

Morocco, **Moroccan**

Morris, Gouverneur (1752–1816) American statesman, signatory of US Constitution

Morrison, Toni (1931–) American novelist, awarded Nobel Prize for Literature 1993

mortar, in the context of weaponry, is the launching device, not the explosive projectiles. It is generally better, and sometimes necessary, to write that troops fired mortar rounds (or bombs or shells, etc.) rather than simply that they fired mortars.

Morte d'Arthur, Le (not *La*) 15th-century prose narrative by Thomas Malory relating the legend of King Arthur

mortise lock

Moselle for the river and wine; in German, **Mosel**

Moser-Pröll, Annemarie (1953–) Austrian skier

Moskva Russian for Moscow

Moslem is an accepted variant, but **Muslim** is generally preferred.

mosquitoes

Mossad Israeli secret service

Moss, Kate (1974–), British supermodel, but **Kate Mosse** (1961–), British writer and broadcaster, co-founder of the Orange Prize

most Unless you are striving for an air of folksiness, *most* as an adverb should be confined to signifying the topmost degree ('the most delicious cake') or as a synonym for *very* ('your offer is most welcome'). As an alternative for *almost* or *nearly* ('he would eat most anything') it is generally not welcome in serious writing.

Mothering Sunday (US **Mother's Day**) In the UK, it is celebrated on the fourth Sunday of Lent, in the US on the second Sunday in May.

mot juste (Fr.) the right word

motto, pl. **mottoes**

moult (US **molt**)

mountebank a charlatan

Mourning Becomes Electra play by Eugene O'Neill (1931)

moussaka Greek dish of lamb, aubergines and tomatoes

moustache (US **mustache**)

mousy (pref.), **mousey** (alt.)

Mozambique, but **Mozambican**

mozzarella Italian white cheese, the best of which is made from buffalo's milk

Mpumalanga South African province, formerly Eastern Transvaal

MRSA short for methicillin-resistant *Staphyloccus aureus*, a type of bacterial infection

MS manuscript; pl. **MSS** (capitalized but without full stops)

MT postal abbreviation of Montana; the traditional abbreviation is **Mont.**

Mubarak, (Muhammad) Hosni (Said) (1928–) Egyptian President 1981–

mucous, mucus, mucosa The first is the adjectival form, the second the noun form. Thus *mucus* is the substance secreted by the *mucous* membranes. A more formal name for the latter is *mucosa*.

Mueller, Lisel (1924–) German-born American poet

Muenster/Munster Either is correct for the cheese from Alsace; see also MUNSTER, MÜNSTER.

muezzin In Islam, an official who calls the faithful to prayer

mufti plain clothes worn by a person who usually wears a uniform

Muhammad (or **Mohammed**) (c. 570–632) founder of Islam

Muhammad Ali (1942–) retired boxing champion, born Cassius Marcellus Clay Jr

Mühlhausen, Germany

mujahideen is the most common spelling in English for Islamic guerrilla fighters, but there are many alternative spellings, including *mujahidin, mujahedin* and *mujahedeen*.

Mukhabarat Iraqi secret police

mukluk, **muktuk** The first is a kind of boot; the second is whale blubber as food.

mulatto offensive term for a person with one black and one white parent; pl. **mulattos**

mullah Muslim teacher

mulligatawny soup

Mumbai Indian city formerly known as Bombay

Munch, Edvard (1863–1944) Norwegian artist

Munster, Münster The first is a province of Ireland comprising six counties: Clare, Cork, Kerry, Limerick, Tipperary and Waterford. The second is a city in North Rhine-Westphalia, Germany.

Muralitharan, Muttiah (1972–) Sri Lankan cricketer, also known as Murali

Murchison Falls, Uganda

Murchison River, Australia

Murfreesboro, Battle of (1863) in the US Civil War; sometimes called the Battle of Stones River

murmur

Murphy's Law If anything can go wrong, it will. Also known as **Sod's Law**

Muscovite person from Moscow. The name comes from the ancient principality of Muscovy.

Muses the nine daughters of Zeus and Mnemosyne who presided over the arts: Calliope (eloquence and epic poetry), Clio (history), Erato (elegiac poetry), Euterpe (music), Melpomene (tragedy), Polyhymnia (lyric poetry), Terpsichore (dancing), Thalia (comedy) and Urania (astronomy)

Musharraf, Pervez (1943–) President of Pakistan 1999–

'Music hath charms to soothe a savage breast' is the correct quotation from the Congreve play *The Mourning Bride* (1697). Not '*the* savage breast' or 'a savage *beast*'

musk-ox (hyphen), but **muskmelon, muskrat, muskroot**

Muslim (pref.), **Moslem** (alt.)

Mussolini, Benito (1883–1945)   Italian dictator, Prime Minister 1922–43

Mussorgsky/Moussorgsky, Modest Petrovich (1839–81) Russian composer

mutatis mutandis (Lat.) with the necessary changes

mutual, common Many authorities continue to insist, with varying degrees of conviction, that *mutual* should be reserved for describing reciprocal relationships between two or more things and not loosely applied to those things shared in common. Thus, if you and I like each other, we have a mutual friendship. But if you and I both like Shakespeare, we have a common admiration. The use of *mutual* in the sense of *common* has been with us since the 16th century and was given a notable boost in the 19th with the appearance of the Dickens novel *Our Mutual Friend*. Most authorities accept it when *common* might be interpreted as a denigration, but even so in its looser sense the word is generally better avoided. It is, at all events, more often than not superfluous, as here: 'They hope to arrange a mutual exchange of prisoners' (*Daily Telegraph*). An exchange of anything can hardly be other than mutual.

muu-muu loose-fitting Hawaiian dress

Muzak (cap.) recorded light background music

MW megawatt; large unit of energy

mW milliwatt; small unit of energy

myalgic encephalomyelitis abbr. ME, a type of chronic malaise

Myanmar, Burma Burma is the former official name of the south-east Asian nation and the one preferred by most publications and other informed users outside Burma. Myanmar was for a time used by many publications, but now its use is mostly confined to the country's government and institutions under its influence. Some authorities write 'Burma/Myanmar'. The United Nations uses just Myanmar.

Mycenae ancient Greek city and civilization; things from or of there are **Mycenaean** or **Mycenean**

My Lai, Vietnam site of notorious massacre of villagers by US troops (1968)

myrrh fragrant gum resin used in perfumery

myself Except when it is used for emphasis ('I'll do it myself') or reflexively ('I cut myself while shaving') *myself* is almost always timorous and better avoided. In the following two examples, the better word is inserted in brackets: 'Give it to John or myself [me]'; 'My wife and myself [I] would just like to say . . .'

MySpace internet social site

myxomatosis viral disease of rabbits

N

NAACP abbr. of the US National Association for the Advancement of Colored People

Nacogdoches, Texas

NAFTA abbr. of the North American Free Trade Agreement, a 1994 trade pact signed by Canada, Mexico and the US

Nagorno-Karabakh Armenian-dominated enclave in the former Soviet republic of Azerbaijan

Nags Head, North Carolina

Naipaul, V. S. (for **Vidiadhar Surajprasad**) (1932–) Trinidad-born British writer; awarded Booker Prize 1971 and Nobel Prize for Literature 2001

naïve, naïvety now frequently written **naive, naivety**

namby-pamby feeble

nameable

Namen (Flemish)/**Namur** (Fr.) Belgian city

nano- prefix meaning one-billionth

naphtha flammable oil; note -*ph*-

Napoleon I (1769–1821) born Napoleon Bonaparte; Emperor of the French 1804–15

narcissism excessive interest in oneself and one's appearance

narcissus bulbous flowering plant of the lily family; pl. **narcissi/narcissuses**

Narragansett Bay, Rhode Island

NASA National Aeronautics and Space Administration

nasal

Nascar National Association for Stock Car Auto Racing (US)

NASDAQ National Association of Securities Dealers Automated Quotations; US stock exchange specializing in technology stocks

Nash (or **Nashe**)**, Thomas** (1567–1601) English dramatist

National Archives, Kew, West London formerly the Public Record Office

National Governors' Association (US)

National Institute for Health and Clinical Excellence abbr. NICE

National Institutes of Health (US) Note *Institutes* plural. It is part of the US Department of Health and Human Services.

National Transportation Safety Board (US)

NATO North Atlantic Treaty Organization. As of 2007, the member countries were: Belgium, Bulgaria, Canada, Czech Republic, Denmark, Estonia, France, Germany, Greece, Hungary, Iceland, Italy, Latvia, Lithuania, Luxembourg, Netherlands, Norway, Poland, Portugal, Romania, Slovakia, Slovenia, Spain, Turkey, United Kingdom, United States.

Natty Bumppo main character in James Fenimore Cooper's *Leatherstocking Tales* (1823–41)

Natural England British conservation authority formed from the amalgamation of all or parts of English Nature, the Countryside Agency and the Rural Development Service

Natural History Museum London; formally it is the **British Museum (Natural History)**

naught, nought Although dictionaries increasingly treat the words as interchangeable, traditionally the first means *nothing* (as in 'his efforts came to naught') while the second is used to signify the figure zero. The game is **noughts and crosses** (known in the US as tick-tack-toe).

nauseous is an adjective describing something that causes nausea ('a nauseous substance'). To feel sick is to be *nauseated.*

Navajo/Navaho Native American tribe; the first is generally preferred, the second accepted

naval, navel The first pertains to a navy and its possessions or operations, the second to belly buttons and like-shaped objects. The oranges are *navel.*

navigable

Nazi a member of the National Socialist German Workers' Party; **Nazism**, not -*ii*-

n.b. (or **NB**) abbr. of *nota bene* (Lat.), 'note carefully'. Note that *n.b.* is spelled with full stops and *NB* without.

NCAA (US) National Collegiate Athletic Association

Ndeti, Cosmas (1971–) Kenyan distance runner

Ndjamena (or **N'Djaména**) capital of Chad

NDPB abbr. of non-departmental public body; type of semi-autonomous government department (UK)

'Ndrangheta organized crime group in Calabria, Italy

Neagh, Loch, Northern Ireland largest lake in British Isles (153 sq m/396 sq km)

Neandertal increasingly is the preferred spelling for the extinct species of human, though the formal scientific rendering *Homo neanderthalensis* still generally keeps the -*thal* spelling. *Neanderthal man*, as a term for the species, is both sexist and old-fashioned.

near disaster 'His quick thinking saved an RAF jet pilot from

a near disaster.' Not quite. The pilot was saved from a
disaster. A near disaster is what he had.

neat's-foot oil a substance used to treat leather

nebbish weak, ineffectual man

Nebuchadnezzar (c. 625–562 BC) King of Babylon 605–562 BC

nebuchadnezzar an exceptionally large bottle of champagne,
equivalent to 20 normal bottles

nebula The plural can be either **nebulae** or **nebulas**.

necessarily, **necessity**

needless to say is a harmless enough expression, but it often
draws attention to the fact that you really didn't need to
say it.

nefarious wicked

negligee

negligible

Negretti & Zambra maker of scientific instruments

Nehemiah Jewish leader in 5th century BC after whom an Old
Testament book is named

Nehru, Jawaharlal (1889–1964) Indian Prime Minister
1947–64

neighbour (US **neighbor**)

Neiman Marcus The US department store group no longer
hyphenates its name.

neither In *neither . . . nor* constructions, the verb should always
agree with the noun nearest it. Thus, 'Neither De Niro nor
his agent was available for comment.' When the noun
nearest the verb is plural, the verb should also be plural:
'Neither the President nor his advisers were available for
comment.' When *neither* is used on its own without the
nor, the verb should always be singular: 'Neither of the
men was ready', 'Neither of us is hungry.' In short, more
often than not a singular verb is called for – but that sin-

gularity is by no means invariable. Try to remember that *neither* emphasizes the separateness of items. It doesn't add them together, at least not grammatically.

nemesis A *nemesis* (from Nemesis, the Greek goddess of vengeance) is not merely a rival or traditional enemy, but one who extracts retributive justice or is utterly unvanquishable.

neodymium a chemical element

neologism a newly coined word

nephritis inflammation of the kidneys

Nephthys Egyptian goddess, companion of the dead

ne plus ultra (Lat.) perfection, the acme

Neptune Roman god of the sea, identified with the Greek god Poseidon, and the eighth planet from the Sun

nerve-racking, not -*wracking*. See RACK, WRACK.

n'est-ce-pas? (Fr.) 'is that not so?'; pronounced *ness-pah*

Netanyahu, Benjamin (1949–) Israeli politician, Prime Minister 1996–9

Netherlands, the The capital is Amsterdam, but the seat of government is The Hague. (As with all place names, *the* is not capitalized with the country name, but is with the city name.)

netsuke Japanese carved ornament

Netzhualcóyotl part of the Mexico City conurbation

Neuchâtel Swiss town and wine

Neufchâtel French town and cheese

Neuilly-sur-Seine suburb of Paris

neurasthenia chronic lethargy

nevertheless (one word)

Newberry Library, Chicago

Newbery Medal formally the **John Newbery Medal**, award for outstanding children's literature

Newcastle-under-Lyme (hyphens), Staffordshire

Newcastle upon Tyne (no hyphens), Tyne and Wear

New England Although it has no official standing, the name takes in six states: Connecticut, Maine, Massachusetts, New Hampshire, Rhode Island and Vermont.

New Hebrides former name of Vanuatu

Newton-le-Willows (hyphens), Merseyside

New York City comprises five boroughs, each coextensive with a state county (in brackets): the Bronx (Bronx County), Brooklyn (Kings County), Manhattan (New York County), Queens (Queens County) and Staten Island (Richmond County).

New Year's Day, New Year's Eve

Niagara Falls on the river separating Ontario and New York State

Niamey capital of Niger

Nibelungenlied German epic poem

niblick golf club used for getting the ball out of bad lies

NICE National Institute for Health and Clinical Excellence (UK)

niceish is the spelling for something that is rather nice.

nickel, not -*le* metal; US five-cent coin

Nicklaus, Jack (1940–) American golfer

Nicolson, Sir Harold George (1886–1968) English diplomat and writer

Nicosia, Cyprus To the Greeks it is Levkosia.

nicotine

Nielsen ratings TV audience measurement system

Nietzsche, Friedrich Wilhelm (1884–1900) German philosopher; the adjective is **Nietzschean**

Nightingale, Florence (1820–1910) English nurse and hospital reformer

Niigata, Honshu, Japan Note *-ii-*.

Niihau Hawaiian island. Note *-ii-*.

Nijinsky, Vaslav (1890–1950) Russian dancer and choreographer

Nijmegen, Netherlands

Nikkei 225 Index principal Japanese stock market index; Nikkei is derived from *Nihon Keizai Shimbun,* a business newspaper

Niña, **Pinta** and **Santa María** the ships in Columbus's fleet during the 1492 crossing of the Atlantic

nincompoop, not *nim-* stupid person

niqab Muslim woman's face veil covering all but the eyes

Nisei literally 'second generation'; term used in North America for native US or Canadian citizens born to immigrant Japanese parents; often loosely used to describe all Japanese expatriates, particularly in the context of Second World War internment.

Nissen hut named after its inventor, British engineer Peter Norman Nissen (1871–1930)

nitty-gritty (hyphen)

nitwit

Nixon, Richard Milhous (not *-house*) (1913–94) US President 1969–74

Nizhny Novgorod, Russia called Gorky during the Communist era

Nobel Prizes are awarded in six categories: chemistry, literature, peace, physics, physiology or medicine, and economics – though the last named is not strictly a Nobel prize. (Its formal title is the Bank of Sweden Prize in Economic Sciences.) Nobel Prizes are named for the Swedish inventor and industrialist Alfred Nobel (1933–96).

noblesse oblige (Fr.) 'nobility creates obligation'; applied to duties that come with rank

nobody (one word), but **no one**

Noh stylized Japanese drama

noisome has nothing to do with noise or noisiness. It is related to *annoy* and means offensive or objectionable and is most often used to describe unpleasant smells.

nolo contendere (Lat.) 'I do not wish to contend'; tantamount to a plea of guilty, but leaves the defendant with the option of denying the same or similar charges in other proceedings

nom de guerre (Fr.) 'war name'; an assumed name; in most contexts, a cliché

nom de plume 'pen name', a writer's pseudonym

nomenklatura secret list of names from which people in the USSR were chosen for advancement

nonagenarian person from 90 to 99 years old

nonce a word coined for a specific occasion; also a sexual deviant

non-Christian, but **unchristian**

non compos mentis (Lat.) not of sound mind

none Although *none* can always take a singular verb, there is no rule recognized by any authority on English grammar that it cannot equally well take a plural one.

nonetheless (or **none the less**)

non sequitur (Lat.) 'it does not follow'; the combination of two or more statements that are jarringly unrelated, as in 'He was born in Omaha and his shoes were brown.'

no one (two words), but **nobody** (one word)

Nord-Pas-de-Calais region of France

nor'easter a strong or stormy wind from the north-east

Norge Norwegian name for Norway

normalcy Although most dictionaries accept it as standard, it is still derided as a casualism by many authorities, who suggest *normality* instead.

Norrköping, Sweden

Northants (no point) abbr. of Northamptonshire

Northern Ireland part of the United Kingdom, comprising six counties: Antrim, Armagh, Down, Fermanagh, Londonderry and Tyrone

North Fork BanCorp New York-based banking company

nosy, not -*ey*

nota bene (Lat.) 'note well'; abbreviated **n.b.** (with full stops) or **NB** (without)

Notes from Underground novel by Dostoyevsky (1864); not *the Underground*

not so much is often followed by *but* when the word should be *as*, as here: 'He was not so much a comic actor, but a real comedian.' Make it 'He was not so much a comic actor as a real comedian.'

notwithstanding (one word)

Nouakchott capital of Mauritania

n'oubliez pas (Fr.) don't forget

noughts and crosses

nouveau riche (Fr.) 'new rich'; mildly disparaging description of someone whose wealth is recently acquired; pl. **nouveaux riches**

Novocaine (cap.)

Novosibirsk, Russia

NOW National Organization for (not *of*) Women, US activist group

nowadays

NSPCC National Society for the Prevention of Cruelty to Children

NTT DoCoMo Japanese telecommunications company
Nuits-Saint-Georges French wine
Nuku'alofa/Nukualofa capital of Tonga
Nullarbor Plain, Western Australia   often misspelled
Nullabor
number Used with the definite article, *number* always takes a
singular verb ('The number of people in the world is ris-
ing'); used with an indefinite article, it always takes a
plural verb ('A number of people are unhappy').
numismatics the study or collection of coins or medals
numskull, not *numbskull*, is the preferred spelling for most,
but not all, authorities.
Nunavut Canadian territory created in 1999
Nunivak second largest Alaskan island (after Kodiak)
Nuremberg (in German Nürnberg) Bavarian city; not -*burg*
Nureyev, Rudolf (1938–93) Russian ballet dancer
Nuuk formerly Godthaab; capital of Greenland
Nyasaland former name of Malawi
Nyerere, Julius (Kambarage) (1922–99) President of
Tanganyika and (after its union with Zanzibar) of
Tanzania 1961–85
Nymphenburg Palace, Munich   in German, Schloss
Nymphenburg

O, oh, oho The first normally appears in a literary or religious context; it is always capitalized and never followed by punctuation. The second is used in more general contexts to denote emotions ranging from a small sigh to an outcry; it is capitalized only at the start of sentences and normally followed by either a comma or an exclamation mark. *Oho*, with or without an exclamation mark, denotes an expression of surprise.

O. Henry pen name of William Sydney Porter (1862–1910), American short-story writer

O_2 arena formerly the Millennium Dome, Greenwich

Oakenclough, Lancashire pronounced *oak-en-klew*

OAS Organization of American States

OAU Organization of African Unity

Oaxaca city and state in southern Mexico; pronounced *wa-haka*

Obadiah Old Testament prophet

Obama, Barack (1961–) Democratic Senator from Illinois 2005– ; full name Barack Hussein Obama

Obasanjo, Olusegun (1937–), President of Nigeria 1999–2007

obbligato in music, an indispensable part

obeisance a show of deference

Oberammergau   village in Bavaria, Germany, where a celebrated passion play is performed every ten years

obiter dictum (Lat.)   a remark made in passing; pl. *obiter dicta*

objet d'art, pl. *objets d'art*

objet trouvé (Fr.)   a found object; pl. *objets trouvés*

oblique

oblivious   Many authorities long maintained that *oblivious* can mean only forgetful. You cannot properly be oblivious of something that you were not in the first place aware of. But in its broader sense of merely being unaware or impervious, *oblivious* is now accepted universally.

obloquy   verbal abuse; pl. **obloquies**

O'Brien, Flann   pen name of Brian O'Nolan (1911–66), Irish writer, who also wrote a column in the *Irish Times* under the pseudonym Myles na Gopaleen

obscurum per obscurius (Lat.)   the obscure by the more obscure

obsidian   glassy volcanic rock

obsolete, obsolescent   Things that are no longer used or needed are *obsolete*. Things that are becoming obsolete are *obsolescent*.

obstetrics, obstetrician

obstreperous   noisy, vociferous

obtuse, abstruse   *Obtuse*, of a person, means slow to understand; *abstruse*, of a concept, means difficult to understand.

obtuse angle   one between 90 and 180 degrees

obviate   does not mean reduce or make more acceptable, as is often thought: 'A total redesign of the system should obviate complaints about its reliability' (*The Times*). It means to make unnecessary.

Occam's/Ockham's razor   paring all presumptions to the minimum; a principle attributed to the English philosopher William of Occam/Ockham (c. 1285–c. 1349)

occult

occur, take place *Take place* is better reserved for scheduled events. When what is being described is accidental, *occur* is the better word.

ochlocracy government by mob rule

ochre (US **ocher**) earthy colour, yellow, red or brown

octet

octocentennial 800th anniversary

octogenarian person from 80 to 89 years old

octopus, pl. **octopuses** (or, in technical writing, **octopodes**)

oculist

Oder-Neisse line boundary between Germany and Poland

Odets, Clifford (1906–63) American playwright

odometer device for measuring distance travelled

odoriferous

ODPM Office of the Deputy Prime Minister; former government department (UK)

Od's bodkins   archaic oath, probably a corruption of 'by God's body'

Odysseus (Greek)/**Ulysses** (Lat.) in Greek mythology, the king of Ithaca; an **odyssey** is a long journey

OECD Organization for (not *of*) Economic Cooperation and Development. The members are Australia, Austria, Belgium, Canada, Czech Republic, Denmark, Finland, France, Germany, Greece, Hungary, Iceland, Ireland, Italy, Japan, Luxembourg, Mexico, Netherlands, New Zealand, Norway, Poland, Portugal, Slovakia, South Korea, Spain, Sweden, Switzerland, Turkey, United Kingdom, United States.

Oedipus complex term coined by Freud to describe a child's (usually a son's) feelings of love for the parent of the opposite sex mingled with dislike for the parent of the same sex

oenology (or **enology**) study of wines. A connoisseur is an **oenophile**.

oesophagus, oesophageal (US **esophagus, esophageal**)

oestrogen, oestrus (US **estrogen, estrus**)

oeuvre an artist's body of work

O'Faoláin, Seán (1900–91) Irish novelist and short-story writer

Ofcom body that regulates the communications industries in Britain

Offaly county in the Republic of Ireland

Offa's Dike (or **Dyke**) 8th-century earthwork roughly following the English–Welsh border

Offenbach, Jacques (1819–80) born Jakob Eberst; German-born French composer

off of The *of* is redundant. Write 'Get off the table,' not 'Get off of the table.'

Ofgen government agency that regulates the electricity and gas markets

Oftel, the agency that regulated the telecommunications industry in Britain, no longer exists; it is now part of Ofcom.

Ofwat formally the Water Services Regulatory Authority; British agency responsible for regulating water and sewerage services

Ogdon, John (**Andrew Howard**) (1937–89) British pianist

ogre

oh, oho See O, OH, OHO.

Oireachtas Irish legislature, consisting of the President and the two assemblies, the Dáil Éireann and Seanad. It is pronounced *ur´-akh-tus*.

Ojos del Salado Andean mountain on the Chilean–Argentinian border; second highest peak in the western hemisphere (22,600 feet/6,910 metres)

Okeechobee lake and inland waterway, Florida

O'Keeffe, Georgia (1887–1986) American artist

Okefenokee Swamp, Florida and Georgia

Okhotsk, Sea of between the Kamchatka Peninsula and the eastern Siberian coast

Okri, Ben (1959–) Nigerian-born novelist, Booker prize-winner 1991

Olazabal, Jose Maria (1966–) Spanish golfer

Oldenburg, Claes (1929–) Swedish-born American sculptor

Old Lady of Threadneedle Street nickname for the Bank of England

Old Peculier an English beer

Olduvai Gorge, Tanzania

Olivetti formally Ing. C. Olivetti & Co. SpA; Italian industrial group, once famous for typewriters

Olmert, Ehud (1945–) Prime Minister of Israel 2006–

Olympic-sized swimming pool An official Olympics swimming pool is fifty metres long. Almost no one owns a private pool that large, so the description in respect to private pools is almost always a gross exaggeration.

Omar Khayyám is the correct spelling of the Persian poet and mathematician (c. 1050–c. 1125). Note *-yy-*.

omelette (US also **omelet**)

omit, **omitted**, **omitting**, **omissible**

omnipotent, **omniscient** The first means all-powerful, the second all-knowing.

on, upon Although some journalists think there is, or ought to be, a distinction between these two, there isn't. The choice is sometimes dictated by idiom ('on no account', 'upon my soul'), but in all other instances it is a matter of preference.

Ondaatje, Michael (1943–) Sri Lankan-born Canadian novelist, Booker joint prizewinner 1992

one can be a grammatically tricky word. It takes a singular verb in straightforward constructions like 'One out of every seven men is bald.' But when extra words are attached to it – *one or more, one of those* – it ceases to govern the verb and the sense of the sentence becomes plural. Thus the sentence 'Inside each folder is one or more sheets of information' should be 'are one or more' and 'Nott is one of those rare politicians who doesn't mind what he says' should be 'don't mind what they say'. A helpful trick to determine whether a singular or plural verb is needed is to invert the word order of the sentence: 'Of those politicians who do not mind what they say, Nott is one.'

one or more is plural. For a discussion, see ONE.

only In general, *only* ought to be attached to the word or phrase it is modifying and not set adrift, as here: 'The bus only ran on Sundays.' Taken literally, the sentence suggests that on other days of the week the bus did something else – perhaps flew? The writer would better have said that the bus 'ran only on Sundays' or 'on Sundays only'. Oftentimes, to be sure, clarity and idiom are better served by bringing *only* to a more forward position ('This will only take a minute', 'The victory can only be called a miracle'). And increasingly, it must be said, authorities are inclined towards leniency with regard to where *only* is permitted. Certainly it is always better to avoid an air of fussiness. But when, as in the example of the bus, a simple repositioning puts the word in the right place without creating a distraction, there is no reason not to make the adjustment.

onomatopoeia the formation of words based on the sounds they denote, as with *buzz*, *bang* and *vroom-vroom*

on to, onto Until the 20th century *onto* as one word was almost unknown in both Britain and America, and its standing remains somewhat dubious in Britain. Today in the United States (and increasingly in Britain), *onto* is used where the two elements function as a compound preposition ('He jumped onto the horse') and *on to* is used where *on* is an adverb ('We moved on to the next subject').

oolong tea a partly fermented China tea

oozy

op. cit., *opere citato* (Lat.) in the work cited

openness Note -*nn*-.

opéra bouffe, **opera buffa** The first is a farcical French opera, the second a farcical Italian one.

Opéra-Comique Paris theatre

operose laborious

ophthalmologist, **oculist**, **optometrist**, **optician** *Ophthalmologist* is often misspelled and even more frequently mispronounced. Note that it begins *oph-* and not *opth-* and that the first syllable is pronounced *off*, not *op*. Thus it is similar in pronunciation and spelling to *diphtheria*, *diphthong* and *naphtha*, all of which are also frequently misspelled and misspoken. *Oculist* and *ophthalmologist* both describe doctors who specialize in diseases of the eye. An *optometrist* is one who is trained to test eyes but is not a doctor. An *optician* is one who makes or sells corrective lenses.

Oppenheimer, J. (for **Julius**) **Robert** (1904–67) American physicist

Oporto, Portugal in Portuguese, **Pôrto**

opossum (or **possum**) The plural can be either **opossum** or **opossums** (or **possum/possums**).

oppressor

optimistic, **pessimistic** Strictly speaking, both words should be used to describe a general outlook rather than a specific view, particularly with regard to the inconsequential. 'He was optimistic that he would find the missing book' would be better as 'was hopeful' or 'was confident'.

optimum does not mean greatest or fastest or biggest, as is sometimes thought. It describes the point at which conflicting considerations are reconciled. The optimum flying speed of an aircraft is the speed at which all the many variables that must be taken into account in flying – safety, comfort, fuel consumption and so on – are most nearly in harmony.

opus magnum, *magnum opus* (Lat.) The first is a great work; the second is an author's principal work.

or When *or* links two or more singular items in a sentence, the verb must always be singular. 'It was not clear whether the President or Vice-President were within hearing range at the time' should be 'was within hearing range'.

oral, **verbal** *Oral* can apply only to spoken words; *verbal* can describe both spoken and written words.

Orange Broadband Prize for Fiction formerly the Orange Prize; literary award for women writers

orange pekoe tea

ordinal numbers first, second, third, etc. See also CARDINAL NUMBERS.

ordinance, ordnance The first is a command or decree; the second refers to military stores and materials.

ordonnance the proper arrangement of parts in a literary, musical, artistic or architectural work

Ordzhonikidze, Russia formerly Dzaudzhikau

Oresteia trilogy by Aeschylus (c. 458 BC)

Orestes in Greek mythology, the son of Clytemnestra and Agamemnon

Öresund strait between Sweden and Denmark

Oriel College, Oxford

originally is often needlessly inserted into sentences where it conveys no additional information, as here: 'The plans were originally drawn up as long ago as 1972' (*Observer*).

Origin of Species, On the seminal book by Charles Darwin (1859), full title *On the Origin of Species by Means of Natural Selection, or the Preservation of Favoured Races in the Struggle for Life*

Orinoco South American river, rising in Venezuela

Orkney Islands, Scotland Properly they can be called Orkney or the Orkney Islands, but not *the Orkneys*. A native or resident is an **Orcadian**.

Orly Airport, Paris

orology the study of mountains

Ortega y Gasset, José (1883–1955) Spanish philosopher

orthoepy the study of pronunciation. Curiously, there are two accepted pronunciations: *or´-tho-ep-ee* and *or-tho´-ip-ee*.

orthography correct or accepted spelling; the study of spelling

orthopaedics (US **orthopedics**) the area of medicine concerned with bones and muscles

Orwell, George pen name of the English writer Eric Blair (1903–50)

Osborne, John (1929–94) English playwright

oscillate swing back and forth

oscilloscope

OSHA Occupational Safety and Health Administration (US)

Osiris Egyptian god of the underworld

Osservatore Romano, L' Vatican newspaper

Ostend Belgian port; in Flemish, **Oostende**

osteo- prefix meaning bone(s)

osteomyelitis infection in the bone or bone marrow

Österreich the name in German for Austria

Oswaldtwistle, Lancashire

Oświęcim the Polish name for **Auschwitz**, Nazi concentration camp in Poland during the Second World War

otorhinolaryngology the branch of medicine dealing with ear, nose and throat disorders

Ottawa, Ontario capital of Canada

Otway, Thomas (1652–85) British playwright

Ouachita (or **Washita**) river and mountains in Arkansas and Oklahoma

Ouagadougou capital of Burkina Faso

oubliette dungeon with access only through a trapdoor in the ceiling

Oudenarde, Battle of (1708) key battle in the War of the Spanish Succession

Ouija board (cap.)

'Ours is not to reason why, ours is but to do or die' is often heard, but is wrong. The lines from Tennyson's 'Charge of the Light Brigade' are 'Their's not to reason why,/Their's but to do and die.' Note that the closing words 'do and die' give the lines an entirely different sense from 'do or die'. Finally, it should be noted that Tennyson's punctuation of *theirs* is irregular (see POSSESSIVES).

outspokenness Note *-nn-*.

ouzo Greek drink

over The notion that *over* is incorrect for 'more than' (as in 'over 300 people were present at the rally') is a widely held superstition. The stricture has been traced to Ambrose Bierce's *Write It Right* (1909), a usage book teeming with quirky recommendations, many of which you will find repeated nowhere. There is no harm in preferring 'more than', but also no basis for insisting on it.

Overbeck, Johann Friedrich (1769–1869) German painter

Overijssel province of the Netherlands

Overlord code name given to the Normandy invasion by Allied forces in 1944

overly Making *over* into *overly* is a little like turning *soon* into *soonly*. Adding *-ly* does nothing for *over* that it could not already do.

overripe, overrule, overrun, etc. Note *-rr-*.

overweening Arrogant or presumptuous expectations are *overweening* ones. There is no word *overweaning*.

Ovid Publius Ovidius Naso (43 BC–AD 17), Roman poet

ovum (Lat.) egg; pl. **ova**

Oxford Movement a movement in the Church of England, begun at Oxford in 1833, seeking a return to certain Roman Catholic doctrines and practices

Oxford University colleges All Souls, Balliol, Brasenose,

Christ Church, Corpus Christi, Exeter, Green, Hertford, Jesus, Keble, Lady Margaret Hall, Linacre, Lincoln, Magdalen, Merton, New College, Nuffield, Oriel, Pembroke, (The) Queen's, St Anne's, St Antony's, St Catherine's, St Cross, St Edmund Hall, St Hilda's, St Hugh's, St John's, St Peter's, Somerville, Trinity, University, Wadham, Wolfson, Worcester

Oxon abbr. of *Oxonia/Oxoniensis* (Lat.); used as abbr. for Oxford, Oxfordshire, of Oxford University

oxymoron the intentional mingling of contradictory ideas or expressions for rhetorical effect, as in 'getting nowhere fast'

Ozawa, Seiji (1935–) Japanese conductor

'Ozymandias' sonnet by Shelley (1818); not *Oxy-*

P

PA postal abbr. of Pennsylvania; formerly **Pa.**, **Penn.**, or **Penna.**

pablum (or **pabulum**) food; in figurative sense it is used to convey the idea of being weak or nutritiously insipid. When capitalized it is a trademark for a US brand of baby food.

pachyderm a thick-skinned animal such as an elephant or a rhinoceros

paddywhack a tantrum

Paderewski, Ignace Jan (1860–1941) Polish concert pianist, composer and Prime Minister 1919–20

Padova the Italian name for Padua

paean, paeon, peon A *paean* is a hymn or song of praise. A *paeon* is a metrical foot in classical poetry. A *peon* is a servant or peasant.

paediatrics, paediatrician (US **pediatrics**, **pediatrician**)

paedophile a person who is sexually attracted to children

paella Spanish dish of rice and chicken or seafood

Paganini, Niccolò (1782–1840) Italian violin virtuoso and composer

Paget's disease bone disorder

Pago Pago pronounced *pango pango*; capital of American Samoa

Pahlavi, Mohammed Reza (1919–80) Shah of Iran 1941–79

pail, **pale** The first is a small bucket; the second means lacking colour. The expression is *beyond the pale*. Historically the Pale signified the areas of Ireland controlled by the English; lands beyond were therefore beyond English control.

Paine, Thomas (1737–1809) British-born American political philosopher and pamphleteer

Paiute Native American people

pajamas US spelling of **pyjamas**

pak choi Chinese vegetable, **bok choi** in the US

Palaeocene (US **Paleocene**) geological epoch

palaeology (US **paleology**) study of antiquities

palaeontology (US **paleontology**) study of fossils

palate, **palette**, **pallet** *Palate* has to do with the mouth and taste. *Palette* is the board used by artists. *Pallet* is a mattress, a machine part or the wooden platforms on which freight is stood.

palaver fuss

Palazzo Vecchio, Florence

Palikir capital of Micronesia

palindrome a word or passage that reads the same forwards and backwards, as in 'A man, a plan, a canal: Panama.'

palisade a fence of stakes or railings

Palladian architecture the style of architecture of Andrea Palladio (1508–80)

palliasse (or **paillasse**) a thin and very basic mattress

Pall Mall, **pell-mell** The first was a game popular in the 17th century. A favoured site for playing it later became the London street *Pall Mall*. For the act of moving crazily or in haste, the word is *pell-mell*. At one time both spellings, including *Pall Mall* the street, were pronounced *pell-mell*, though the street is now generally pronounced *pal-mal*.

pallor, not *-our*

Palme, Olof (1927–86) Swedish politician

Palmers Green, London (no apos.)

PalmPilot one word, for the hand-held organizer

palomino type of horse; pl. **palominos**

palsy

Pamuk, Orhan (1952–) Turkish novelist, awarded Nobel Prize for Literature 2006

panacea is a universal remedy, a cure for all woes, and is not properly applied to the treatment for a single short-coming.

pandemonium

P&O should be printed closed up. It stands for Peninsular and Oriental Steamship Company.

panegyric a formal speech of praise

Pangloss an excessively optimistic character in Voltaire's *Candide*, hence any optimistic person

panjandrum self-important person, pompous official

Pankhurst, Emmeline (1858–1928) English activist for women's rights. Her daughters, **Dame Christabel Pankhurst** (1880–1958), **Sylvia Pankhurst** (1882–1960) and **Adela Pankhurst** (1885–1961), were similarly dedicated to women's causes.

Pão de Açucar Portuguese for Sugarloaf Mountain, Rio de Janeiro

Paolozzi, Eduardo (1924–2005) Scottish sculptor

Papal Nuncio a prelate acting as an ambassador of the Pope

paparazzi is plural; a single roving photographer who stalks celebrities is a **paparazzo**.

papier mâché

Pap test a test for uterine cancer and other disorders devised by Dr George Papanicolaou (1883–1962), a Greek-American doctor

papyrus writing material; pl. **papyruses** or **papyri**

Paracelsus (1493–1541) Swiss physician and alchemist; real name Theophrastus Philippus Aureolus Bombastus von Hohenheim

paradisaical, not -*iacal* having the nature of paradise

paraffin

paragon model of excellence

parakeet

parallel, paralleled, paralleling

paralyse (US **paralyze**), **paralysis**

Paraná South American river

paranoia, paranoiac

paraphernalia

paraplegic, quadriplegic The first describes paralysis of the legs and lower body; the second indicates paralysis of all four limbs.

paraquat lethal herbicide

paraphrase

parasite

parasol

parbleu! (Fr.) exclamation of surprise

Parcheesi (cap.) US name for **ludo**

pardonnez-moi (Fr.) 'pardon me'; note hyphen

par excellence (Fr.) the best of its type

pariah person of low standing; a social outcast

Paribas short for Compagnie Financière de Paris et des Pays-Bas; French bank

pari passu (Lat.) with the same speed, at an equal rate

parka type of hooded jacket

Parkinson's disease is the traditional name, but increasingly the non-possessive **Parkinson disease** is displacing it, particularly in medical texts.

Parkinson's Law 'Work expands to fill the time available for its completion'; stated by C. Northcote Parkinson (1909–93), British writer

parky chilly

parlay, parley The first is to use one gain to make another ('He parlayed his winnings into a small fortune'). The second is a conference.

Parliamentary Commissioner for Administration formal title of the UK government ombudsman

Parmesan cheese (cap.) in Italian, *parmigiano* (no cap.)

Parmigiano, Il (1504–40) Italian painter; real name Girolamo Francesco Maria Mazzola

Parnassus, Mount a Greek mountain; in Greek mythology, sacred to the Muses

paroxysm

parquet flooring

Parr, Catherine (1512–48) sixth wife of Henry VIII

parricide, patricide The first is the murder of a parent or close relative; the second is the killing of a father.

Parry, Sir William Edward (1790–1855) British admiral and explorer

Parsee a follower of **Parseeism**, an Indian religion related to Zoroastrianism

Parsifal opera by Wagner (1879)

Parsons Green, London (no apos.)

Parthian shot a remark or blow made while retreating

parti pris (Fr.) a prejudice

Parti Québécois Canadian political party

parturition act of giving birth

partly, partially Although they are often interchangeable, their meanings are slightly different. *Partially* means incompletely and *partly* means in part. 'The house was made partially of brick and partially of stone' would be better as 'partly of brick and partly of stone'.

parvenu (masc.)/**parvenue** (fem.) an upstart; a person who has risen above his original social class; pl. **parvenus** (masc.)/**parvenues** (fem.)

Pasadena, California city near Los Angeles; home of the Rose Bowl, or Tournament of Roses, an important college football match

paso doble (Sp.) a type of dance

Pasolini, Pier Paolo (1922–75) Italian writer, actor and film director

passable, passible The first means capable of being passed ('The road was passable') or barely satisfactory ('The food was passable'); the second, in theology, means capable of feeling or suffering.

Passchendaele, not -*dale* Belgian village, scene of a bloody battle in the First World War

passe-partout a passkey; adhesive tape used in picture framing

Passepartout, Jean character in Jules Verne's *Around the World in Eighty Days* (1873)

passers-by

past Often a space-waster, as in this example: 'Davis said the dry conditions had been a recurrent problem for the past 30 years.' In this sentence, and in countless others like it, 'the past' could be deleted without any loss of sense. Equally tautological and to be avoided are such expressions as *past records, past history, past experience, past achievements* and *past precedents*. See also LAST, LATEST.

Pasteur, Louis (1822–95) French chemist

pastiche a work in a style that imitates that of another work

pastille

pastrami

pâté de foie gras

Patek Philippe Swiss watch manufacturer

paterfamilias (one word) male head of household

Paterson, New Jersey

pâtisserie

Pattenmakers' Company London livery company; not *Pattern-*. A patten is a type of shoe or clog.

paucity scarcity

Pauli, Wolfgang (1900–58) Austrian-born physicist, awarded Nobel Prize for Physics 1945

Pavarotti, Luciano (1935–2007) Italian tenor

pavilion, not *-ll-*

pax vobiscum (Lat.) peace be with you

Pays-Bas French name for the Netherlands

Pb chemical symbol for lead; short for *plumbum*

PCBs polychlorinated biphenyls, organic substances used in hydraulics and electrical systems; banned in most Western countries

peaceable, peaceful *Peaceful* means tranquil and serene. *Peaceable* is a disposition towards the state of peacefulness.

peak, peek The first is a point or summit; the second means to steal a look.

Pearse, Padraic (1879–1916) Irish writer and nationalist

Peary, Robert Edwin (1856–1920) American admiral and explorer, first to reach the North Pole (1909)

pease pudding

peccadillo a minor fault; pl. **peccadilloes**

pedal, **peddle** The first applies to devices or actions involving foot power – the pedal on a piano, to pedal a bicycle. The second is a verb only, meaning to sell goods in an informal or itinerant manner. The person who sells such goods is a **pedlar** (US **peddler**).

pedant, **pedagogue** The two are synonyms. They describe someone who makes an ostentatious show of his learning or is dogmatically fussy about rules. Some dictionaries still give *pedagogue* as a synonym for teacher or educator, but its pejorative sense has effectively driven out the neutral one.

pederasty (or **paederasty**) sexual relations between an adult male and a boy

Peeblesshire note -*ss*-; former Scottish county

peek, **peak** The first means to steal a look; the second is a point or summit.

peekaboo (no hyphens)

Peekskill, New York

Peel, Sir Robert (1788–1850) British Prime Minister 1834–5, 1841–6

peers The British peerage comprises, in descending order, the ranks duke, marquess, earl/countess, viscount and baron/baroness. Male peers below the rank of duke may be referred to as Lord (i.e., the Earl of Avon may be called Lord Avon), and peeresses below the rank of duchess may be referred to as Lady. However, not every lord is a peer. The eldest son of a duke, marquess or earl, for instance, may use one of his father's minor titles as a courtesy title and call himself the Marquess of X or Earl of Y, but he is not a peer and would not be eligible to sit in the House of Lords. Younger sons of dukes and marquesses may put Lord in front of their names: Lord

John X. Their wives are then called Lady John X. Daughters of dukes, marquesses and earls will similarly put Lady before their names: Lady Mary Y. Wives of peers, and of knights and baronets, are referred to as Lady X or Lady Y; that is, their first names are not used. Sir John Bloggs's wife is simply Lady Bloggs, not Lady Mary Bloggs. Life peers are people of distinction who are elevated to the peerage but whose titles die with them.

Pei, I. M. (for **Ieoh Ming**) (1917–) Chinese-born American architect

Peirce, Charles Sanders (1839–1914) American philosopher, pronounced *purse*

Pekinese (or **Pekingese**) breed of dog

pekoe a tea

Pelagianism (cap.) a heresy

pelargonium flowering plant popularly known as the geranium

Pelé nickname of Edson Arantes do Nascimento (1940–), Brazilian soccer player widely acclaimed as the best ever

Peloponnese, Peloponnesus southern peninsula of Greece; in Greek it is **Pelopónnisos**

pelota another name for the game of jai alai

pell-mell in a state of confusion; see also PALL MALL

Pembroke, Dyfed; **Pembroke College**, Cambridge; **Pembroke College**, Oxford all pronounced *pem-brook*

pemmican dried meat

penance

PEN Club short for Poets, Playwrights, Editors, Essayists and Novelists; an international association

pendant (noun), **pendent** (adj.)

Penetanguishene, Ontario

penicillin

Peninsular and Oriental Steamship Company British shipping company commonly known as **P&O**

Penney, J. C. US department store group, now **JCPenney** (one word)

penniless

penn'orth (British, mostly historical) a penny's worth

Penrhyndeudraeth, Gwynnedd

Pensacola, Florida

Pentateuch the first five books of the Old Testament: Genesis, Exodus, Leviticus, Numbers and Deuteronomy

pentathlon, modern The five events are swimming, fencing, pistol shooting, cross-country running and cross-country riding.

Pentecost the Christian Whit Sunday, the seventh Sunday after Easter; the Jewish Shavuot, the sixth and seventh days of Sivan

peon, **paean**, **paeon** A *peon* is a servant or peasant; a *paean* is a hymn or song of praise; a *paeon* is a metrical foot in ancient Greek and Latin poetry.

peony a flowering plant

PepsiCo (one word) **Inc.** US company that owns Pepsi-Cola

Pepys, Samuel (1633–1703) pronounced *peeps*; English Admiralty official, remembered for his diary

per Many usage guides suggest, and a few insist, that Latinisms like *per* should be avoided when English phrases are available – that it is better to write 'ten tons a year' than 'ten tons per year'. That is certainly reasonable enough in general, but I would suggest that when avoidance of the Latin would result in clumsy constructions such as 'output a man a year', you shouldn't hesitate to use *per*.

per ardua ad astra (Lat.) to the stars through adversities

P/E ratio short for **price-to-earnings ratio**; a stock market measure in which a value of a stock is determined by dividing the stock's price by the company's earnings per share

per cent, percentage point If interest rates are 10 per cent and are raised to 11 per cent, they have gone up by one percentage point, but by 10 per cent in value (i.e., borrowers must now pay 10 per cent more than previously). In everyday contexts the distinction is not always vital, but in contexts in which the percentage rise is large and confusion is likely, the distinction is crucial.

perceptible

Perceval, Spencer (1762–1812) British Prime Minister 1809–12; only British Prime Minister to be assassinated

perchance (arch.) possibly

Perelman, S. J. (for **Sidney Joseph**) (1904–79) American humorist

peremptory brusque

perestroika (Russ.) restructuring

Perez de Cuellar, Javier (1920–) Peruvian diplomat, Secretary-General of the United Nations 1982–92

perfectible, perfectibility

perforce without choice

perigee the lowest or nearest point in an orbit; opposite of **apogee**

Pérignon, Dom champagne

perinatal pertaining to the period immediately before and after birth

peripatetic wandering

periphrasis using more words than necessary; circumlocution; pl. **periphrases**

perishable
periwinkle
Perlman, Itzhak (1945–) Israeli violinist
permissible
pernickety
Perón, (Maria) Eva (Duarte de) (1919–52) nickname Evita; second wife of **Juan Perón** (1895–1974), President of Argentina 1946–55, 1973–4
perpetrate, perpetuate Occasionally confused. To *perpetrate* is to commit or perform. To *perpetuate* is to prolong or, literally, to make perpetual. The Boston Strangler perpetrated a series of murders. Those who write about him perpetuate his notoriety.
Persephone in Greek mythology, queen of the underworld; identified with the Roman goddess Proserpina
Perseus in Greek mythology, the son of Zeus who killed Medusa
persevere, perseverance
persiflage idle banter
persimmon
personal, personally When it is necessary to emphasize that a person is acting on his own rather than on behalf of a group or that he is addressing people individually rather than collectively, *personal* and *personally* are unexceptionable. But usually the context makes that clear and the word is used without purpose, as here: 'Dr Leonard has decided to visit personally the Oklahoma parish which is the center of the dispute.' If he visits, Dr Leonard can hardly do it otherwise than personally. Many other common terms – *personal friend, personal opinion, personal favourite* – are nearly always equally redundant.

personnel

perspicacity, **perspicuity** The first means shrewdness, the second lucidity.

peso basic monetary unit of several South American countries

pertinacious persistent

pertinent relevant

peruse It is a losing battle no doubt, but perhaps worth pointing out that *peruse* does not mean to look over casually. It means to read or examine carefully.

Pétain, Henri Philippe (1856–1951) French general and politician, head of the Vichy government 1940–4

Peter Principle the idea that people are promoted until they reach a level at which they are incompetent

petit (or **petty**) **bourgeois** a small businessman; member of the lower middle class, the **petite** (or **petty**) **bourgeoisie**

Petri dish (cap.) item of laboratory equipment

Petrograd originally St Petersburg, Petrograd 1914–24, then Leningrad, reverted to St Petersburg 1991

Petrovsk former name of Makhachkala, Russia

Pettenkofer, Max Joseph von (1818–1901) German chemist

Pettersen, Suzann (1981–) Norwegian professional golfer

pettifog quibble over petty matters; practise legal trickery

peu à peu (Fr.) little by little

Peugeot French automobile

peut-être (Fr.) perhaps

Pevsner, Sir Nikolaus (1902–83) German-born British art historian and expert on architecture

pfennig former German coin worth 1/100th of a mark

PFLP Popular Front for the Liberation of Palestine

PGA Professional Golfers Association (no apos.)

pH potential of hydrogen, a measure of acidity or alkalinity

Phalange political party in Lebanon

phalanx cohesive group of people, pl. **phalanxes**; bone in the finger or toe, pl. **phalanges**

pharaoh, not -*oah*

pharmacopoeia a book containing descriptions of medicines and drugs

phenomenon, pl. **phenomena**

Phidias (c. 498–c. 432 BC) Greek sculptor, involved in the design of the Parthenon and famous for the statue of Athene it housed

philanderer an unfaithful person

Philip Morris US tobacco and diversified products company

Philippi ancient city in Macedonia

Philippians book of the New Testament

philippic a verbal denunciation

Philippine Sea

Philippines, Republic of the note -*l*-, -*pp*-; island state in the Pacific Ocean; capital Manila. A person from the Philippines is a **Filipino** if male, a **Filipina** if female. **Filipino** is also the name of the national language.

Philips Dutch electrical company; formally, NV Philips Gloeilampenfabrieken

Philips Arena, Atlanta

philistine a person who is indifferent or hostile to matters of culture

Phillips screws and screwdrivers named for their originator, Henry F. Phillips

Phillips Collection, Washington, DC

Phillips curve in economics, a measure showing the relationship between inflation and unemployment

Phillips Petroleum US oil group

Phillips Son & Neale (no comma) London auction house

Philomel/Philomela poetic name for the nightingale
phlebitis inflammation of the veins
Phnom Penh capital of Cambodia
phony
Phyfe, Duncan (1786–1854) born Duncan Fife; Scottish-born American furniture maker
phyllo pastry Use **filo.**
phylum taxonomic division of plants and animals; pl. **phyla**
Physic, Regius Professor of Cambridge University; not *Physics*
physiognomy facial characteristics
physique
pi ratio of circumference to diameter of a circle, an irrational number calculated to five decimal places as 3.14159; also the 16th letter of the Greek alphabet
piano, pianissimo, pianississimo In music, the first (abbr. *p.*) means soft, the second (abbr. *pp.*) means very soft and the third (abbr. *ppp.*) even more soft.
Picard, Jean (1620–82) French astronomer
Picasso, Pablo (1881–1973) Spanish artist
picayune petty, trifling
Piccadilly
piccalilli a kind of relish
Piccard, Auguste (1884–1962) Swiss physicist
piccolo a small flute pitched an octave higher than a normal flute; pl. **piccolos**
picnicked, picnicking, picnicker
pico- prefix meaning one-trillionth
Pico della Mirandola, Count Giovanni (1463–94) Italian philosopher
pidgin, creole *Pidgin* is a language spontaneously devised by two or more peoples who have no common language.

Pidgins are generally very rudimentary. If contact between the different peoples is prolonged and generations are born for whom the pidgin is their first tongue, the language will usually evolve into a more formalized system of speech called a *creole*. Most languages that are commonly called pidgins are in fact creoles.

pièce de résistance (Fr.) most outstanding item, particularly applied to the finest dish in a meal

piecemeal

pied-à-terre (Fr.) (hyphens) a small secondary residence; pl. *pieds-à-terre*

Piedmont region of Italy; in Italian, **Piemonte**

Pied Piper of Hamelin

Piero della Francesca (c. 1418–92) Italian artist

pierogi (or **pirogi**) Polish dumpling; pl. same

Pierre, South Dakota pronounced *peer*; the state capital

Pierre, DBC (closed up, no full stops) (1961–) pen name of Peter Warren Finlay, Australian-born Mexican novelist; Booker prizewinner 2003

Piers Plowman, The Vision of William Concerning epic poem by William Langland (c. 1360–99)

Pietermaritzburg, South Africa capital of Natal

pigeonhole (one word)

piggyback

Pikes Peak (no apos.) summit (14,100 feet/4,341 metres) in Rocky Mountains, Colorado; named after Zebulon Montgomery Pike, its discoverer

Pilates (cap.) trademarked exercise system

Pilsener (or **Pilsner**) a German beer

Pilsudski, Józef (1867–1935) Polish statesman

pimento, pl. **pimentos** **Pimiento** and **pimientos** are accepted alternatives.

PIN personal identification number

pineal gland

Pinero, Sir Arthur Wing (1855–1934) English comedic playwright

Ping-Pong (caps)

Pinocchio Note -*cc*-.

Pinochet, Augusto (1915–2006) President of Chile 1973–90

pinscher, Dobermann (US **Doberman**) breed of dog

pint a liquid measure equal to 16 ounces in the United States, 20 ounces in Britain

Pinturicchio nickname of Bernardino di Betto Vagio (1454–1513), Italian painter

Pinyin system for romanizing Chinese names. Pinyin was devised in 1953 but has been in widespread international use only since about 1977. See also CHINESE NAMES.

piquant pungent, alluring

pique resentment. 'Fit of pique' is a cliché.

Piraeus port of Athens

Pirandello, Luigi (1867–1936) Italian author and playwright; awarded Nobel Prize for Literature 1934

Piranesi, Giovanni Battista (or **Giambattista**) (1720–78) Italian artist and architect

piranha species of fish

Pirelli Italian tyre manufacturer

pirouette graceful turn on one foot

Piscataway, New Jersey

Pissaro, Camille (1830–1903) French painter

pistachio nut-bearing tree; pl. **pistachios**

pistil part of a flower

pitiable, pitiful, pitiless, but **piteous**

Pitti Palace, Florence in Italian, **Palazzo Pitti**

Pittsburgh, Pennsylvania, not -*burg*

pixels picture elements, the little squares from which computer graphics are composed

pixie, not *pixy* a sprite

Pizarro, Francisco (c. 1475–1541) Spanish *conquistador*, conquered Peru, founded Lima

pizzeria, not *pizza-* restaurant where pizzas are made

Plaid Cymru Welsh nationalist political party; pronounced *plide kum´-ree*

plan ahead always tautological. Would you plan behind?

Planck, Max (1858–1947) German physicist, awarded Nobel Prize for Physics 1918

planetarium, pl. **planetariums/planetaria**

planetesimal orbiting body with planet-like qualities, but too small to qualify as such

Plantagenets dynasty of English monarchs from Henry II to Richard III, 1154–1485

plaster of paris (no cap.)

Plasticine (cap.)

plat du jour (Fr.) dish of the day; pl. *plats du jour*

plateau, pl. **plateaus** (or **plateaux**)

platen the roller on a typewriter

plate tectonics, not *tech-* the science of the Earth's crust and its movements

Platt-Deutsch/Plattdeutsch German dialect, also called Low German

platypus, pl. **platypuses**

plausible, plausibility

'Play it, Sam,' is the correct line from the film *Casablanca*; Humphrey Bogart never actually said, 'Play it again, Sam.'

playwright, not *–write*

PLC (UK) Public Limited Company, one whose shares are sold publicly and quoted on the stock market; equivalent to the American Inc. or German AG. Many companies write 'plc' or 'Plc', but there is no logical reason for so doing.

plead innocent is wrong, at least in the English-speaking world. Under the British and American judicial systems, one pleads guilty or not guilty.

plebeian common, vulgar, of the lower classes

plebiscite vote of the people

Pleiades in Greek mythology, the seven daughters of Atlas and Pleione; a cluster of stars in the constellation Taurus

Pleistocene geological period

plenary full, complete. A **plenary session** of a council is one attended by all the members.

plenitude, not *plenti-* an abundance

plenteous abundant

Plessy v. Ferguson 1896 US Supreme Court case that upheld the view that children of different races could be educated separately as long as the quality of education was equal

plethora is not merely a lot, it is an excessive amount, a super-abundance. For a word that is often similarly misused, see SPATE.

pleurisy inflammation of the membrane covering the lungs

Plexiglas (cap.), not *-ss*

Plimsoll line/mark point marked on a ship's side indicating the legal limit of submersion when the ship is loaded

plimsolls rubber-soled canvas shoes

PLO Palestine Liberation Organization

PLR Public Lending Right (UK); system by which payments are made to authors based on the number of times their books are borrowed from public libraries

plum, plumb If it is edible or growing the word is *plum* (plum pudding, sugarplum, plum tree), and when used figuratively of something choice (a plum job), but in all other senses the word is *plumb* (plumb line, plumb the depths).

plummy of a voice, affected, rich

plus is a preposition, not a conjunction, and therefore does not influence the number of the verb. Two and two are four, but two plus two *is* four.

Plutarch Ploutarchos (c. 46–c. 120), Greek historian, biographer and philosopher

plutocrat person who has influence or power because of wealth

p.m./PM, *post meridiem* (Lat.) after noon

Pocahontas (c. 1595–1617) North American Indian princess, known for saving the life of John Smith

Pocatello, Idaho

pocket borough a British parliamentary borough controlled by one person or group; common before parliamentary reforms of 1832

Podhoretz, Norman (1930–) American journalist and writer

Poe, Edgar Allan (1809–49) American poet and short-story writer

poet laureate For the plural, **poets laureate** and **poet laureates** are both generally accepted.

pogrom methodical massacre of a minority group

poinsettia winter-flowering plant

pokey, poky The first is US slang for jail; the second means small, cramped or slow.

Poliakoff, Stephen (1954–) British dramatist

poliomyelitis commonly shortened to polio, once called (somewhat misleadingly) infantile paralysis

politburo/Politburo the chief committee of a Communist Party

Polizei (Ger.) police

Pollaiuolo, Antonio (1429–98) Italian painter, sculptor and goldsmith

Pollock, Jackson (1912–56) American artist

Pollok House, **Pollok Country Park**, **Pollokshaws Road**, Glasgow

Pollyanna an optimistic person, particularly one who is foolishly so; after the heroine of a 1913 American children's novel by Eleanor Porter

polonaise a slow Polish dance, or the music for it

poltergeist

Poltoratsk former name of Ashgabat, capital of Turkmenistan

polyandry state or practice of a woman having more than one husband at the same time

polygamy state or practice of having more than one marriage partner at the same time

polypropylene type of plastic

pomegranate round fruit with many seeds

Pomeranian a toy breed of dog

Pompeian of Pompeii, the Roman city destroyed by the eruption of Mount Vesuvius in AD 79

Pompey Gnaeus Pompeius Magnus (106–48 BC), Roman soldier and statesman

Pompidou Centre, Paris formally Le Centre National d'Art et de Culture Georges Pompidou; also called Centre Beaubourg

pompom (or **pompon**) a ball or tuft of material

Ponce de Léon, Juan (1460–1521) Spanish explorer, discovered Florida

Pontchartrain, Lake, Louisiana

Ponte Vecchio famous bridge over the Arno, Florence

Pont l'Évêque French town and type of cheese named after it

Pontypridd, Mid Glamorgan pronounced *pon-ty-preeth*

pooh-bah person who holds many offices at once, from the character Pooh-Bah in Gilbert and Sullivan's *The Mikado* (1885)

pooh-pooh to dismiss or make light of

Popescu-Tăriceanu, Călin (1952–) Prime Minister of Romania 2004–

poppadom (or **poppadum**) Indian thin, crisp bread made of ground lentils fried in oil

populace, populous The first describes a general population. The second means heavily populated.

porcupine

pore, pour Occasionally *pour* appears where *pore* is intended. As a verb, *pore* means to examine carefully ('He pored over the documents') or, more rarely, to think deeply. *Pour* indicates a flow, either literally ('He poured the water down the drain') or figuratively ('The rioters poured through the streets').

port, starboard When facing forward on a ship, port is to the left, starboard to the right.

Port-au-Prince (hyphens) capital of Haiti

portentous, not *-ious*

Porthmadog, Gwynedd formerly Porthmadoc

portico a porch supported by pillars; pl. **porticoes/porticos**

Portland cement, Portland stone (cap.)

portmanteau word a word blending two others, e.g., smog = smoke + fog

Portmeirion, Wales fanciful Italianate village built by Sir Clough Williams-Ellis, and a brand of pottery that originated there

Port Moresby capital of Papua New Guinea

Porto-Novo (hyphen) capital of Benin

Portuguese

Port-Vila (hyphen) capital of Vanuatu

Portzamparc, Christian de (1944–) Moroccan-born French architect; on second reference he is Mr (or Monsieur) Portzamparc, not de Portzamparc

Poseidon Greek god of the sea; identified with the Roman god Neptune

position Often a pointer to verbosity. 'They now find themselves in a position where they have to make a choice' would be immeasurably better as 'They now have to make a choice.'

possessives Three especially common faults are worth mentioning here:

1. Failure to put an apostrophe in the right place. This is particularly frequent with plural words such as *men's*, *women's* and *children's*, which all too often appear as *mens'*, *womens'* and *childrens'*.

2. Failure to put in an apostrophe at all. This practice – spelling the words *mens*, *womens* and *childrens* and so on – is particularly rife among retailers. It is painful enough to behold there, inexcusable elsewhere.

3. Putting an apostrophe where none is needed. Possessive pronouns – *his*, *hers*, *ours*, *theirs* and so on – do not take an apostrophe. But sometimes one is wrongly inserted, as here: 'I don't think much of your's' (*Independent* headline).

(See also 'Ours is not to reason why . . .')

possible is wrongly followed by *may* in constructions such as the following: 'It is possible that she may decide to go after all' (*Daily Telegraph*). Make it either 'It is possible that she will decide to go after all' or 'She may decide to go after all.' Together the two words are wrong and unnecessary.

post-haste (hyphen) with speed

posthumous after death

postilion rider who guides a team of horses when there is no coachman

postmeridian, *post meridiem* The first means related to or happening in the afternoon. The second, also pertaining to the period after noon, is the Latin term better known to most of us in the abbreviation p.m. or PM. Note the different terminal spellings.

post-partum after birth

postprandial after dinner

potage thick soup

potpourri, pl. **potpourris**

Potteries, the group of six towns in Staffordshire, all associated with china and pottery production: Stoke-on-Trent, Burslem, Fenton, Hanley, Longton and Tunstall

Poughkeepsie, New York

Poulenc, Francis (1899–1963) French composer

Poulters' Company London livery company; not *Poulterers'*

Poulton-le-Fylde (hyphens), Lancashire

pour, pore The first means to flow or rain heavily; the second means to examine carefully.

pourboire (Fr.) a gratuity, a tip

pour encourager les autres (Fr.) to encourage the others

Poussin, Nicolas (1594–1665) French painter

Powell, Anthony (1905–2000) British novelist; pronounced *pole*

powwow a conference

Powys   Welsh county containing the former counties of Montgomeryshire, Radnorshire and Breconshire; pronounced *pow* (rhymes with cow)-*iss*

Powys, John Cowper (1872–1963) English poet and novelist; the names are pronounced *cooper* and *po-iss*

PPI   abbr. of Producer Price Index; in economics, a measure of changes in commodity prices

practical, practicable   Anything that can be done and is worth doing is practical. Anything that can be done, whether or not it is worth doing, is practicable.

practice, practise   In British usage, the first is a noun (a sound practice, the practice of medicine), the second a verb (I practise my music, you practise as a doctor). In the United States, *practice* is used for both noun and verb.

praemonitus praemunitus (Lat.)   forewarned is forearmed

praeseodymium   chemical element

Praetorian Guard   élite Roman army unit

Praha   Czech spelling of Prague

Praia   capital of Cape Verde, an island nation west of Senegal

precautionary measure is a common phrase, but can nearly always be shortened simply to *precaution.*

precipitate, precipitous   Both words come from the same root, the Latin *praecipitare* ('to throw headlong'). *Precipitous* means very steep: cliff faces are precipitous. *Precipitate* indicates a headlong rush, one that may be foolish. The most common error is to use *precipitous* to describe actions ('his precipitous departure from the Cabinet'). *Precipitous* can describe only physical characteristics.

precondition, preplanning, prerecorded, etc.   Almost always redundant: 'A lot of headaches can be avoided with a little careful preplanning' (*Chicago Tribune*). All planning must be done in advance. *Pre-* adds nothing to its meaning and should be deleted, as it should have been in these examples: 'There are, however, three pre-conditions to be met before negotiations can begin' (*Guardian*); 'The company's music performance reflected both the volatility and opportunities for growth in the worldwide market for prerecorded music' (advertisement in *The Economist*).

precursor, not -*er*

predilection special liking

preface introduction to a book, written by its author. See also FOREWORD.

prehensile able to grasp

premier, **première** Used as a noun, the first, chiefly in the UK, is a government official of top rank, especially a prime minister. The second is a first performance of an artistic work.

Preminger, Otto (1906–86) Austrian-born American film director

premises is always plural when referring to property. There is no such thing as a business premise.

premiss (US **premise**) an assumption

prepositions The lingering belief that sentences should not end with prepositions is entirely without foundation.

prerogative an exclusive right

Prescelly Mountains, Wales

prescribe, proscribe *Prescribe* means to set down as a rule or guide. *Proscribe* means to denounce or prohibit. If you get bronchitis, your doctor may prescribe antibiotics and proscribe smoking.

present, presently Like *current* and *currently*, these two often appear needlessly in sentences, as here: 'A new factory, which is presently under construction in Manchester, will add to capacity.' The sentence says as much without *presently* as with it.

Presidents' Day (apos.) US bank holiday, third Monday of February

presumptive, presumptuous The first is sometimes used when the second is intended. *Presumptuous* means impudent and inclined to take liberties, or acting in a manner that is excessively bold and forthright. *Presumptive* means giving grounds to presume and is primarily a technical term (heir presumptive). The wrong use is seen here: 'She considered the question with the equanimity of someone who has long been immune to presumptive prying' (*Sunday Telegraph*).

pretension but **pretentious**

prevalent, prevalence

prevaricate, procrastinate Occasionally confused. *Prevaricate* means to speak or act evasively, to stray from the truth. *Procrastinate* means to put off doing.

prevent often appears incorrectly in sentences such as this: 'They tried to prevent him leaving.' It should be either 'They tried to prevent his leaving' or 'They tried to prevent him from leaving.' (See GERUNDS (2).)

preventive, preventative 'One way to ease their difficulties, they decided, was to practise preventative medicine' (*The Economist*). *Preventative* is not incorrect, but *preventive* is shorter.

Pribilof Islands, Alaska

PricewaterhouseCoopers accountancy company

Prideaux, Cornwall pronounced *pridducks*

'Pride goes before a fall' is wrong. The quotation, from the Bible, is 'Pride goeth before destruction, and an haughty spirit before a fall.'

prima facie at first sight, on the face of it

primeval, not -*evil* from the earliest times

primogeniture the practice by which an entire inheritance passes to the first-born male child

primus inter pares (Lat.) first among equals

Princess Royal, the (1950–) formerly Princess Anne; strictly, she should not be referred to as Anne even after the first reference.

Princes Street, Edinburgh

Princes Town, Trinidad

principal, principle *Principle* comes from the Latin word for beginning and is usually applied to fundamental beliefs or truths ('It's not the money, it's the principle') or to fundamental understandings ('They have signed an agreement in principle'). It is always a noun. *Principal* can be a noun meaning chief or of first importance ('He is the school's principal') or an adjective with the same meaning ('The principal reason for my going . . .').

pristine does not mean spotless. It means original or primeval or in a state virtually unchanged from the original.

privilege

prix fixe (Fr.) fixed price; pl. ***prix fixes***

Prix Goncourt pre-eminent French literary award

p.r.n., short for *pro re nata* (Lat.) 'as necessary'; used by doctors on prescriptions to indicate that a drug should be administered as necessary and not on a fixed schedule

proboscis an animal's trunk, long snout or feeding tube; pl. **proboscises**

proceed, but **procedure**

procrastinate, prevaricate The first means to postpone doing; the second means to be evasive.

Procrustean producing or striving to produce absolute con-
formity, usually through severe or absolute means; from
Procrustes, a mythological Greek robber who made his
victims fit a bed by stretching them or cutting off their
limbs

Procter & Gamble US household products company. Often
misspelled *Proctor*

prodigal does not mean wandering or given to running away,
a sense sometimes wrongly inferred from the biblical
story of the Prodigal Son. It means recklessly wasteful or
extravagant.

progenitor ancestor

prognosis, pl. **prognoses** See DIAGNOSIS.

programme (US **program**), but use *program* in UK also for
contexts involving computers.

Prohibition (cap.), the US ban on alcohol, lasted from 1920
to 1933. It was brought in by the 18th amendment to the
Constitution and the Volstead Act, and repealed by the
21st amendment.

Prokofiev, Sergei (1891–1953) Russian composer

Promised Land, the (caps)

promissory note a written promise to pay

prone, prostrate, recumbent, supine *Supine* means lying face
upwards (it may help to remember that a supine person
is on his spine). *Prone* and *prostrate* are regarded by most
dictionaries and usage authorities – but by no means all
– as meaning lying face downwards. (A few say that they
can also apply to a person or thing lying face up.)
Prostrate should, in any case, suggest throwing oneself
down, either in submission or for protection; someone
who is merely asleep should not be called prostrate.
Recumbent means lying flat in any position, but, like

repose, it should indicate a position of ease and comfort. For the other sense of *prone*, see LIABLE, LIKELY, APT, PRONE.

pronunciation, not *pronoun-*

propaganda

propagate

propellant is the noun, **propellent** the usual spelling of the adjective.

proper nouns Many writers stumble when confronted with finding a plural form for a proper noun, as in the two following examples, both from *The Times* and both wrong: 'The Cox's were said by neighbours to be ... happily married'; 'This is the first of a new series about the Rush's.' The rule for making plurals of proper nouns is precisely the same as for any other nouns. If you have no trouble turning 'one fox' into 'two foxes' or 'one church' into 'two churches', you should have no trouble making 'the Rush family' into 'the Rushes' and 'the Cox couple' into 'the Coxes'. In short, for names ending in *s*, *sh*, *ch* or *x*, add *es*: *Lewises, Lennoxes, Clemenses*. For all others, simply add *s*: *Smiths, Browns, Greens, the two Koreas*. The rule is invariable for Anglo-Saxon names. For others, there are a few exceptions, among them *Rockies, Ptolemies, Alleghenies, Mercuries* and (in some publications) *Germanies*. At all events, the addition of an apostrophe to make a noun plural is always wrong.

prophecy, prophesy The first is the noun, the second the verb. Thus: 'I prophesy war; that is my prophecy.'

propinquity nearness or similarity

proprietor, but **proprietary**

pro re nata abbr. p.r.n, 'as necessary'; used by doctors on prescriptions to indicate that a drug should be taken when needed and not on a fixed schedule

prosciutto Italian ham; pl. **prosciutti** (or **prosciuttos**)

prosthesis artificial limb; pl. **prostheses**

prostrate should be used only with the sense of throwing oneself down in submission or for protection.

protagonist Literally the word means 'first actor' (from the Greek *protos* and *agonistes*) and by extension may be applied to the person who most drives the action in any affair. The word is not the opposite of *antagonist*; it does not necessarily have anything to do with heroic or admirable behaviour or bear any relationship to the Latin *pro-*, meaning 'for' or 'on behalf of'. A protagonist may champion a cause, and in practice often does, but that isn't implicit in the word.

protégé (masc.), **protégée** (fem.) one under the protection or tutelage of an experienced person

pro tem. abbr. of *pro tempore* (Lat.), for the time being

protester

protocol

prototype is the word for an original that serves as a model for later products of its type. Thus *first prototype*, *experimental prototype*, *model prototype* and most other qualifying descriptions are generally redundant.

proved, proven In general *proved* is the preferred past tense form ('the accused was proved innocent') and *proven* the preferred form for adjectival uses ('a proven formula').

provenance place of origin

Provence-Alpes-Côte d'Azur French region

proverbial Unless there is some connection to an actual proverb, the word is wrongly used and better avoided.

provided, providing Most authorities consider the first preferable to the second in constructions such as 'He agreed to come provided he could get the day off work,' but either would be correct. 'If' is often better still.

prudent, prudish The first means cautious and thoughtful; the second describes a person who is easily offended by sexual matters.

Pryor, Richard (1940–2005) American comedian and actor

Przewalski's horse, Przewalski's gazelle two rare species, both named for Nikolai Przewalski (or Przhevalsky), Russian explorer (1839–88)

pseudonym pen name

psittacosis sometimes called parrot fever; a disease of birds that can be passed to people

ptarmigan

pterodactyl

Pty abbr. of *Proprietary*; Australian, New Zealand and South African equivalent of PLC or Inc.

publicly, not -*ally*

Public Record Office, London; not *Records* now called the **National Archives**

Publishers Weekly (no apos.) American book trade magazine

Puccini, Giacomo (1858–1924) Italian composer of operas

Pudd'nhead Wilson, The Tragedy of novel by Mark Twain (1894)

puerile childish

puerperal pertaining to childbirth, as in *puerperal psychosis*

Puerto Rico formerly a US territory, now a self-governing commonwealth

Puget Sound, Washington

Pulitzer Prizes named for Joseph Pulitzer (1847–1911), annual American awards for journalism, literature and musical composition

pumice volcanic rock

pumpernickel coarse wholemeal rye bread

punctilious carefully correct in behaviour

Punxsutawney, Pennsylvania town noted for its Groundhog Day ceremonies

Purim Jewish holiday; pronounced *poo-rim*, not *pyur-im*

Purley, district of London, part of Croydon, but **Purleigh**, Essex

purlieu, **purlieus** The first denotes a boundary or limit; the second denotes outlying areas or environs.

purposely, **purposefully** The first means intentionally. The second means with an objective in mind. 'She purposely nudged me' means it was no accident. 'She purposefully nudged me' means she did it to make a point or draw my attention to something.

Pushkin, Alexander (1799–1837) Russian poet

pusillanimous cowardly

putrid, but **putrefy**, **putrefaction**

putsch violent attempt to overthrow a government

Puttnam, David (1941–) British film producer; now formally Lord Puttnam

Pwllheli, Gwynedd pronounced *pool-thell-ee*

pygmy, pl. **pygmies**

pyjamas (US **pajamas**)

Pynchon, Thomas (1937–) American novelist

Pyongyang capital of North Korea

pyorrhoea (US **pyorrhea**) infection of the gums, more formally called periodontal disease

Pyrenees, but **Pyrenean**

Pyrrhic victory is not a hollow triumph. It is one won at huge cost to the victor.

Pythagoras (582–507 BC) Greek philosopher and mathematician; the adjectival form is **Pythagorean**

Qaddafi (or **Gadaffi**), **Muammar** (1942–) Libyan head of state 1969– . Either spelling is acceptable, but *Gaddafi* is more commonly used than *Qaddafi*. He has no official title or position.

Qaeda, Al (from the Arabic *al-qā'ida*) is the most common spelling in English for the terrorist group, but there are many variants, including *Al Qaida, al-Qaeda* and *al-Qaida*.

Qahira, El (or **Al Qahirah**) Egyptian name for Cairo

Qantas Although the full name is no longer used, for historical purposes it may be worth noting that Qantas is short for Queensland and Northern Territory Aerial Service. Not *Air* and not *Services*

Qatar Persian Gulf emirate, capital Doha; the airline is **Qatar Airways**

QED (no full points) abbr. of *quod erat demonstrandum* (Lat.), 'which was to be demonstrated'

Qom alt. spelling for **Qum**, Iranian holy city

Q-Tip is a trademark.

quadrennium a period of four years. Nearly everyone will understand you better if you just say 'a period of four years'.

quadriplegia, not *quadra-*, for paralysis of all four limbs

quadruped, not *quadra-*, *quadri-*, for a four-legged animal. The adjectival form is *quadrupedal.*

Quai d'Orsay the French Foreign Ministry, so called because it is on a street of that name in Paris

Quakers, the, are formally known as the Society of Friends.

Qualcomm wireless technology company

quandary, not *quandry* or *quandery* state of indecision

quand même (Fr.) 'all the same'

Quant, Mary (1934–) fashion designer

quantum leap has become a cliché and is better avoided. A separate objection is that its general sense of a revolutionary step forward is at variance with its strict scientific sense of a movement or advance that is discrete and measurable, but not necessarily, or even usually, dramatic.

Qu'Appelle Canadian river

quark hypothetical subatomic particle

quasar is derived from, and means, 'quasi-stellar object'.

quaternary of or pertaining to groups of four. When capitalized, it describes the geological period, part of the Cenozoic era, when humans first appeared.

quatrefoil in architecture, a four-pointed tracery

quattrocento abbr. of Italian *millequattrocento*, the 15th century, used especially in reference to Italian art and culture

quaver to tremble (when speaking)

queasy

Québécois (or **Quebecer**) someone from Quebec. The Canadian political party is always Parti Québécois.

Queen Elizabeth II (1926–) Her formal title, though seldom used, is Elizabeth the Second, by the Grace of God, of the United Kingdom of Great Britain and Northern

Ireland and of Her Other Realms and Territories, Queen, Head of the Commonwealth, Defender of the Faith. She became queen in 1952; her coronation was in 1953.

Queens (no apos.) borough of New York

Queensberry rules, not -*bury* code of conduct for boxing; formally they are the Marquess of Queensberry Rules

Queensboro Bridge, New York City, but **Queensborough Community College**

Queens College, City University of New York; **Queen's College**, Oxford; **Queens' College**, Cambridge

quelque chose (Fr.) something, a trifle

¿que pasa? (Sp.) what's up?

querulous fretful, peevish

query, inquiry, enquiry A *query* is a single question. An *inquiry* or *enquiry* may be a single question or an extensive investigation. Either spelling is correct, but in the UK *inquiry* is preferred for formal investigations.

que será, será (Sp.) 'whatever will be, will be'; the same expression in Italian is *che sarà, sarà.*

qu'est-ce que c'est? (Fr.) what is it/this?

question, leading A leading question is not a challenging or hostile one, as is sometimes thought, but the opposite. It is a question designed to encourage the person being questioned to make the desired response. A lawyer who says to a witness, 'So you didn't see the murder, did you?' has asked a leading question.

question mark has become an overworked embellishment of the expression 'a question hanging over', which is itself wearyingly overused. Consider: 'The case . . . has raised a question mark over the competence of British security' (*The Times*). Would you say of a happy event that it had raised an exclamation mark over the proceedings or that a pause in negotiations had a comma hanging over them?

questionnaire Note -*nn*-.

Quetzalcoatl Aztec god

queue, queuing

Quezon City capital of the Philippines 1948–76

quid pro quo (Lat.) tit for tat, a fair trade-off

quiescent inactive

Quiller-Couch, Sir Arthur (1863–1944) Couch pronounced *kootch*; British scholar and author, whose novels were written under the pseudonym Q

qu'importe? (Fr.) what does it matter?

quincentenary 500th anniversary

Quinnipiac University, Connecticut

quinoa plant producing edible seeds and leaves

Quinquagesima roughly the 50th day before Easter, the Sunday before Lent

quinquennial can mean either lasting for five years or occurring once every five years. Because of the inherent ambiguity the word is almost always better replaced with a more specific phrase.

quinsy archaic name for tonsillitis

quintessence, quintessential most perfect essence

quisling one who collaborates with a foreign enemy; after **Vidkun Quisling** (1887–1945), pro-Nazi Norwegian Prime Minister appointed by Germany

Quito capital of Ecuador

qui vive, on the in a state of watchfulness

Qum (or **Qom**) holy city in Iran

quod erat demonstrandum (Lat.) abbr. QED, 'which was to be demonstrated' *quod vide* (Lat.) abbr. q.v., 'which see'; used for textual cross-references

Quonochontaug, Rhode Island

Quonset hut prefabricated metal shelter

quorum minimum number of people present at a meeting to make the proceedings valid; pl. **quorums**

Quoyburray, Orkney pronounced *kwy* (rhymes with eye)-*bur-ee*

Qur'an alt. spelling of Koran; Muslim holy book

Quy, Cambridgeshire rhymes with eye

q.v., *quod vide* (Lat.) 'which see'; used for textual cross-references

qwerty keyboard standard English typewriter/computer keyboard, so called because the first six of the first row of letter keys spell qwerty.

R

rabbet type of groove used in carpentry

rabbi, rabbinical

Rabelais, François (c. 1494–c.1553) French satirist

Rabin, Yitzhak (1922–95) Israeli Prime Minister 1974–7, 1992–5

raccoon

Rachmaninoff (or **Rachmaninov**), **Sergei** (1873–1943) Russian composer and pianist

rack, wrack *Wrack* is an archaic variant of *wreck*. *Rack* means to put under strain. The expressions are *nerve-racking*, *rack and ruin* and to *rack one's brains*.

racket (pref.)/**racquet** (alt.) bat used in tennis, squash and badminton. For the loud noise, the spelling is always *racket*.

racy

radiator, not -*er*

radius The plural can be either *radii* or *radiuses*.

Raeburn, Sir Henry (1756–1823) Scottish artist

raffia fibre used for mats

Rafsanjani, Ali Akbar (Hashemi) (1934–) President of Iran 1989–97

ragamuffin

ragout in French, *ragoût*

raise Cain, to complain strongly

raison d'être (Fr.) reason for being

Rajasthan, India, not -*stan*

raki alcoholic drink of Eastern Europe and the Middle East

Ralegh, Sir Walter (1552–1618) English courtier, explorer and author; *Raleigh* was once the conventional spelling, but *Ralegh* is now generally preferred in serious and academic writings. However, for the city in North Carolina, the bicycles and the cigarettes, use **Raleigh**.

Ramadan ninth month of the Muslim year, and the fast that takes place in that month

Ramblers' Association

Ramses (sometimes **Rameses**) name of 12 pharaohs of ancient Egypt

rand South African currency; the plural is also rand

Ranelagh Gardens former pleasure gardens in London, now part of Chelsea Hospital Gardens

ranges of figures Sentences such as the following are common: 'Profits in the division were expected to rise by between $35 and $45 million.' Although most people will see at once that the writer meant to indicate a range of $10 million, literally she was saying that profits could rise by as little as $35 or as much as $45 million. If you mean 'between $35 million and $45 million' it is always better to say so.

Ransome, Arthur (1884–1967) British author of children's stories

Raphael (1483–1520) Italian painter; real name Raffaello Santi (or Sanzio)

'Rappaccini's Daughter' story by Nathaniel Hawthorne (1844)

Rappahannock River, Virginia

rappel (UK **abseil**), **rappelled**, **rappelling**

rapprochement (Fr.) reconciliation

rapt, wrapped One is rapt in thought, not wrapped. *Rapt* means engrossed, absorbed, enraptured.

rara avis (Lat.) 'a rare bird'; an unusual or wonderful person or thing; pl. *rarae aves*

rarefy, rarefaction, but **rarity**

Rasselas, Prince of Abyssinia, The History of novel by Samuel Johnson (1759)

Rastafarianism religious sect; see also HAILE SELASSIE

ratatouille vegetable stew

rational, rationale The first means sensible or sound ('a rational decision'); the second describes a justification ('the rationale for his actions').

rattan type of cane

ravage, ravish The first means to lay waste. The second means to rape or carry off – or, a touch confusingly, to enrapture. Clearly in all senses, for both words, care needs to be exercised to avoid confusion.

Ravenna, Italy

Rawalpindi, Pakistan

Ray, Satyajit (1921–92) Indian film director

Rayburn cast-iron range cooker company

razed to the ground is a common but mistaken expression. The ground is the only place to which a structure can be razed. It is enough to say that a building has been razed.

razzmatazz

react is better reserved for spontaneous responses ('He reacted to the news by fainting'). It should not be used to indicate responses marked by reflection.

real Brazilian currency; pl. **reais**

realpolitik politics based on the achievable

reason . . . is because is a common construction that almost always points to an overwritten sentence. Consider an example: 'The reason she spends less and less time in England these days is because her business interests keep her constantly on the move.' Remove 'the reason' and its attendant verb 'is', and a crisper, more focused sentence emerges: 'She spends less and less time in England these days because her business interests keep her constantly on the move.'

reason why, like *reason is . . . because* (see above), is generally redundant. Consider two examples: 'Grover said her contract had been terminated, but no one at the company would tell her the reason why'; 'His book argues that the main reason why inner-city blacks are in such a sorry state is not because whites are prejudiced but because low-skilled jobs near their homes are disappearing.' An improvement can nearly always be effected by removing one word or the other – e.g., 'the reason' from the first example, 'why' from the second.

recce slang for reconnaissance; pronounced *recky*

receptacle

recherché far-fetched

reciprocal, **reciprocity**

reckless, not *wreckless*, unless you are describing a setting in which there are no wrecks

reconnaissance

reconnoitre (US **reconnoiter**)

recuse in the US, challenge a judge or juror

reducible

reductio ad absurdum (Lat.) a method of deflating an argument by proving it absurd

reebok type of antelope

Reekie, Auld (Scot.) 'Old Smoky', nickname for Edinburgh

reflector

refute means to show conclusively that an allegation is wrong. It does not mean simply to dispute or deny a contention.

regalia is plural

Regent's Park, London (apos.)

reggae West Indian music

register office (UK), not *registry*

Registrar, Oxford University, but **Registrary**, Cambridge University

regretfully, **regrettably** The first means with feelings of regret ('regretfully they said their farewells'); the second means unfortunately ('regrettably I did not have enough money to buy it').

rehabilitate

Reichstag German parliament building

Reims, France, is the usual spelling, though **Rheims** is sometimes used. It is pronounced *reemz* in English but *ranz* in French.

relatively, like *comparatively*, should not be used unless there is some sense of a comparison or relationship. Often it can be removed without loss from sentences like 'The group has taken the relatively bold decision to expand its interests in Nigeria.'

religieuse (Fr.) a nun; pl. *religieuses*

religieux (Fr.) a monk; pl. *religieux*

Remarque, Erich Maria (1898–1970) German-born American novelist

Rembrandt Harmensz (or **Harmenszoon**) **van Rijn** is the full name for the Dutch painter (1606–69)

remembrance, not *-berance* **Remembrance Sunday** (UK) is the Sunday nearest 11 November.

— 351 —

remissible able to be pardoned

remittance

remittent of a fever, with fluctuating body temperature

remunerate, not *renum-* pay

Renaissance, the in European art, roughly the period 1300–1500

rendezvous is the spelling for both the singular and plural.

renegade

renege go back on; **reneged, reneging**

Renoir, Pierre Auguste (1841–1919), French painter; father of **Jean Renoir** (1894–1979), film director

renown, not *reknown*

Rensselaer Polytechnic Institute, Troy, New York, and Hartford, Connecticut

Rentokil pest control company; not *-kill*

repartee

repellent

repetition, repetitive

replete is not merely full but overfull, stuffed.

replica is an exact copy. A scale model is not a replica. Only something built to the same scale as the original and using the same materials is a replica. It therefore follows that 'exact replica' is always redundant.

repository

reprehensible

reproducible

Repubblica, La Italian newspaper; note *-bb-*

Resnais, Alain (1922–) French film director

respirator, not *-er*

respite, temporary or **brief** It is in the nature of respites to be both. It is enough to say that somebody or something enjoyed a respite.

restaurateur, not -*rant*-

restive properly means obstinate, refusing to move or budge. A crowd of protesters may grow restive upon the arrival of mounted police, but a person sitting uncomfortably on a hard bench is better described as restless.

résumé

resuscitate, resuscitator

retraceable

retroussé (masc.)/**retroussée** (fem.) turned up, particularly applied to noses

retsina Greek white wine flavoured with resin

Reuters news agency (no apos.)

reveille military wake-up call

Revelation, Book of, not -*ions*

reversible

revert back is always redundant. Delete *back*.

revertible

re- Somewhat mystifyingly, many publications show a formidable resistance to putting hyphens into any word beginning with *re-*. Yet often the presence or absence of a hyphen can usefully and immediately denote a difference in meaning, as between *recollect* (remember) and *re-collect* (collect again), or between *recede* (withdraw) and *re-cede* (give back again, as with territory). My advice, for what it is worth, is always to insert a hyphen if you think it might reduce the chance of even momentary misunderstanding.

Reykjavik capital of Iceland

RGS Royal Geographical Society

Rhadamanthus in Greek mythology, a judge of the dead

Rhein German spelling of Rhine

Rhineland-Palatinate   German   state;   in   German,
   Rheinland-Pfalz
rhinestone artificial diamond
rhinoceros, pl. **rhinoceroses**
rhododendron flowering shrub
Rhondda, Mid Glamorgan
Rhône, French river; **Rhône-Alpes**, French region
rhumb line imaginary line used to chart a ship's course
rhythm, rhythmic
RIBA Royal Institute (not *Institution*) of British Architects
Ribbentrop, Joachim von (1893–1946) German politician
ribonucleic acid abbr. RNA
Ricardo, David (1772–1823) English political economist and
   politician
Rice, Condoleezza (1954–)   American political adviser,
   Secretary of State 2005–
Richelieu, Armand Jean du Plessis, Cardinal, Duc de
   (1585–1642) French Prime Minister 1624–42
Richter scale standard measure of earthquake magnitudes. It
   is named for Charles Richter (1900–85) of the
   California Institute of Technology, who invented it in
   the 1930s. The scale increases at a rate that is exponen-
   tial rather than linear, making each level of increment
   vastly greater than most people appreciate. According to
   Charles Office and Jake Page in *Tales of the Earth*, a magnitude 8.3 earthquake is 50 times larger than a
   magnitude 7.3 quake and 2,500 times larger than a magnitude 6.3 quake. In practical terms, this means that
   Richter magnitudes are largely meaningless to most
   readers and comparisons involving two or more Richter
   measurements are totally meaningless. It is considerate
   to the reader to provide, wherever possible, some basis

of comparison beyond the bare Richter numbers. It is also worth bearing in mind that the Richter scale measures only the magnitude of an earthquake at its point of origin, and says little or nothing about the degree of devastation at ground level.

rickettsia microorganism that can transmit various diseases to humans

RICO common abbreviation for Racketeer Influenced and Corrupt Organizations Act, US law designed to attack organized crime

ricochet, ricocheted, ricocheting

RICS Royal Institution of Chartered Surveyors

rideable (US **ridable**)

Riefenstahl, Leni (1902–2003) German actress and film director

Riesling (cap.) German white wine

Rievaulx Abbey, North Yorkshire pronounced *ree-vo*

riffraff

Rigoletto opera by Verdi (1851)

rigor mortis stiffening of joints and muscles after death

Rijksmuseum, Amsterdam

Rikers Island (no apos.), New York

Riksdag Swedish parliament

Riley, the life of comfortable, carefree existence

Rilke, Rainer Maria (1875–1926) Austrian poet

'Rime of the Ancient Mariner, The', not *Rhyme* poem by Samuel Taylor Coleridge (1798)

Rimsky-Korsakov, Nikolai (or **Nicholas**) (1844–1908) Russian composer

Ringling Brothers and Barnum & Bailey Circus, US

Rio de Janeiro, Brazil

Rio Grande, not Rio Grande River

Rio Tinto-Zinc British mining company; note position of hyphen

'Rip Van Winkle' story by Washington Irving (1819)

risotto Italian rice dish

rissole deep-fried minced meat or fish ball or patty

Rive Gauche (Fr.) the Left Bank, most commonly used of the Seine in Paris

Riyadh capital of Saudi Arabia; in Arabic, **Ar Riyad**

Rizzio, David (1540–66) court musician to, and favourite of, Mary, Queen of Scots

RNA ribonucleic acid

Roanoke, Virginia

Robbins, Jerome (1918–98) American choreographer; born Jerome Rabinowitz

Robespierre, Maximilien François Marie Isidore de (1758–94) French revolutionary

Robins, A. H. US pharmaceuticals company

Rochefoucauld, François, Duc de La (1613–80) French writer known for his maxims

Rockefeller, John D. (for **Davison**) (1839–1937) American business tycoon; note middle name was Davison, not Davidson

Rockefeller Center but **Rockville Centre**, New York

rock 'n' roll

rococo highly ornamented

Rodgers, Jimmie (1897–1933) US country music singer

Rodgers, Richard (1902–79) American composer; collaborated often with lyricists Lorenz Hart and Oscar Hammerstein II

Rodin, Auguste (1840–1917) French sculptor

Roebling, John Augustus (1806–69) American engineer, designer of Brooklyn Bridge

Roedean School, Brighton

Roederer, Louis champagne

Roeg, Nicolas (1928–) British film director; note unusual spelling of first name

Rogers, Ginger (1911–95) actress and dancer; real name Virginia Katherine McMath

Rogers, Richard (1933–) British architect; now formally Lord Rogers of Riverside

Rogers Centre (not *-er*), Toronto formerly SkyDome; sporting arena

Rogge, Jacques (1942–) Belgian sports administrator, president of the IOC

Roissy informal name of Charles de Gaulle Airport, Paris

Rolls-Royce (hyphen)

roly-poly

ROM read-only memory, a type of computer memory

roman-à-clef (Fr.) a novel about real people but using fictitious names; pl. **romans-à-clef**

roman-fleuve (Fr.) a long novel, or series of novels, chronicling several generations of a family; pl. **romans-fleuves**

Romania, not *Ru-*

Roman numerals See Appendix.

Romanov dynasty that ruled Russia 1613–1917

Romansch (or **Romansh**) language spoken in parts of Switzerland

Romberg, Sigmund (1887–1951) Hungarian-born American composer of operettas

Rommel, Erwin (1891–1944) German field marshal, commander of the Afrika Korps in the Second World War

Roppongi nightclub district of Tokyo

Roquefort a French cheese, from the village of Roquefort-sur-Soulzon

Rorschach test psychological test involving ink blots devised by Swiss psychiatrist and neurologist Hermann Rorschach (1884–1922)

Roseau capital of Dominica

Rosebery, Lord (1847–1929) British Prime Minister 1894–5; note single *r* in Rosebery. His full name was Archibald Philip Primrose, Earl of Rosebery.

Rosenberg, Julius (1918–53) and his wife **Ethel** (1915–53) Americans executed as Russian spies

Rosenborg Castle, Copenhagen

Rosenkavalier, Der opera by Richard Strauss (1911)

Rosetta Stone

Rosh Hashanah (or **Hashana**, **Hoshana**, **Hoshanah**) Jewish New Year, usually late September or early October

Rosmersholm play by Henrik Ibsen (1886)

RoSPA Royal Society for the Prevention of Accidents

Rossetti, Dante Gabriel (1828–82) English poet and painter, one of the founders of the Pre-Raphaelite Brotherhood; brother of **Christina Rossetti** (1830–94), poet

Rossini, Gioacchino Antonio (1792–1868) Italian composer

Rostand, Edmond, not -*mund* (1868–1918) French playwright and poet

Rostropovich, Mstislav (1927–2007) Russian cellist

rosy, not *rosey*

Rotavator (cap.)

Rothko, Mark (1903–70) Russian-born American painter

Rothschilds family of European financiers. Among the more distinguished members are: **Nathaniel Mayer Victor, Baron Rothschild** (1910–90), English scientist and public servant; **Edmund Leopold de Rothschild**

(1916–2007), British banker; and **Baron Élie Robert de Rothschild** (1917–).

Rottweiler breed of dog. Note two *t*s, one *l*.

Rouault, George Henri (1871–1958) French expressionist painter

Roubiliac, Louis François (1695–1762) French sculptor

rouble (or **ruble**) Russian unit of currency

Rousseau, Henri (1844–1910) French painter, known as **Le Douanier**

Rousseau, Jean-Jacques (1712–78) Swiss-born French political theorist

Routledge & Kegan Paul British publisher, subsequently **Routledge**; now an imprint of the Taylor & Francis Group

Rowlandson, Thomas (1756–1827) English caricaturist

Roy, Arundhati (1961–) Indian novelist and activist, Booker prizewinner 1997

Royal and Ancient Golf Club, the formal name of the famous golf course at St Andrews

Royal Dutch/Shell Group Anglo-Dutch oil company

Royale, Ségolène (1953–) French Socialist politician

Royal Geographical Society

Royal Institution of Chartered Surveyors, London not *Institute*

Royal Welch Fusiliers, Royal Welch Regiment British regiments, united in 2006 to form the **Royal Welsh**

RSVP, *répondez s'il vous plaît* (Fr.) 'please reply'; the term is not used in France

RTE Radio Telefís Éireann, Irish broadcasting corporation

RTL Radio Télévision Luxembourg

Rubáiyát of Omar Khayyám, The Persian verses translated by Edward Fitzgerald (1859)

rubella German measles

Rubens, Bernice (1929–2004)   British novelist, Booker prizewinner 1970

Rubens, Peter Paul (1577–1640) Flemish painter

rubeola medical term for measles

Rubinstein, Artur (1886–1982)   Polish-born American pianist

Rüdesheimer German wine

Rukeyser, Louis (1933–2006)   American economic commentator

'Rule, Britannia'   British patriotic song; note comma

rumba a lively dance of Cuban origin

rumbustious boisterous

Rumpelstiltskin dwarf in a story by the Brothers Grimm

Runnymede meadow in Surrey where King John signed the Magna Carta in 1215

Ruritania fictional country in *The Prisoner of Zend*a, a novel by Anthony Hope (1894), and by extension a romantic, unreal country

Rushdie, Salman (1947–)   British-Indian novelist, Booker prizewinner 1981; formally Sir Ahmed Salman Rushdie

Ruy Lopez a type of opening move in chess

Ruysdael/Ruïsdael, Jacob van (1628–82)   Dutch artist; pronounced *royz-dale*

Ruzyně Airport, Prague

Ruyton-XI-Towns, Shropshire

Rwanda central African republic, capital Kigali

Ryme Intrinseca, Dorset

Ryukyu Islands, Japan

Ryun, Jim (1947–)   American distance runner and Republican politician

S

Saarbrücken, Germany

Saarinen, Eero (1910–61), Finnish-born American architect, and son of **Gottlieb Eliel Saarinen** (1873–1950), also a noted architect

Saarland German state

Sables d'Olonne, Les, France

sabotage, saboteur

saccharin, saccharine The first is an artificial sweetener; the second means sugary.

Sackville-West, Vita (1892–1962) English writer

sacrilegious abusing something sacred or greatly respected. Sometimes misspelled *sacreligious* on the mistaken assumption that *religious* is part of the word. It isn't.

Saddam Hussein (1937–2006) President of Iraq 1979–2003. His name in full was Saddam Hussein Abd al-Majid al-Tikrit.

Sadler's Wells London theatre

safflower oil-producing plant

Saffron Walden, Essex

Sagittarius a sign of the Zodiac

sago, pl. **sagos**

Sahara means desert, so in the common expression Sahara Desert the second word is redundant.

Saigon former name of Ho Chi Minh City, Vietnam

St Albans, Hertfordshire, but **St Alban's Head**, Dorset

St Andrews (no apos.), Scotland site of St Andrews University and golf's most revered course, the Royal and Ancient Golf Club

St Andrew's Day (apos.) 30 November

St Anne's, Lancashire; **St Anne's College**, Oxford

St Antony's College, Oxford

St Barthélemy French West Indies

St Benet's Hall, Oxford, but **St Bene't's Church**, Cambridge

St Briavels, Gloucestershire

St Catharine's College, Cambridge, but **St Catherine's College**, Oxford

St Catherines, Ontario

St Christopher and Nevis See St Kitts and Nevis.

St Croix US Virgin Islands, pronounced *kroy*; formerly Santa Cruz

St Devereux, Herefordshire

St Dogmaels, Pembrokeshire

St Dominick, Cornwall

St Edmund Hall, Oxford, but **St Edmund's College**, Cambridge

Saint-Exupéry, Antoine (Marie Roger) de (1900–44) French aviator and author

Saint-Germain-des-Prés, Paris

St Germans (no apos.), Cornwall

St Helens (no apos.), Merseyside

St Helens, Mount volcano in Washington state, which famously erupted in 1980

St Helier, Jersey

St James Garlickhythe London church

St James's, not *James'*, for the London palace, park and square. Diplomats likewise are posted to the **Court of St James's**. But it is **St James Park** (no apos.) for the home of Newcastle United.

St John Ambulance Brigade, not *John's*

St Just-in-Roseland, Cornwall

St Katharine's Dock, London, not *Kather-*

St Katherines (no apos.), Aberdeenshire

St Kitts and Nevis is the common name for the Caribbean state formally known as the Federation of St Christopher and Nevis; capital Basseterre. Residents are known as Kittians or Nevisians.

St Leonards-on-Sea, East Sussex

St Louis, Missouri pronounced *lewis*, not *looey*

St Maarten/St Martin Caribbean island divided into Dutch and French sides, respectively

St Martin-in-the-Fields Church, London, but **St Martin's** on second reference

St Mary-le-Bow (hyphens) but **St Mary le Strand**, London churches

St Michael's Mount, Cornwall

St Neots, Cambridgeshire, but **St Neot**, Cornwall

St Olaves, Norfolk

St Owens (no apos.) **Cross**, Herefordshire

St Petersburg, Russia; formerly Leningrad

St Pierre and Miquelon French islands off the east coast of Canada; formally they are a territorial collectivity

St Sampson, Guernsey

St Swithin's (or **Swithun's**) **Day** 15 July. According to legend, rain on that day will be followed by 40 days of more rain.

St Thomas' Hospital, London

St Vincent and the Grenadines Caribbean state; capital Kingstown

sake Japanese rice wine

Sakharov, Andrei (1921–89) Russian physicist and dissident; awarded Nobel Peace Prize 1975

Saki pen name of H. H. Munro (1870–1916), English writer

saleable (US **salable**) for something that can be sold

Sallie Mae, nickname for the US Student Loan Marketing Board

salmonella poisonous bacterium, named for its discoverer, American Dr D. J. Salmon (1850–1914)

Salonika, Greece, not Thessaloniki

salsify edible root; pl. **salsifies**

SALT strategic arms limitation talks. The expression 'SALT talks', though redundant, is sometimes unavoidable.

saluki breed of dog

salutary, not -*tory* conducive to health. For a discussion of its usage, see HEALTHY, HEALTHFUL, SALUTARY.

Salvadoran, not -*ean* a person or thing from El Salvador

salvos (or **salvoes**) sudden series of shots, literal or figurative

Sam Browne, not *Brown* type of belt with a supporting strap worn diagonally across the chest

samizdat underground publication of banned texts in the former Soviet Union

Samson, not *Sampson* biblical figure of great strength

Samuel Johnson Prize award for non-fiction writing

samurai (sing. and pl.)

Sanaa (or **Sana'a**) capital of Yemen

sanatorium, pl. **sanatoriums/sanatoria**

Sanchez-Vicario, Arantxa (1971–) Spanish tennis player

sanctimonious claiming moral superiority

Sand, George pen name of Amandine Aurore Lucile Dupin, Baronne Dudevant (1804–76), French writer

sandal for the type of shoe. Not *sandle*

sandalwood

Sandinistas/Sandinists revolutionary party in Nicaragua; named after General Augusto César Sandino (1895–1934), a Nicaraguan revolutionary

sangfroid 'cold blood', unflappability

Sangre de Cristo Mountains, Colorado and New Mexico

sangria Spanish drink

sanitary, not -*tory*

San Joaquin Valley, California

San Luis Obispo, California; not *Louis*

San Salvador capital of El Salvador

sans-culotte (Fr.) 'without breeches'; an extreme revolutionary or republican. French revolutionaries were so called because they wore pantaloons rather than breeches.

San Siro football stadium shared by AC Milan and Internazionale; official name Stadio Giuseppe Meazza after the 1930s Italian football legend

sans serif (or **sanserif**) a typeface without serifs, which are the projections added to some strokes of letters in traditional typefaces

Santa Ana wind; also the name of a town in California

Santa Isabel former name of Malabo, capital of Equitorial Guinea

Santayana, George (1863–1952) Spanish-born American poet, novelist and philosopher

Santo Domingo formerly Ciudad Trujillo; capital of the Dominican Republic

Saône French river

São Paulo largest city in Brazil

São Tomé and Príncipe west African republic, capital São Tomé. Natives are known as São Toméans.

sapphire note -*pp*-; precious stone

Sappho (c. 620 –c. 565 BC) Greek poet

Sara Lee, not *Sarah*, for the US food company

sarcoma a malignant tumour in connective tissue, bone or muscle; pl. **sarcomas/sarcomata**

sarcophagus stone coffin; pl. **sarcophagi**

Sardegna Italian for Sardinia

sardonic mocking, cynical

Sargasso Sea area of the Atlantic Ocean where masses of floating seaweed are found

Sargent, John Singer (1856–1925) American painter

Sarkozy, Nicolas (1955–) French politician, President of France 2007–

SARS Severe Acute Respiratory Syndrome, a viral disorder

sarsaparilla a sweet drink, formerly a tonic, flavoured with plant extracts

Sartre, Jean-Paul (1905–80) French philosopher, dramatist and novelist

Sarum signature of the Bishop of Salisbury

SAS Scandinavian Airlines System

Saskatchewan Canadian river and province

Saskatoon city in Saskatchewan

sasquatch North American abominable snowman

sassafras North American tree, source of flavouring

Sassoon, Siegfried (Lorraine) (1886–1967) British poet

satellite

satirical using satire – exaggerated humour – to make fun of faults

Sauchiehall Street, Glasgow pronounced *sockiehall*

saucisse (Fr.) sausage; a *saucisse de Toulouse* is a pork sausage

saucy, not *-ey*

sauerbraten (Ger.) braised beef marinated in herbs and vinegar

sauerkraut pickled cabbage

Saugatuck river in Connecticut and town in Michigan

Sauk Centre, Minnesota birthplace of Sinclair Lewis; note spelling of *Centre*

Sault Sainte Marie towns in Michigan and Ontario, and canal linking Lake Huron and Lake Superior

Sausalito, California

Sauternes a sweet French wine and the village in Gironde from which it comes. The name of the wine is sometimes lower-cased and, in the US, spelled **sauterne**.

sauve qui peut (Fr.) 'save who can'; wild flight; every man for himself

savannah (or **savanna**) tropical and subtropical grassland

Savannah, Georgia, but **Savana Island**, US Virgin Islands, and **Savanna** for towns in Illinois and Oklahoma. The river is also **Savannah**.

SAVE Britain's Heritage heroic preservation organization

Savile Row, not -*ll*- street famous for men's tailoring, London

savoir-faire, **savoir-vivre** Both are French, of course. The first indicates know-how, the second social grace.

Savonarola, Girolamo (1452–98) Italian religious and political reformer

Saxony-Anhalt German state; in German **Sachsen-Anhalt**

saxophone musical instrument invented by Adolphe Sax (1814–94), a Belgian

Scafell Pike the highest peak in England at 3,206 feet/977 metres. There is a separate neighbouring eminence called **Sca Fell** (two words).

Scala, La opera house in Milan; formally, Teatro alla Scala

scalene triangle one with no equal sides

scallywag (US **scalawag**) a rascal

scaloppina (It.) escalope; pl. *scaloppine*

Scandinavia, not *Scanda-*

Scapigliatura, La 19th-century Italian literary movement; literally, 'the dishevelled ones'

Scarborough, North Yorkshire, but the **Earl of Scarbrough**

scarce, scarcely

scared, scarred The first means frightened, the second disfigured.

scarfs, scarves Either is correct for the plural of *scarf.*

Scarlatti, Alessandro (1659–1725) and **Scarlatti, Domenico** (1683–1757) father and son composers from Italy

scary, not *-ey*

sceptic, scepticism (US **skeptic, skepticism**) a doubtful, questioning person and his doubtfulness. Not to be confused with **septic**, meaning infected.

Schadenfreude (Ger.) pronounced *shah-den-froy-duh*; deriving pleasure from the misfortunes of others

Schaffhausen, Switzerland in French, **Schaffhouse**

Schaffner, Franklin (1920–89) American film director

Scheherazade fictional sultan's wife, narrator of *The Arabian Nights*; title of compositions by Rimsky-Korsakov and Ravel

Schenectady, New York pronounced *skuh-nek´-tuh-dee*

Scheveningen suburb of The Hague

Schiaparelli, Elsa (1890–1973) Italian-born French fashion designer

Schiller, (Johann Christoph) Friedrich von (1759–1805) German poet, playwright and historian

schilling former Austrian unit of currency

Schiphol Airport, Amsterdam

Schirra, Wally (1923–2007) American astronaut; formally he was Walter M. Schirra, Jr

schistosomiasis parasitic disease of tropical regions; also known as **bilharzia**

Schleiermacher, Friedrich Daniel Ernst (1768–1834) German philosopher

schlemiel (Yiddish) a fool

Schlesinger, Arthur M. (for **Meier**) (1888–1965) American historian, and father of **Arthur M.** (for **Meier**) **Schlesinger, Jr** (1917–2007), American historian

Schleswig-Holstein province of Germany

Schlieffen, Alfred, Count von (1833–1913) Prussian field marshal and military strategist

Schliemann, Heinrich (1822–90) German archaeologist who excavated Mycenae and Troy

schmaltz maudlin sentimentality

Schmeling, Max (1905–2005) German heavyweight boxer

Schnabel, Artur (1882–1951) Austrian-born American pianist

Schnabel, Julian (1951–) American painter

schnapps a strong alcoholic drink similar to gin

Schnauzer breed of dog

schnitzel veal cutlet

Schnitzler, Arthur (1862–1931) Austrian playwright and novelist

Schoenberg (or **Schönberg**), **Arnold** (1874–1951) Austrian composer

Schomburg Center for Research in Black Culture, New York

Schönbrunn Palace, Vienna

Schopenhauer, Arthur (1788–1860) German philosopher

Schröder, Gerhard (1944–) Chancellor of Germany 1998–2005

Schubert, Franz (1797–1828) Austrian composer

Schulberg, Budd (1914–) American screenwriter. Note unusual spelling of Budd.

Schulz, Charles M. (for **Monroe**) (1922–2000) American comic-strip cartoonist, creator of *Peanuts*

Schumacher, Michael (1969–) German motor-racing driver; Formula 1 champion a record seven times

Schuman, Robert (1886–1963) Luxembourg-born French statesman who devised the Schuman Plan, which led to the setting-up of the European Coal and Steel Community

Schumann, Robert (1810–56) German composer

schuss downhill run in skiing

Schuylkill River, Pennsylvania pronounced *skoo´-kill*

schwa, not *schwah*, for the phonetic symbol ə representing an indeterminate unstressed sound akin to *uh*, as with the second and fourth vowel sounds of *memorandum* (i.e., *mem-ə-ran-dəm*)

Schwabing district of Munich

Schwarzenegger, Arnold (1947–) Austrian-born American body-builder, actor and Republican politician; governor of California 2003–

Schwarzkopf, Dame Elisabeth (1915–2006) Austrian-British soprano

Schwarzkopf, H. Norman (1935–) American general, commander of Operation Desert Storm in the first Gulf War

Schwarzwald (Ger.) the Black Forest

Schweitzer, Albert (1875–1965) German theologian, medical missionary, philosopher and musician; established Lambaréné mission, French Equatorial Africa; awarded Nobel Peace Prize 1952

Schweiz, die German name for Switzerland; **schweizerdeutsch** (one word) for Swiss German

Schygulla, Hanna (1943–) German actress

Science Museum, London formally the National Museum of Science and Industry

Scilly, Isles of pronounced *silly*; group of islands off Cornwall; adj. **Scillonian**

scintilla a tiny amount

Scofield, Paul (1922–) British actor

Scorsese, Martin (1942–) American film director

Scotch, **Scottish**, **Scots** Except for *Scotch whisky* and well-established expressions such as *Scotch broth* and *Scotch mist*, *Scottish* and *Scots* are preferred. In particular a person from Scotland is *Scottish*, not *Scotch*. The British army unit is the Scots Guards. The dog is a Scottish terrier.

Scotch tape (US, cap.) In the UK, use Sellotape.

scot-free of an escape, 'without penalty'

Scott, Dred a Missouri slave who unsuccessfully sued for his freedom on the grounds that his owner had taken him into free territory. The Supreme Court case of 1857 that resulted is called *Dred Scott v. Sanford*.

Scott, Elisabeth (1898–1972) architect of the Shakespeare Memorial Theatre, Stratford-upon-Avon

Scribner's US publisher, formerly Charles Scribner's Sons

scrutiny, scrutinize To *scrutinize* something means to look at it with particular attentiveness. Thus qualifying words like *close* or *careful* are nearly always superfluous.

SCSI small computer system interface, a type of port on small computers

scurrilous does not mean merely angry or insulting. It means grossly obscene or abusive. An attack must be exceedingly harsh to be scurrilous.

Scylla and Charybdis In Greek mythology, Scylla (pronounced *silla*) was a six-headed monster who lived beside a treacherous whirlpool called Charybdis (pronounced *kuh-rib´-dis*) off the coast of Sicily, so being between Scylla and Charybdis signifies a highly unattractive dilemma.

SDI Strategic Defence Initiative, commonly called 'star wars'; plan propounded by President Reagan in 1983 to erect a shield of weapons in space over the US to keep out incoming missiles

Seaborg, Glenn (1912–) American nuclear chemist and physicist; awarded Nobel Prize for Chemistry 1951

Seanad Éireann upper house of Irish parliament, pronounced *shin-add' air-ann'*

Sears, Roebuck US mail-order retailer; note the comma

SEATO South-East Asia Treaty Organization

Sebastopol/Sevastopol The first is the historical spelling, the second the modern spelling for the Crimean city and Black Sea port, now part of Ukraine.

secede withdraw from membership of an organization

second largest and other similar comparisons often lead writers astray, as in 'Japan is the second largest drugs market in the world after the United States'; what is meant is that Japan is the largest drugs market in the world after the United States, or the second largest drugs market in the world.

Securities and Exchange Commission (note *and*) the regulatory body for US stock markets; but note that it is the Securities Exchange Act (US)

sedentary of a lifestyle, spending a lot of time seated

Sedgemoor, Battle of (1685) in which forces of James II defeated the Duke of Monmouth

Segovia, Andrés (1894–1987) Spanish guitarist

se habla español (Sp.) Spanish spoken here

seigneur lord of the manor, feudal lord; hence DROIT DE SEIGNEUR

seismograph, seismometer, seismogram Occasionally, and perhaps understandably, confused. A *seismometer* is a sensor placed in the ground to record earthquakes and other vibrations. A *seismograph* is the instrument that records the seismometer's readings. A *seismogram* is the printout or chart that provides a visual record of seismic activity.

seize

Sejm Parliament of Poland

Selassie, Haile See HAILE SELASSIE.

self-confessed, as in 'a self-confessed murderer', is usually tautological. In most cases, *confessed* alone is enough.

Selfridges (no apos.) London department store

Sellotape (cap.)

Selznick, David O. (for **Oliver**) (1902–65) American film producer

semblance

Sendero Luminoso (Sp.) Shining Path, Peruvian revolutionary group

Senegal west African republic; capital Dakar

Senhor, Senhora, Senhorita (Port.) Mr, Mrs, Miss; first syllable pronounced *sun*

Senna, Ayrton (1960–94) Brazilian Formula 1 racing driver

'Sennacherib, The Destruction of' poem by Byron (1815)

Sennett, Mack (1884–1960) born Michael Sinnott; Canadian-born American film producer and director

Señor, Señora, Señorita (Sp.) Mr, Mrs, Miss

sensual, sensuous The words are only broadly synonymous. *Sensual* applies to a person's baser instincts as distinguished from reason. It should always hold connotations of sexual allure or lust. *Sensuous* was coined by Milton to avoid those connotations and to suggest instead the idea of being alive to sensations. It should be used when no suggestion of sexual arousal is intended.

Seoul capital of South Korea. An alternative name in Korea is Kyongsong.

Sephardi a Jew of Spanish, Portuguese or North African origin; pl. **Sephardim**; see also ASHKENAZI

seppuku ritual suicide in Japan; hara-kiri

septicaemia (US **septicemia**) blood poisoning

septuagenarian, not *septa-* person 70–79 years old

Septuagesima third Sunday before Lent, 70th day before Easter

sepulchre (US **sepulcher**)

sequacious lacking independent thought

seraglio a harem

serendipity happy chance

Serengeti National Park, Serengeti Plain, Tanzania; not *-getti*

sergeant

seriatim, not *-tum* in a series, one after another

serving, servicing *Servicing* is better reserved for the idea of installation and maintenance, or paying interest on a debt. *Serving* is the better word for describing things that are of general and continuing benefit.

sesquipedalian long-winded, containing many syllables

Session, Court of supreme court of Scotland; not *Sessions*

Seurat, Georges Pierre (1859–91) French painter

Seuss, Dr (real name Theodor Seuss Geisel) (1904–91) American children's writer and illustrator

seven deadly sins They are avarice, envy, gluttony, lust, pride, sloth and wrath.

7-Eleven is the trademark name for the convenience stores chain.

7UP is the trademark name for the soft drink.

Seven Wonders of the World Of the ancient world, they were the Hanging Gardens of Babylon, the Great Pyramids of Egypt, the Colossus of Rhodes, the Mausoleum at Halicarnassus, the Temple of Artemis at Ephesus, the statue of Zeus at Olympia, and the Pharos at Alexandria.

Sèvres porcelain

Sexagesima second Sunday before Lent, about sixty days before Easter

Seychelles island republic in the Indian Ocean; capital Victoria; adj. **Seychellois**

sforzando in music, an abrupt stress on a note or chord

S4C Sianel Pedwar Cymru (Welsh), Channel Four Wales

's-Gravenhage formal name for The Hague; pronounced *skrah-ven-hah'-guh*

shaikh Use **sheikh**.

Shake 'N Bake American grocery product

Shakespearean, Shakespearian The first is the usual spelling in America and the second is the usual spelling in Britain.

shaky (not -*ey*), **shakiness**

shallot a plant related to the onion

'Shalott, The Lady of' poem by Tennyson (1832); not *Shallot*

Shamir, Yitzhak (1915–) born Yitzhak Jazernicki; Prime Minister of Israel 1983–4, 1988–92

Shandong Chinese province, formerly spelled **Shantung**; capital Jinan

Shangri-La, not -*la*, for the Himalayan paradise created by James Hilton in the 1933 novel *Lost Horizon*

Shankill Road, Belfast; not -*hill*

Shanks's pony (US also **Shanks's mare**) on foot

Shanxi Chinese province; capital Taiyuan

SHAPE abbr. of Supreme Headquarters, Allied Powers, Europe

Sharapova, Maria (1987–) Russian tennis player

sharia (or **shariah**) Islamic law

Shar Pei breed of dog

Sharpeville Massacre fatal shooting of 67 black South African demonstrators by police in the black township of Sharpeville, near Johannesburg, on 21 March 1960

Shatt al-Arab river that forms a section of the border between Iran and Iraq

Shays' Rebellion, not *Shay's* uprising by American farmers in 1786–7 led by Daniel Shays of Massachusetts

Shea Stadium, New York home of the New York Mets baseball team

Shedd Aquarium, Chicago

Sheetrock, for a type of plasterboard, is a trademark.

shekel Israeli unit of currency

Shelley, Mary Wollstonecraft (1797–1851) English writer, and second wife of **Percy Bysshe Shelley** (1792–1822), English poet

shenanigans mischief

Shepard, Sam (1943–) born Samuel Shepard Rogers; American actor and playwright

Shepherd, Cybill (1949–) American actress

Shepherd Market, but **Shepherd's Bush**, both London

Sherborne, Dorset Pupils of the boys' public school there are called **Shirburnians**.

Sheremetyevo Airport, Moscow

sheriff

Sherpa (cap.) a Himalayan people living in Tibet and Nepal

's-Hertogenbosch city in the Netherlands, commonly called Den Bosch

Shetland or **the Shetland Islands** are the accepted designations for the Scottish islands. *The Shetlands* is frowned on by some and thus better avoided. See also ORKNEY.

Shevardnadze, Eduard (1928–)   President of Georgia 1995–2003

shibboleth a word, phrase or linguistic quirk common to all members of a particular group and by which they can be distinguished from others

Shiite (or **Shi'ite**) member of the Shia branch of Islam

Shikoku Japanese island

shiksa (Yiddish) disparaging term for a non-Jewish girl

shillelagh Irish cudgel; pronounced *shi-lay´-lee*

Shinawatra, Thaksin (1949–)   former Prime Minister of Thailand, deposed in a coup in 2006

Sholokov, Mikhail (1905–84)   Russian novelist; awarded Nobel Prize for Literature 1965

Shooters Hill, London

Shostakovich, Dmitri (1906–75) Russian composer

shriek

shrivelled, shrivelling

Shriver, Lionel (1957–)   born Margaret Ann Shriver; American novelist, Orange prizewinner 2005

shrove past tense of *shrive*, to give absolution

Shrove Tuesday the day before Ash Wednesday. **Shrovetide** is the three days before Ash Wednesday.

shtum (or **schtum**) silent

Shubert Theatre, New York

Shultz, George (1920–) American statesman

Shute, Nevil pen name of Nevil Shute Norway (1899–1960), British novelist

Sibelius, Johan Julius Christian (1865–1957)   Finnish composer

sibilant hissing

sibylline prophetic

sic (Lat.) thus; used, usually in square brackets, to show that a word or passage is being quoted exactly despite any errors or infelicities it may contain

Sichuan Chinese province formerly known as **Szechwan** or **Szechuan**; capital Chengdu

sic transit gloria mundi (Lat.) so passes the glory of the world

Sidgwick & Jackson British publisher, now an imprint of Macmillan

Sidney, Sir Philip (1554–86) English poet

Sidney Sussex College, Cambridge

SIDS Sudden Infant Death Syndrome; cot death

siege

Siegfried Line defensive fortification built by Germany along its western border before the Second World War

Siena, Italy, but **sienna** for the earth-coloured pigment

Sierra Leone republic in west Africa; capital Freetown

Sierra Nevada, not *Sierra Nevada Mountains*; *sierra* is Spanish for 'mountains' so already present in the name

sieve

signatory

Sign of Four, The, not *the Four* Sherlock Holmes story (1890)

Signor, Signora, Signorina (It.) Mr, Mrs, and Miss

Sikkim former Himalayan kingdom annexed by India in 1975

Sikorsky a type of helicopter

silhouette

silicon chip, not *-cone*

sillabub variant spelling of **syllabub**, a creamy dessert

Sillitoe, Alan (1928–) English novelist

s'il vous plaît (Fr.) please

simile, metaphor Both are figures of speech in which two things are compared. A *simile* likens one thing to another, dissimilar one: 'He ran like the wind.' A *metaphor* acts as if the two compared things are identical and substitutes one for the other; thus comparing the beginning of time to the beginning of a day produces the metaphor 'the dawn of time'.

Simon & Schuster publisher

simpatico (It.)/*simpático* (Sp.) friendly, congenial

simulacrum a likeness or copy; a deceptive substitute; pl. *simulacra*

Sinai, not *the*

since A common error is seen here: 'Since April the company stopped giving discounts to students.' *Since* indicates action starting at a specified time in the past and continuing to the present. The verbs in sentences in which it appears must also indicate action that is continuing. Make it either 'In April the company stopped' or 'Since April the company has stopped'.

sinecure a profitable or advantageous position requiring little or no work

Sinepuxent Bay, Maryland

sine qua non (Lat.) a necessary condition

sinfonietta a small orchestra; a simple or light symphony

singe, singed, singeing

Singin' in the Rain, not *Singing* classic MGM musical (1952)

Sinhalese main population group of Sri Lanka

Sinn Fein (Gaelic) literally 'we ourselves', Irish nationalist movement and political party; pronounced *shinn fane*

siphon is the usual spelling, but **syphon** is also acceptable.

sirocco (or **scirocco**) hot wind originating in the Sahara and blowing over southern Europe

Sistani, Grand Ayatollah Ali al- (1930–) senior Shia Muslim cleric in Iraq

Sisyphus, not *-ss-* In Greek mythology, Sisyphus, king of Corinth, was condemned for eternity to push a heavy stone up a hill, only to have it roll down again. Hence **Sisyphean** describes some endless task.

Sithole, Revd Ndabaningi (1920–2000) Zimbabwean clergyman and politician

sitz bath type of hip bath

Sixth Avenue, New York former but still widely used name for the Avenue of the Americas

sizeable (US **sizable**)

Skagerrak note *-rr-*; channel of the North Sea lying between Norway and Denmark

skedaddle make off at speed

skein pronounced *skane*; flock of geese in flight or bundle of thread or yarn

skeptic, skepticism (US) (UK **sceptic, scepticism**)

ski, skied, skiing

Skidmore, Owings and Merrill American architectural firm

skidoo (or **skiddoo**) US, to depart hastily

skilful (US **skillful**)

skilless Note *-ll-*. This clumsy word, meaning to be without skills, is better avoided.

skirmish

skulduggery, not *skull-*

sleight of hand, not *slight*

sloe a bluish-black wild plum. Hence *sloe-eyed, sloe gin*

slough Pronounced to rhyme with *cow*, it means a swamp or bog; pronounced to rhyme with *rough*, it means to shed skin.

smart alec (US **aleck**) a know-all

smidgen (or **smidgin** or **smidgeon**) a tiny amount

Smith, Zadie (1975–) British novelist, Orange prizewinner 2006

Smithsonian Institution, Washington, DC

smoky

Smollett, Tobias (1721–71) British novelist

Smuts, Jan Christian (1870–1950) Prime Minister of South Africa 1919–24, 1939–48

Smyrna former name of Izmir, Turkish city on the Aegean Sea

SNCF Société Nationale des Chemins de Fer, French national railway company

sneaked, snuck The day may well come when *snuck* supersedes *sneaked* – it probably already has done so in American speech – but it is worth bearing in mind that many authorities continue to regard it as non-standard. Use *sneaked* instead.

snippet

Soane's Museum, Sir John, London. Note apos.

so as to The first two words can generally be deleted without loss, as they might have been here: 'The rest of the crowd stuffed hot dogs into their faces so as to avoid being drawn into the discussion.'

sobriquet pronounced *so´-bri-kay*; a nickname

Society of Friends formal name of the Quakers

Sofia capital of Bulgaria; in Bulgarian, *Sofiya*

Soho, London, but **SoHo**, Manhattan, where it is short for South of Houston Street

soi-disant (Fr.) self-styled

soigné (Fr. masc.)/**soignée** (Fr. fem.) well groomed

sojourn stay temporarily

soliloquy in a play, an actor's speech when alone on stage; pl.
   soliloquies
Solomon R. Guggenheim Museum, New York City
solos
soluble, **solvable** The first is something that can be dissolved; the second is something that can be solved.
Solzhenitsyn, Alexander (1918–) Russian novelist
somersault
some time, **sometime** In the UK it is usually two words:
   'They will arrive some time tomorrow.' When *some* is
   used as an adjective equivalent to *a short* or *a long* or *an*
   indefinite, it should always be two words: 'The
   announcement was made some time ago.' *Sometime* can
   also mean former, as in 'the sometime model turned
   photographer'.
     These considerations may help you to make the
   distinction:
     1. *Some time* as two words is often preceded by a
   preposition ('for some time', 'at some time') or followed
   by a helping word ('some time ago').
     2. When spoken, greater stress is placed on *time*
   when *some time* is two words.
Sommet Center, Nashville pronounced *so-may*
Somoza, Anastasio (1925–80) President of Nicaragua
   1967–72 and 1974–9
Sondheim, Stephen (1930–) American composer and
   lyricist
son et lumière (Fr.) night-time sound and light show
Sophocles (495–406 BC) Greek playwright
sophomore in the US, a second-year student; the adjective is
   sophomoric
Sorbonne, Paris formally Académie Universitaire de Paris

Sorenstam, Annika (1970–) Swedish professional golfer

sortie a quick attack, especially by the besieged on their besiegers; also, one mission by a single military aircraft

Sotheby's auctioneers; formerly Sotheby Parke Bernet & Co.; now Sotheby's Holdings Inc.

Sotomayor, Javier (1967–) Cuban high jumper

souchong Chinese tea

soufflé light, puffy dish made with egg whites

souk market in Arab countries

soupçon a very small amount

sou'wester rain hat with a broad brim at the back, or a southwest wind

Sovereign Bancorp Inc. Pennsylvania-based bank

Soviet Union, the, formally ceased to exist in 1991. It comprised 15 Union Republics: Armenia, Azerbaijan, Byelorussia, Estonia, Georgia, Kazakhstan, Kyrghyzstan, Latvia, Lithuania, Moldavia, Russia, Tajikistan, Turkmenistan, Ukraine and Uzbekistan.

Soyinka, Wole (1934–) Nigerian writer; awarded Nobel Prize for Literature 1986; full name Akinwande Oluwole Soyinka

SPAB Society for the Protection of Ancient Buildings (UK)

spate properly describes a torrent, not a flurry.

special, especial The first means for a particular purpose, the second to a high degree. A special meal may be especially delicious.

specie coins, as opposed to paper money; pronounced *spee-shee*

species, genus The first is a subgroup of the second. The convention is to capitalize the genus but not the species. Thus, *Homo sapiens*. The plurals are **species** and **genera**.

specious, spurious The first means apparently plausible but actually wrong. The second means fake.

Spenser, Edmund (1552–99) English poet

Spetsai, Greece

spicy, not *-ey*

Spielberg, Steven (1946–) American film director and producer

spigot a small plug; in the US, a tap

spiky, not *-ey*

spinnaker type of sail

spinney small woodland

Spinoza, Baruch de (1632–77) Dutch philosopher

Spitsbergen Norwegian island in the Svalbard archipelago in the Arctic Ocean

spittoon a receptacle for spitting into

split infinitives The belief that it is a serious breach of grammar to split an infinitive (that is, to put an adverb between 'to' and a verb as in 'to boldly go') is without foundation. It is certainly not a grammatical error. If it is an error at all, it is a rhetorical fault – a question of style – and not a grammatical one. It is practically impossible to find a recognized authority who condemns the split infinitive.

spoliation, not *spoil-* the state of being spoiled

spontaneous, spontaneity

spoonfuls, not *spoonsful* or *spoons full*

Spratly Islands, South China Sea

springbok an antelope

squeegee device for cleaning windows

Srebrenica, Bosnia and Herzegovina site of infamous massacre of 8,000 citizens by Serbian forces in 1995

Sri Lanka island state off India; formerly called Ceylon;

capital Colombo; but note the airline is **SriLankan** (one word) **Airlines**

SS abbr. of Schutzstaffel, infamous Nazi special police force

SSSI site of special scientific interest (UK)

staccato in music, with each note sharply detached from the others

Stakhanovite in the former Soviet Union, a worker held up to the nation as a paragon

stalactite, **stalagmite** Stalactites point downwards, stalagmites upwards.

stalemate is a permanent deadlock – one so intractable that no further action is possible. A chess match that reaches stalemate is not awaiting a more decisive outcome; the stalemate *is* the outcome. *Standoff, deadlock* or *impasse* are all better words if remedial action is still possible.

Stamford, **Stanford** Occasionally confused. *Stamford* is the name of notable communities in Lincolnshire and the state of Connecticut. *Stanford* is the university in Palo Alto, California. The intelligence test is the *Stanford-Binet test.*

stanchion an upright post forming a support

Stanislavsky system method of acting named for Konstantin Stanislavsky, a Russian drama teacher

Stansted Airport

staphylococcus a type of bacterium; pl. **staphylococci**

starboard the right-hand side of a ship when looking forward

Stasi short for Staatssicherheitsdienst, Ministry for State Security in East Germany before reunification

stationary, **stationery** The first means standing still, the second is writing paper and envelopes.

staunch (US **stanch**, for the verb only)

Stendhal (1783–1842), not -*dahl* pen name of Marie Henri Beyle, French writer

Sterne, Laurence (1713–68) English clergyman and writer

stethoscope

stevedore a dockworker

Stevens, Wallace (1879–1955) American poet

Stevenson, Adlai (1900–65) Democratic politician, ran unsuccessfully for President in 1952 and 1956

Stevenson, Robert Louis (1850–94) Scottish writer

Stieglitz, Alfred (1864–1946) American photographer

stiletto a spiky high heel or a knife; pl. **stilettos**

still life, pl. **still lifes**

stilton for the cheese, but **Stilton** for the English village where it originated

Stockhausen, Karlheinz (1928–2007) German composer

Stockton, Earl of title created for Harold Macmillan (1894–1986)

Stoke-on-Trent, Staffordshire

Stolichnaya brand of vodka

stony

Storey, David (1933–) English novelist and playwright, Booker prizewinner 1976

Storting Norwegian parliament

Stradivarius a violin or other stringed instrument made by Antonio Stradivari (c. 1645–1737)

straitjacket garment used to restrain a violent mental patient

straitlaced with a strict or prudish moral code

Stranraer, Dumfries and Galloway pronounced *stran-rar´*

Strasbourg, France in German, **Strassburg**

Strategic Defence Initiative (SDI) commonly called 'star wars'; plan propounded by President Ronald Reagan to erect a shield of space weapons over the US to stop incoming missiles

Stratford-on-Avon, Stratford-upon-Avon Most gazetteers and other reference sources give *Stratford-upon-Avon* as the correct name for the birthplace of William Shakespeare, but it is worth noting that the local authority calls itself Stratford-on-Avon District Council.

stratum, strata The plural form is sometimes used when the singular is intended, as in 'They dug into another strata and at last found what they were looking for.' A single level is a *stratum*. *Strata* signifies more than one.

Strauss, Johann, the Younger (1825–99) Austrian composer known for waltzes, polkas, marches and operettas. His father, **Johann Strauss the Elder** (1804–49), brothers **Eduard** (1835–1916) and **Josef** (1827–70) and son **Johann Strauss III** (1866–1939) were also composers. None of them should be confused with the next entry.

Strauss, Richard (1864–1949) German composer of operas and other musical works

Stravinsky, Igor (1882–1971) Russian-born American composer

Streep, Meryl (1951–) American actress

Streisand, Barbra (1942–) American singer and actress; not *-bara*

strewth Australian expletive

Strindberg, August (1849–1912) Swedish playwright and writer

Stroessner, Alfredo (1912–2006) President of Paraguay 1954–89

Stroganoff (cap.) strips of meat cooked in a sour-cream sauce

strived, **strove** Either is acceptable.

strychnine a kind of poison

Stuka (cap.) German dive bomber in the Second World War

stupefy   to stun; hence **stupefied**, **stupefaction**. Don't confuse the spelling with *stupid*.

Sturm und Drang (Ger.) storm and stress

Stuttgart, Germany

Stuyvesant, Peter (1592–1672) Dutch governor of New Netherlands (1646–64), which later became New York

stylus a hard point, a pen; pl. **styluses/styli**

stymie thwart or immobilize

Styrofoam is a trademark.

Styx the river flowing around Hades; adj. **Stygian**

submersible

suborn does not mean undermine, as is sometimes thought; it means to induce someone to commit a wrongful act.

subpoena a writ ordering a person to appear in court

sub rosa (Lat.) 'under the rose'; in secret

sub silentio (Lat.) in silence

substitute should be followed only by *for*. You substitute one thing for another. If you find yourself following the word with *by* or *with* or any other preposition, you should choose another verb.

subterranean

succès d'estime (Fr.) an undertaking that makes little or no profit but wins critical acclaim

succès fou (Fr.) a huge success, a smash hit

succubus a female evil spirit that has sexual relations with a man; a male spirit that has intercourse with a sleeping female is an **incubus**

Sucre official capital of Bolivia, although the seat of government is La Paz

Sudetenland   German-speaking area of Czechoslovakia annexed by Hitler in 1938

sudoku   Japanese number game. It is an abbreviation of *suuji wa dokushin ni kagiru*, 'the numbers must be single'.

Suetonius (Gaius Suetonius Tranquillus) (c. 70–c. 160) Roman historian and biographer

suggestible   easily

sui generis (Lat.) in a class of its own

suing, not *sueing*

sukiyaki   Japanese dish

Suleiman I (c. 1490–1566) called 'the Magnificent'; Sultan of the Ottoman Empire 1520–66

Sullavan, Margaret (1911–60) Hollywood actress; not *Sulli-*

Sully Prudhomme   pen name of René François Armand Prudhomme (1839–1907), French poet; awarded Nobel Prize for Literature 1901

sulphur (US **sulfur**)

Sulzberger, Arthur Ochs (1926–)   American newspaper publisher

Sunni   branch of Islam

SunTrust Banks   US banking group; note *SunTrust* one word, *Banks* plural

Sun Yat-sen (1866–1925)   Chinese statesman and revolutionary

Suomen Tasavalta   Finnish for 'Republic of Finland'

supersede   is one of the most frequently misspelled words. Note the final syllable is *-sede*, not *-cede*.

Surayud Chulanont, General (1943–)   Prime Minister of Thailand 2006– ; on second reference he is General Surayud

Suriname, Surinam   Confusion still sometimes arises concerning the name of this small South American country.

The spelling *Surinam* can now safely be regarded as historic and *Suriname* as the preferred modern spelling. The Suriname River and Suriname toad also take the modern spellings. Suriname was formerly Dutch Guiana.

surreptitious clandestine

surrounded means completely encircled. To say that something is 'surrounded on three sides' is a poor use of the word.

surveillance close observation

survivor, not -*er*

susceptible easily affected

Susquehanna River in the eastern US

Sussex former English county, now divided into East Sussex and West Sussex

sustenance nourishment, support

susurrate whisper

suttee Hindu practice of widow throwing herself on her husband's funeral pyre

Suu Kyi, Aung San (1945–) Burmese political activist, awarded Nobel Peace Prize 1991

Suva capital of Fiji

Suvarnabhumi Airport, Bangkok

Suwannee River southern US; immortalized in songs as the Swanee

Sverige Swedish for Sweden

Swayze, Patrick (1952–) American actor

Sweet 'N Low sugar substitute

Swinburne, Algernon Charles (1837–1909) English poet

Swissair (one word) former Swiss airline

Swithin's (or **Swithun's**) **Day, St** 15 July; according to legend, rain on that day will be followed by 40 days of the same

sycamore tree

Sydney, New South Wales

sylvan (or **silvan**) wooded

syllabub (or **sillabub**) type of dessert

symbiosis a relationship that benefits both parties; adj. **symbiotic**

Synge, J. M. (for **John Millington**) (1871–1909) Irish playwright

synonym a word with the same meaning as another in the same language

syphilis, not -*ll*-

syphon is acceptable, but **siphon** is generally preferred.

Szczecin, Poland formerly Stettin

Szechwan/Szechuan former spellings for the Chinese province that is now spelled **Sichuan**; the cuisine of the region, however, remains known in English by either of the earlier spellings

Szilard, Leo (1898–1964) Hungarian-born American physicist

Szymborska, Wislawa (1923–) Polish author; awarded Nobel Prize for Literature 1996

T

tableau, pl. **tableaux**

table d'hôte set meal at a fixed price

tablespoonfuls

tabula rasa (Lat.) a blank slate, the mind at birth

tachycardia abnormally fast heartbeat

taffeta fabric

tagliatelle type of pasta

Taipei capital of Taiwan

Taittinger champagne

Taiwan formerly Formosa; officially the Republic of China, though that title is seldom used outside Taiwan itself

Tajik for the language, **Tajikistani** for something that is from or of Tajikistan

Taj Mahal celebrated mausoleum at Agra, India

Takashimaya Company Limited leading Japanese retail group

Takeshita, Noburu (1924–2000) Japanese Prime Minister 1987–9

Taklimakan Chinese desert

Tale of a Tub, A (not *The*) satire by Jonathan Swift (1704)

Tales of Hoffmann, The opera by Jacques Offenbach (1881)

Taliban (or **Taleban**) Sunni Muslim insurgent force in Afghanistan

Tallahassee capital of Florida

Tallahatchie river in Mississippi

Tallinn capital of Estonia

Talmud sacred Hebrew writings, the main body of laws for Judaism, comprising two parts: the Mishna, containing the laws themselves, and the Germara, containing later commentaries and elaborations

Tamaulipas, Mexico

tambourine percussion instrument

Tamburlaine the Great play by Christopher Marlowe (1587–8); the Mongol conqueror himself is now usually spelled **Tamerlane** (1336–1405)

tameable

Tammany Hall fraternal society of the Democratic Party in New York

tam-o'-shanter Scottish cap, named after the hero in the Burns poem 'Tam o'Shanter'

T'ang (or **Tang**) Chinese dynasty, ruled 618–907

Tanguy, Yves (1900–55) French-born American painter

Tantalus in Greek mythology, a son of Zeus for whom food and drink forever move out of reach whenever he tries to attain them

tantamount almost equivalent to

Tanzania African nation formed by the merger of Tanganyika and Zanzibar in 1964; capital Dodoma

Taoiseach the Prime Minister of Ireland; pronounced *tea´shuck*

taradiddle (or **tarradiddle**) nonsense

tarantella southern Italian dance; not to be confused with *tarantula*, the type of spider

Tar Heels (two words) people and things associated with North Carolina, and the sporting teams of the University of North Carolina

tariff

tarpaulin

tartar, **tartare**, **Tatar** The first is dental plaque or a violent, intractable person, the second is a sauce and the third a member of a Turkic-speaking people in central Asia.

Tartuffe play by Molière (1664)

Tashkent capital of Uzbekistan

TASS short for Telegrafnoye Agenstvo Sovyetskovo Soyuza; Soviet news agency; now called ITAR-TASS News Agency

Tate Gallery The London art museum now consists of four separate branches: Tate Britain and Tate Modern in London, and Tate Liverpool and Tate St Ives in the provinces.

tattoo

Taufa'ahau Tupou IV (1918–2006) King of Tonga 1965–2006

tautology, **redundancy**, **pleonasm**, **solecism** Although various authorities describe various shades of distinction between the first three words, those distinctions are generally slight and frequently contradictory. Essentially all three mean using more words than necessary to convey an idea. Not all repetition is inexcusable. It may be used for effect, as in poetry, or for clarity, or in deference to idiom. 'Opec countries', 'SALT talks' and 'HIV virus' are all technically redundant because the second word is already contained in the preceding abbreviation, but only the ultra-finicky would deplore them. Similarly in 'wipe that smile off your face' the last two words are tautological – there is no other place a smile could be – but the sentence would not stand without them. Finally, *solecism* describes any violation of idiom or grammar. Redundancies, tautologies and pleonasms are all solecisms.

taxiing the act of moving a plane into position
taxonomy the science of classification of organisms
Tay-Sachs disease genetic disorder that affects the nervous system
Tbilisi formerly Tiflis; capital of Georgia
Tchaikovsky, Peter Illich (1840–93) Russian composer
Teamsters, International Brotherhood of US trade union
Teatro alla Scala formal name of the Milan opera house commonly called *La Scala*
Tebbit, Norman (1931–) British Conservative politician; now Lord Tebbit
techie a technology expert
Technicolor (cap.)
tectonics, not *tech-* study of the structure and movement of the Earth's crust
Te Deum Latin hymn
tee-hee the sound of laughter
Teesside
teetotaller (US **teetotaler**)
Tegucigalpa capital of Honduras
Tehachapi Mountains, California
Tehran capital of Iran
Tehuntepec, Isthmus of narrowest part of Mexico
Teignmouth, Devon pronounced *tin´-muth*
Teilhard de Chardin, Pierre (1881–1955) French scientist, priest and philosopher
Telefónica Spanish telecommunications company
Telemachus in Greek mythology, the son of Odysseus and Penelope
Telstar early communications satellite (launched 1962)
temblor, not *trem-* an earthquake
temporary respite is redundant; all respites are temporary.

tempus fugit (Lat.) time flies
tendentious biased
Tenerife, Canary Islands
Tennyson, Alfred, Lord (1809–92) English poet; Poet Laureate 1850–92
Tenochtitlán Aztec capital on site of modern Mexico City
Teotihuacán site of ancient Mexican city
tepee, not *tee-* Native American tent
tequila
tera- prefix meaning 1 trillion
Terence Publius Terentius Afer (c. 190–159 BC), Roman comedy writer
teriyaki Japanese marinated meat dish
terminus, pl. **termini/terminuses**
terracotta
terra firma dry land
terra incognita (Lat.) unknown territory
terrazzo stone flooring material
terrine an earthenware dish and the food, especially pâté, prepared in it
Tesla, Nikola (1857–1943) Croatian-American scientist and inventor
Tess of the D'Urbervilles novel by Thomas Hardy (1891)
tetchy touchy, ill-tempered
tête-à-tête
Tevere Italian name for the river Tiber
Tewkesbury, Gloucestershire, but **Tewksbury,** Massachusetts
TGV *Train à Grande Vitesse,* high-speed French train
Thackeray, William Makepeace (1811–63) English novelist
thalassic pertaining to the sea
thalassocracy dominance of the seas

than Three small but common problems need noting.

1. In comparative constructions *than* is often wrongly used, as here: 'Nearly twice as many people die under 20 in France than in Great Britain' (cited by Gowers). Make it 'as in Great Britain'.

2. *Than* is wrongly used after *hardly* in sentences such as this: 'Hardly had I landed at Liverpool than the Mikado's death recalled me to Japan' (cited by Fowler). Make it 'No sooner had I landed than' or 'Hardly had I landed when'.

3. It is often a source of ambiguity in sentences of the following type: 'She likes tennis more than me.' Does this mean that she likes tennis more than I do or that she likes tennis more than she likes me? In such cases, it is better to supply a second verb if it avoids ambiguity, e.g., 'She likes tennis more than she likes me' or 'She likes tennis more than I do.'

Thanksgiving Day fourth Thursday in November in the United States, second Monday in October in Canada

that (as a conjunction) Whether you say 'I think you are wrong' or 'I think that you are wrong' is partly a matter of idiom but mostly a matter of preference. Some words usually require *that* (*assert, contend, maintain*) and some usually do not (*say, think*), but there are no hard rules. On the whole, it is better to dispense with *that* when it isn't necessary.

that, which To understand the distinctions between *that* and *which* it is necessary to understand restrictive and non-restrictive clauses. A non-restrictive or non-defining clause is one that can be regarded as parenthetical: 'The tree, *which had no leaves*, was a birch.' The italicized words are effectively an aside and could be deleted. The real point of the sentence is that the tree was a birch; its leaflessness is incidental. A restrictive, defining clause is one that is essential to the sense of the sentence. 'The tree *that had no leaves* was a birch.' Here the leaflessness is a defining characteristic; it helps us to distinguish that tree from other trees. In correct usage *that* is always used to indicate restrictive clauses and *which* to indicate non-restrictive ones. Restrictive clauses should never be set off with commas and non-restrictive clauses always should.

'Their's not to reason why,/Their's but to do and die' are the correct lines, and original (but incorrect then too) punctuation, from Tennyson's 'Charge of the Light Brigade' (1854).

Theophrastus (c. 372–286 BC) Greek philosopher

therapeutic

Thermopylae a pass in Greece between the mountains and the sea, used throughout history as an invasion route; site of a famous battle in 480 BC

thesaurus a book listing words in groups of synonyms; pl. **thesauri/thesauruses**

thesis, pl. **theses**

Theron, Charlize (1975–) South African-born actress

Thimphu capital of Bhutan

thinking to oneself, as in 'I thought to myself: "We're lost," ' is always tautological; there is no one else to whom one can think. Delete 'to myself'. Similarly vacuous is 'in my mind' in constructions like 'I could picture in my mind where the offices had been.'

thingummy, thingamabob, thingamajig, etc.

thinness, thinnest

Third World (caps)

Thirty Years/Years' War (1618–48) war between Catholic

and Protestant factions fought principally in Germany

Thomas, Dylan (1914–53) Welsh poet

thorax, pl. **thoraces/thoraxes**

Thoreau, Henry David (1817–62) American naturalist, poet and writer

Thornburgh, Dick (1932–) US Republican politician, Governor of Pennsylvania 1979–87 and US Attorney General 1988–91

Thorndike, Dame Sybil (1882–1976) English actress

thorny, not -*ey*

Thorvaldsen, Albert Bertel (1770–1844) Danish sculptor of statues on an epic scale

though, although The two are interchangeable except at the end of a sentence, where only *though* is correct ('He looked tired, though'), and with the expressions *as though* and *even though*, where idiom precludes *although*.

Thousand and One Nights, The, or ***The Arabian Nights***

Threadneedle Street, Old Lady of nickname for the Bank of England

Three Mile Island nuclear power station, Harrisburg, Pennsylvania

threshold

thrived/throve Either is acceptable, but most authorities prefer the latter.

Through the Looking-Glass and What Alice Found There is the full, formal title of the 1871 Lewis Carroll classic. Note the hyphen in *Looking-Glass*.

Thruway (US) is the correct official spelling in many highway contexts (New York State Thruway Authority, Governor Thomas E. Dewey Thruway).

Thucydides (c. 460–c. 400 BC) Greek historian of the Peloponnesian War

Tiananmen Square, Beijing

Tibullus, Albius (c. 54–19 BC) Roman elegiac poet

tic douloureux disorder of the facial nerves. Its formal medical designation is trigeminal neuralgia.

tickety-boo

tiddlywinks

Tiepolo, Giovanni Battista (1696–1770) Italian artist

Tierra del Fuego South American archipelago

Tiffany, Charles Lewis (1812–1902) American jeweller and founder of the famous New York jewellery store; father of **Louis Comfort Tiffany** (1848–1933), American designer, known for design and production of Tiffany glass and Tiffany lamps

Tigonankweine Range mountains in western Canada

tilde pronounced *till'-duh*; the mark (~) used in Spanish to denote the sound *ny*, as in *señor* or *cañon*

Tilden, Bill (1893–1933) American tennis player, three times world champion

timber, timbre The first is wood; the second refers to sound.

Timbuktu small city in Mali; the name is used to signify any very remote place

time often has a curious magnetic effect, attracting extra words to sentences, as in: 'The property was occupied for a short length of time.' Make it 'for a short time'. Occasionally, *time* itself is superfluous, as in constructions of this sort: 'The report will be available in two weeks' time.' *Time* adds nothing to the sentence but wordiness.

time, at this moment in Unless you are striving for an air of linguistic ineptitude, never use this expression. Say *now*.

Timor Leste Asian republic, capital Dili

tin lizzie a Model T Ford, not any old car

tinnitus persistent ringing in the ears

Tin Pan Alley district of Manhattan where music publishers once congregated

tinsel

tintinnabulation ringing sound of bells

Tintoretto (1518–94) Italian artist; real name Jacopo Robusti

Tipperary town and county in the Republic of Ireland

tipsy, not -*ey* mildly intoxicated

tiramisu Italian dessert

Tirol German for **Tyrol**, region of Austria

'Tis Pity She's a Whore, not *a Pity* play by John Ford (1633)

Titian (c. 1490–1576) Italian painter; in Italian, Tiziano Vecellio

titillate to excite, especially sexually

titivate to smarten up

Tito, Marshal (1892–1980) born Josip Broz; Prime Minister of Yugoslavia 1945–53, President 1953–80

TLS *The Times Literary Supplement*

tmesis interposing a word between the syllables of another, as in *abso-bloody-lutely*

TNT a well-known explosive. The initials are short for trinitrotoluene.

to all intents and purposes is unnecessarily wordy. 'To all intents' is enough.

toboggan

toby jug (no caps)

Tocqueville, Alexis (Charles Henri Maurice Clérel) de (1805–59) French politician and historian

together with, along with *With* in both expressions is a preposition, not a conjunction, and therefore does not govern the verb. This sentence is wrong: 'They said the man, a motor mechanic, together with a 22-year-old arrested a day earlier, were being questioned' (*The*

Times). Make it 'was being questioned'.

Togolese of or from Togo

Tojo, Hideki (1884–1948) Japanese Prime Minister 1941–4, executed as war criminal

Tolkien, J. R. R. (for **John Ronald Reuel**) (1892–1973) English philologist and author of fantasies

Tolstoy, Count Leo (1828–1910) Russian novelist

tomato, pl. **tomatoes**

tomorrow

Toms River, New Jersey

ton, tonne There are two kinds of ton: a long ton (used principally in the UK), weighing 2,240lb/1,016kg, and a short ton (used in the US and Canada) weighing 2,000lb/907kg. A *tonne* is the British term for what in America is normally called a metric ton; it weighs 2,204lb/1,000kg.

tonnages of ships *Deadweight tonnage* is the amount of cargo a ship can carry. *Displacement tonnage* is the weight of the ship itself. *Gross tonnage* measures the theoretical capacity of a ship based on its dimensions. When using any of these terms, it is only fair to give the reader some idea of what each signifies.

tonsillitis

Tontons Macoute civilian militia in Haiti; supporters of the Duvalier regimes

Tony Awards US theatrical awards named for the actress and producer Antoinette Perry. They have been awarded since 1947; pl. **Tonys**

topsy-turvy

Torino Italian for Turin

tormentor, not -*er*

tornadoes

Torquemada, Tomás de (1420–98)   Spanish monk who
organized the Inquisition

torsos

tortuous, torturous *Tortuous* means winding and circuitous
('The road wound tortuously through the mountains').
When used figuratively it usually suggests deviousness
('a tortuous tax-avoidance scheme'). The word is thus
better avoided if all you mean is complicated or
convoluted. *Torturous* is the adjectival form of *torture*
and describes the infliction of extreme pain.

Torvill, Jayne (1957–) British figure skater, generally in part-
nership with **Christopher Dean** (1958–   )

Toscanini, Arturo (1867–1957) Italian conductor

total Three points to note:

1. *Total* is redundant and should be deleted when
what it is qualifying already contains the idea of a totality, as here: '[They] risk total annihilation at the hands
of the massive Israeli forces now poised to strike at the
gates of the city.'

2. The expression *a total of*, though common, is also
generally superfluous: 'County officials said a total of 84
prisoners were housed in six cells.' Make it 'officials said
84 prisoners'. An exception is at the start of sentences
when it is desirable to avoid spelling out a large number,
as in 'A total of 2,112 sailors were aboard' instead of 'Two
thousand one hundred and twelve sailors were aboard.'

3. 'A total of 45 weeks was spent on the study' is wrong.
As with 'a number of' and 'the number of', the rule is to
make it 'the total of . . . was', but 'a total of . . . were'.

totalled, totalling (US **totaled, totaling**)

to the tune of A hackneyed circumlocution. 'The company is
being subsidized to the tune of $500 million a year'

would be more succinct as 'The company receives a subsidy of $500 million a year.'

Toulouse-Lautrec, Henri de (1864–1901) French painter; full name Henri Marie Raymond de Toulouse-Lautrec-Monfa

toupee (no accent)

Tourette syndrome (pref.), **Tourette's syndrome** (alt.) neurological disorder named for the French physician Georges Gilles de la Tourette (1859–1904)

Tournai, Belgium, but **Tournay**, France

tournedos (sing. and pl.) choice cut or cuts of beef

tout à l'heure (Fr.) soon, just now, a moment ago

tout de suite (Fr.) immediately

tout le monde (Fr.) everybody

tovarich/tovarish Either is acceptable for the Russian word for comrade. In Russian, *tovarishch*

toward, towards The first is the preferred form in America, the second in Britain, but either is correct. *Untoward* ('inconvenient'), however, is the only accepted form in both.

toxaemia (US **toxemia**) blood poisoning

traceable

tradable (or **tradeable**)

trademark/trade name A *trademark* is a name, symbol or other depiction that formally identifies a product. A *trade name* is the name of the maker, not of the product. Cadillac is a trademark, General Motors a trade name.

Tralee, Ireland

tranquillity, tranquillize, tranquillizer (US **tranquility, tranquilize, tranquilizer**)

transatlantic Most dictionaries and style guides (but by no means all) prefer *transatlantic* to *trans-Atlantic*.

Similarly, *transalpine, transarctic, transpacific*

Transdniestra breakaway part of Moldova

trans fat (two words) a type of unsaturated fat

transgressor, not *-er*

transitive verb In grammar, a verb that takes a direct object.

translucent is sometimes wrongly treated as a synonym for *transparent*. A *translucent* material is one through which light passes but through which images cannot be clearly seen, as with frosted glass. Note also the spelling; it is not *-scent*.

transsexual, transvestite The first is a person born into one sex who feels he or she really belongs in the other; the second a person who dresses in the clothes of the opposite sex.

transship, transshipment

Trappist monk

trattoria Italian restaurant; pl. **trattorie**

Traviata, La opera by Giuseppe Verdi (1853)

treble, triple There is no fixed distinction between the two. *Treble* is established in the UK in certain expressions (*treble chance, treble a stake*), but is seldom encountered in the US.

trek, trekked

Trentino-Alto Adige region of Italy

TriBeCa short for Triangle Below Canal Street, New York

Triborough Bridge, New York

Trinidad and Tobago Caribbean republic; capital Port-of-Spain. Natives are Trinidadians or Tobagonians, depending on which island they come from.

Trintignant, Jean-Louis (1930–) French actor

triptych painting on three panels hinged together

trireme ancient Greek ship with three banks of oars

triskaidekaphobia fear of the number 13

Tristan da Cunha British island colony in the South Atlantic

Tristram Shandy, Gentleman, The Life and Opinions of novel by Laurence Sterne (1760–7)

trivia is, strictly speaking, a plural, and a few dictionaries recognize it only as such. 'All this daily trivia is getting on my nerves' should be 'All these daily trivia are getting on my nerves.' There is no singular form (the Latin *trivium* now has only historical applications), but there are the singular words *trifle* and *triviality*. The other option, if the plural form seems ungainly, is to convert *trivia* into an adjective: 'All these trivial daily matters are getting on my nerves.'

troglodyte cave dweller

troika a group of three

Troilus and Cressida play by Shakespeare (c. 1601). The poem by Geoffrey Chaucer is '**Troylus and Criseyde**'. In Boccaccio's *Il Filostrato* the spelling is **Criseida**.

Trollope, Anthony (1815–52) English novelist, son of **Frances Trollope** (1780–1863), novelist and travel writer

trompe-l'oeil (Fr.) 'deceive-the-eye'; painting designed to deceive the viewer into thinking that the object depicted is not painted but real; pronounced *tromp loy*

Trooping the Colour The annual event celebrating the Queen's official birthday in June (as opposed to her actual birthday in April) is not *the Trooping of the Colour*, as it is often written, even in Britain, but just *Trooping the Colour*.

troubadour a medieval French lyric poet

trousseau, pl. **trousseaus/trousseaux**

Trovatore, Il opera by Giuseppe Verdi (1853)

Trudeau, Garry (1948–)   American cartoonist, creator of *Doonesbury*

Trudeau, Pierre (**Elliott**) (1919–2000)   Prime Minister of Canada 1968–79, 1980–4

true facts is always either redundant or wrong. All facts are true. Things that are not true are not facts.

Truffaut, François (1932–84) French film director

Truman, Harry S. (1884–1972) Democratic politician, US President 1945–53. The S stands for nothing as Truman had no middle name, and for that reason some authorities spell it without a full stop.

try and, as in constructions such as 'We'll try and come back next week,' is regarded as colloquial by many authorities and thus is better avoided in serious writing. Use 'try to' instead.

tsetse fly pronounced *tetsi*

tsunami

Tsvangirai, Morgan (1952–)   opposition leader in Zimbabwe, president of Movement for Democratic Change

TUC Trades Union Congress (UK)

Tuckahoe, New York

Tucson, Arizona pronounced *too´-sun*

Tuileries, the, Paris

Tumucumaque, Serra de mountain range in northern Brazil

tumult, turmoil Both describe confusion and agitation. The difference is that *tumult* applies only to people, but *turmoil* applies to both people and things. *Tumultuous*, however, can also describe things as well as people ('tumultuous applause', 'tumultuous seas').

turbid, turgid The first means muddy or impenetrable; the second means inflated, grandiloquent, bombastic.

Turkmenistan former republic of the Soviet Union, now an
independent state; capital Ashgabat (or Ashkhabad)

Turner Prize annual award for contemporary art

turpitude does not signify rectitude or integrity, as is sometimes thought, but rather baseness or depravity. 'He is a
man of great moral turpitude' is not a compliment.

turquoise

Tuskegee, Alabama home of **Tuskegee University** (formerly
Tuskegee Institute)

Tussaud's, Madame London waxworks museum

Tutankhamun (or **Tutankhamen**) (c. 1359–c. 1340 BC)
Egyptian pharaoh

tutti-frutti

TWA Trans World Airlines (no hyphens), former American
airline

Twain, Mark pen name of Samuel Langhorne Clemens
(1835–1910), American author

Tylers' and Bricklayers' Company London livery company;
not *Tilers'*

Tymoshenko, Yulia (1960–) Prime Minister of Ukraine 2005

Tyndale (or **Tindale**), **William** (c. 1494–1536) English
biblical scholar

tyrannosaur any dinosaur of the genus *Tyrannosaurus*. The
largest tyrannosaur was *Tyrannosaurus rex*.

tyrannous

Tyrol region of Austria and Italy; not *the Tyrol*; in German,
Tirol; in Italian, **Tirolo**

tyro, tiro a novice; pl. **tyros, tiros**

Tyrrhenian Sea stretch of the Mediterranean between Italy,
Corsica, Sardinia and Sicily

Tyus, Wyomia (1945–) American sprinter

U

U a Burmese honorific, roughly equivalent to Mr

UAE United Arab Emirates

UAL United Airlines (US)

UAR United Arab Republic, title used by Egypt and Syria together from 1958 to 1961, and by Egypt alone from 1961 to 1971

Übermensch (Ger.) superman

ubiquitous found everywhere; **ubiquity**

U-boat short for *Unterseeboot*, German term for submarine

UBS PaineWebber Inc. investment company

Uccellina National Park, Tuscany

Uccello, Paolo (1397–1475) born Paolo di Dono; Italian painter

UCLA University of California at Los Angeles

UDI unilateral declaration of independence

Udmurtiya Russian republic

UDR Ulster Defence Regiment

UEFA Union of European Football Associations

Ueno Park station and district, Tokyo

Uffizi Gallery, Florence in Italian, Galleria degli Uffizi

UHF ultra high frequency

UHT ultra heat tested (not *ultra high temperature*), process for long-life milk products *uisge beatha* Gaelic for whisky

UKAEA United Kingdom Atomic Energy Authority

ukase an edict

Ukraine former republic of Soviet Union, now an independent state, capital Kiev

ukulele stringed instrument. Not *uke-*

Ulaanbaatar (or **Ulan Bator**) capital of Mongolia

Ullmann, Liv (1939–) Norwegian actress

Ullswater, Cumbria

ulna the larger bone in the forearm; pl. **ulnas/ulnae**

Ulster province of Ireland, not coextensive with Northern Ireland; three counties are in the Republic of Ireland

ultimatums

ululate to howl or hoot

Uluru is the formal, and generally preferred, name for Ayers Rock in Australia. Pronounced *oo-luh-roo*. It is part of Uluru-Kata Tjuta National Park. The resort alongside it is Yulara.

Ulysses/Odysseus Two names for the same person: a leader of the Greeks in the Trojan war. The first is Latin, the second Greek.

Umayyad Dynasty rulers of a Muslim empire from 661 to 750

umbilicus the umbilical cord

unadulterated pure, with nothing added

un-American, **un-French**, etc

unanimous, unanimity

una voce (Lat.) with one voice, unanimously

unbiased

unbribable

unchristian, but **non-Christian**

UNCTAD United Nations Conference on (not *for*) Trade and

Development, agency set up in 1964 with the purpose of smoothing trade differences between nations and promoting economic development

unctuous oily

underdog (one word)

Underground (cap.)   London underground railway, the Tube

Under Milk Wood (three words) Dylan Thomas play (1954)

under way (two words)

un-English, **un-British**, etc.

UNESCO   United Nations Educational, Scientific and Cultural Organization

unexceptionable, **unexceptional**   Something that is *unexceptional* is ordinary, not outstanding ('an unexceptional wine'). Something that is *unexceptionable* is not open to objections ('In Britain, *grey* is the preferred spelling, but *gray* is unexceptionable').

Ungaretti, Giuseppe (1888–1970) Italian poet

unget-at-able Note 'unget' is one word.

unguent soothing cream or lotion

UNHCR Office of the United Nations High Commissioner for Refugees

unicameral legislature a legislature having just one chamber

UNICEF United Nations Children's Fund (formerly United Nations International Children's Emergency Fund)

UNIDO   United Nations Industrial Development Organization

unilateral, **bilateral**, **multilateral** are slightly numbing words and are often unneeded anyway, as in 'Bilateral trade talks are to take place next week between Britain and Japan.' Trade talks between Britain and Japan could hardly be other than two-sided. More often than not, the context makes clear how much laterality is involved.

uninterested, disinterested The first means not caring; the second means neutral.

Union of Soviet Socialist Republics abbr. USSR; in Russian, Soyuz Sovyetskikh Sotsialisticheskikh Respublik; ceased to exist in 1991; see also SOVIET UNION

unique means the only one of its kind. A thing cannot be 'more unique' or 'one of the most unique'.

unison all together

UNISON British trade union

Unisys US computer company

United Airlines, not *Air Lines* abbr. UAL

United Arab Emirates formerly the Trucial States; composed of Abu Dhabi, Ajman, Dubai, Fujaira, Ras al Khaima, Sharja and Umm al Qaiwain

United Arab Republic abbr. UAR; title used by Egypt and Syria together 1958–61, and by Egypt alone 1961–71

UnitedHealth Group American health services company

United Kingdom formally, the United Kingdom of Great Britain and Northern Ireland; comprising England, Scotland, Wales and Northern Ireland

University College London (no comma) abbr. UCL

unknown is often used imprecisely, as here: 'A hitherto unknown company called Ashdown Oil has emerged as a bidder for the Wytch Farm oil interests.' A company must be known to someone, if only its directors. It would be better to call it a little-known company.

unlabelled (US **unlabeled**)

unless and until One or the other, please.

unlicensed

unmanageable

unmistakable

unmovable

unnameable

unnatural Note -*nn*-.

unnecessary Note -*nn*-.

unnerved Note -*nn*-.

unnumbered Note -*nn*-.

unparalleled

unpractical/impractical The words are synonyms.

unravelled (US **unraveled**)

unrideable (pref.), **unridable** (alt.)

UNRRA United Nations Relief and Rehabilitation Administration

unselfconscious

unshakeable (pref.), **unshakable** (alt.)

Unsworth, Barry (1930–) British novelist, Booker joint prizewinner 1992

until, till, 'til, 'till The first two are legitimate and interchangeable. The second two are wrong and, indeed, illiterate.

untimely death is often somewhat fatuous; few deaths are timely.

ununbiium, ununhexium, unnunnilium, ununquadium, uniununium chemical elements all discovered or first produced between 1994 and 2000

unwieldy

up-and-coming (hyphens)

Upanishads ancient Hindu metaphysical treatises

UPI United Press International

Upper Volta former name of Burkina Faso

Uppsala, Sweden

upsilon, not -*ll*- twentieth letter of the Greek alphabet

upsy-daisy or **ups-a-daisy**

uraemia (US **uremia**) toxic blood condition associated with
    kidney failure
Urdang, Laurence (1927–) American lexicographer
urethra urinary duct; pl. **urethrae** or **urethras**
Uriah Heep character in Dickens's *David Copperfield*
Uribe, Álvaro (1952–) President of Colombia 2002–
URL abbr. of Uniform Resource Locator, technospeak for a
    web address on the internet
Urquhart Scottish family name; pronounced *erk´-ert*
Ursa Major, **Ursa Minor** constellations meaning respectively
    Big Bear and Little Bear
ursine like or of a bear
Ursuline order of nuns
Uruguay South American republic; capital Montevideo
USAF United States Air Force
usage, **use** The words are largely interchangeable. In general,
    usage appears in contexts involving languages ('modern
    English usage') and *use* in most other cases.
US Airways formerly USAir
USB short for Universal Serial Bus, a computer bus standard
US Bancorp American banking group
use, **usage** *Usage* normally appears only in the context of
    formal practices, particularly in regard to linguistics
    ('modern English usage'), and *use* does duty for all other
    senses, but most dictionaries recognize the words as
    interchangeable in nearly all contexts. See also UTILIZE.
USP unique selling point
USSR See UNION OF SOVIET SOCIALIST REPUBLICS.
usufruct the right to use another's property so long as no
    damage is done, as with walking on a path across
    farmland
usury the practice of lending money at a grossly inflated rate

of interest; the adjectival form is **usurious**

Uther Pendragon legendary father of King Arthur

utilize, use *Utilize* is the preferred term for making use of something in a task for which it wasn't intended ('He utilized a coat hanger to repair the car') or for extracting maximum value ('The farmers utilized every square inch of the hillside'). In other senses *use* is generally better.

Utrillo, Maurice (1883–1955) French artist

Utsunomiya, Honshu, Japan

Uttar Pradesh Indian state; capital Lucknow

utterance

Utzon, Jørn (1918–) Danish architect, best known for designing Sydney Opera House

uvula the piece of flesh hanging at the back of the mouth above the throat

uxoricide the murder of a wife by her husband, and the man who commits such a crime

Uzbekistan former Soviet republic, now an independent country; capital Tashkent

V

vacillate waver

vade-mecum (Lat.) 'go with me'; a handbook carried on the person for constant use

vagary an inexplicable change; pl. **vagaries**

vagrant, **vagrancy**

Vaishnava Hindu devotee of Vishnu

Vajpayee, Atal Bihari (1924–) Prime Minister of India 1996, 1998–2004

valance, **valence** The first is a short curtain, the second a term from chemistry to describe molecular bonding.

Val-d'Isère ski resort in French Alps

valediction a farewell speech; adj. **valedictory**

Valenciennes lace

Valera, Éamon de (1882–1975) US-born Prime Minister of Ireland 1919–21, 1932–48, 1957–9, and President 1959–73

valetudinarian a person, particularly an invalid, obsessed with his or her health

Valhalla in Norse mythology, a great hall of slain warriors

valiant

Valium (cap.) brand of tranquillizer

Valkyrie in Norse mythology, one of the 12 handmaidens of Odin

Valladolid province and city in Castile, Spain

Valle d'Aosta region of Italy

Valletta capital of Malta

vamoose to flee or leave hurriedly

Van Alen, William (1883–1954) American architect, designed the Chrysler Building, New York; note unusual spelling of Alen

Vanbrugh, Sir John (1664–1726) English architect and playwright

Van Buren, Martin (1782–1862) US President 1837–41

Van de Graaf, Robert J. (for **Jemison**) (1901–67) American physicist and inventor of the Van de Graaf accelerator

van der Post, Sir Laurens (1906–96) South African writer and explorer

Vandross, Luther (1951–2005) American entertainer

Van Dyck (or **Vandyke**), **Sir Anthony** (1599–1641), was born Anton Van Dijck, but that spelling is almost never encountered outside his native Belgium. In America his name is usually rendered as *Sir Anthony Vandyke*, though *Van Dyck* (the spelling favoured in Britain) is also sometimes found. In both countries, objects associated with him are spelled *Vandyke* – e.g., a *Vandyke beard*, *Vandyke brown*, a *Vandyke collar*.

Vänern largest lake in Sweden

van Eyck, Jan (c. 1380–1440) Flemish painter

van Gogh, Vincent (1853–90) Dutch painter

Vanuatu island republic in the South Pacific, formerly the New Hebrides; capital Port-Vila (or Port Vila, without hyphen)

vaquero Spanish for cowboy

Vargas, Getulio Dornelles (1883–1954) President of Brazil 1930–45, 1951–4

varicella medical name for chickenpox
varicose veins
variegated
various different is inescapably repetitive.
VDU visual display unit, a computer screen
Veblen, Thorstein (1857–1929) American economist
Vecchio, Palazzo, Florence The famous bridge across the Arno is the **Ponte Vecchio**.
VE Day (or **V-E Day**) 8 May 1945, date of Allied victory in Europe in the Second World War
veins, but **venous**
Velázquez (or **Velásquez**), **Diego Rodriguez de Silva y** (1599–1660) Spanish painter
veld (pref.), **veldt** (alt.) grassland
vellum the finest type of parchment
venal, **venial** *Venial*, from the Latin *venialis* ('forgivable'), means excusable; a venial sin is a minor one. *Venal* means corruptible. It comes from the Latin *venalis* ('for sale') and describes someone who is capable of being bought.
vendetta
vendible saleable
veneer
venerable
venerate, **worship** Although in figurative senses the words are interchangeable, in religious contexts *worship* should apply only to God. Roman Catholics, for instance, worship God but venerate saints.
Venezuela South American republic, capital Caracas
vengeance
Veni, vidi, vici (Lat.) 'I came, I saw, I conquered'; attributed to Julius Caesar by Suetonius

venomous

venous pertaining to veins

ventilator

ventre à terre (Fr.) 'belly to the ground'; full out, at top speed

ventricles for the heart valves, not *ventricals*

Venus flytrap (no apos.) carnivorous plant

veranda is the preferred spelling, but **verandah** is acceptable.

verbal agreement, because it can mean either a written or a spoken agreement, can be ambiguous. Where the manner of agreeing is important, it is generally better to describe it as an oral or a written agreement.

verbatim in exactly the same words

verboten (Ger.) forbidden

verdant green

Verdi, Giuseppe (1813–1901) Italian opera composer

verdigris green rust on copper or brass

verisimilitude air of truth, the quality of being realistic

Vermeer, Jan (1632–96) Dutch painter

Vermeille, Côte, France

vermicelli type of pasta

vermilion (one *l*) for the colour, but **Vermillion** (two *l*s) for the towns in Kansas and South Dakota

vermouth

vernal pertaining to the spring, as in *vernal equinox*

Veronese, Paolo (1528–88) Italian painter, born Paolo Cagliari

Verrazano-Narrows Bridge, New York City

Verrocchio, Andrea del (1436–88) Italian painter and sculptor

Versailles palace near Paris

vertebra, pl. **vertebrae**

Verwoerd, Hendrik (1901–66) Dutch-born South African

Prime Minister 1958–66

very should be made to pay its way in sentences. Too often it is used where it adds nothing to sense ('It was a very tragic death'), or is inserted in a futile effort to prop up a weak word that would be better replaced by something with more punch ('The play was very good').

Vespucci, Amerigo (1454–1512) Italian navigator and explorer after whom America was named

vestibule entrance room or hall

Veterans Administration (no apos.) former name of the US Department of Veterans Affairs

vetoes

Veuve Clicquot champagne

vexatious annoying

VHF very high frequency

via, meaning 'by way of', indicates the direction of a journey and not the means by which the journey is achieved. It is correct to say, 'We flew from London to Sydney via Singapore,' but not 'We travelled to the islands via seaplane.'

viable does not mean feasible or promising, senses in which it is frequently used. It means capable of independent existence. A foetus is viable if it can live outside the womb.

Via Dolorosa, Jerusalem 'way of sadness'; route taken by Jesus to the Crucifixion

Vianchang capital of Laos, formerly called Vientiane

vicarious experienced through another person's feelings

vicereine female viceroy; the wife of a viceroy

vichyssoise soup; note -*ss*-

vicious cruel; not to be confused with **viscous**, which means sticky

vicissitude a change of circumstance. Although there is no compelling reason for it, the word is almost always used in the plural.

victualler (US **victualer**) a provider of food and drink; pronounced *vittler*

vie, vying

Vientiane, capital of Laos, is now called **Vianchang**.

Vietcong, Vietminh (one word)

Vietnam (one word) South-east Asian nation, capital Hanoi

Vieux Carré French quarter of New Orleans

vigilance, vigilant A **vigilante** is one of a self-appointed group who, without any official standing, attempt to keep order in their neighbourhood.

vignette a decoration or sketch; an image with no definite border; a literary sketch

vilify defame; not *-ll-*

Villa-Lobos, Heitor (1887–1959) Brazilian composer; not *Hector*

Villaraigosa, Antonio (1953–) mayor of Los Angeles 2005–

Ville Lumière, La (Fr.) 'city of light', nickname of Paris

Villette novel by Charlotte Brontë (1853)

vinaigrette salad dressing

vin ordinaire (Fr.) an inexpensive wine

Virgil anglicized name of Publius Vergilius Maro (70–19 BC), Roman poet

Virgin Atlantic Airways

Virgin Islands comprise the British Virgin Islands (capital Road Town) and the US Virgin Islands (capital Charlotte Amalie).

virtuoso, pl. **virtuosi** or **virtuosos**

vis-à-vis (Fr.) face to face, with regard to

Visconti, Count Luchino (1907–76) Italian stage and film director

viscous sticky

Vishnu Hindu god

visitable

vis major (Lat.) 'greater force'; pl. *vires majores*

visor sun shield

VISTA, Volunteers in Service to America, is now **AmeriCorps*VISTA**.

vita brevis, ars longa (Lat.) 'life is short, art is long'

vitiate contaminate, ruin

Viti Levu main island of Fiji, site of Suva, the capital

vitreous, **vitriform** The first describes something made of or having the quality of glass. The second means to have the appearance of glass.

vituperate bitterly insult. The adjective is **vituperative**.

vivacious, **vivacity**

vivat regina! (Lat.) long live the queen

vivat rex! (Lat.) long live the king

viva voce an oral examination

vivify to bring to life

viz. abbr. of *videlicet* (Lat.), 'namely', 'that is to say'

Vizcaíno, Sebastián (c. 1550–1615) Spanish explorer

VJ Day 15 August 1945, the date of Japan's surrender in the Second World War

Vlaanderen Flemish for Flanders

Vladivostok, Russia

Vlaminck, Maurice de (1876–1958) French artist and writer

Vlissingen, Netherlands

vocal cords, not *chords*. Vocal cords are so called because of their shape and structure, not because of their tonal qualities.

vociferous outspoken

Vodafone telecommunications company

voilà (Fr.) see there

Volapük artificial language that once rivalled Esperanto in popularity

volatile changeable, unpredictable

vol-au-vent puff pastry filled with savoury foodstuffs and sauce

volcano, pl. **volcanoes**

volcanology, vulcanology Both mean the scientific study of volcanoes. The first is the preferred American spelling, the second the preferred British one.

Volcker, Paul (1927–) American banking executive and government official, chairman of the Federal Reserve 1979–87

Volgograd Russian city; formerly Stalingrad and before that Tsaritsyn

Volkswagen German car company; formally Volkswagenwerk AG

Volstead Act US act passed in 1919 to enforce Prohibition

Völsunga Saga Scandinavian epic

Voltaire (1694–1778) pen name of François-Marie Arouet, French writer; **Voltairean** is the somewhat awkward adjectival form of the name

volte-face (hyphen) a complete change or reversal, especially an unexpected one

voluptuous

von Braun, Wernher (1912–77) German-born American rocket scientist

von Karajan, Herbert (1908–89) Austrian conductor

Vonnegut, Kurt (1922–2007) American novelist

von Sternberg, Josef (1894–1969) Austrian-born American film director

von Stroheim, Erich (1885–1957) German-born Hollywood
    actor and director
Von Willebrand's disease genetic disorder that affects blood
    clotting
voodoo
voortrekker Afrikaans for a pioneer
Vorderasiatisches Museum, Berlin
vortexes, vortices For the plural of *vortex*, either is correct.
vox populi (Lat.) voice of the people
Voyageurs National Park, Minnesota
voyeur one who enjoys watching others engage in sexual acts
Vuillard, Édouard (1868–1940) French artist
vulpine having the nature of a fox
vying competing

WAAC Women's Army Auxiliary Corps (UK)
WAAF Women's Auxiliary Air Force (UK)
wacky
Waikiki beach and district, Honolulu
wainscot, wainscoting type of panelling
Waitemata Harbour, Auckland, New Zealand
waiver, waver The first is a relinquishment of a claim; the
second means to hesitate.
Wajda, Andrzej (1926–) pronounced *vai´-da*; Polish film
director
Walden Pond small lake in Massachusetts associated with
Henry David Thoreau
Waldenses puritanical Christian sect originating in 12th-
century Lyon
Waldheim, Kurt (1918–2007) Austrian politician, Secretary-
General of the United Nations 1972–82 and President of
Austria 1986–92
Walesa, Lech (1943–) President of Poland 1990–5; awarded
Nobel Peace Prize 1983
walkie-talkie
wallaby species of small kangaroo
Wallace, Alfred Russel (not *-ll)* (1823–1913) British
naturalist

Wallace and Gromit British cartoon-film characters

Wallenberg, Raoul (1912–47?) Swedish diplomat who helped to save thousands of Hungarian Jews from being sent to concentration camps in the Second World War

Wallis, Sir Barnes Neville (1887–1979) British aeronautical engineer and inventor

Wallis and Futuna Islands South Pacific island cluster, formerly a French overseas territory, now formally a French overseas collectivity; capital Mata-Utu

Walloon, a French-speaking Belgian, but **Wallonia** for the region

Wal-Mart US discount stores group. The company's full name is Wal-Mart Stores Inc.

Walpurgis night (or **Walpurgisnacht**) night of 30 April, when witches were once thought to gather

Walton, Izaak (not *Isaac*) (1593–1683) English biographer and naturalist

Wampanoag Native American group, part of the Algonquin people

Wardour Street, London

Warrnambool, New South Wales

Warszawa the Polish spelling of Warsaw

Wassermann test blood test for syphilis, named after the German bacteriologist August von Wassermann (1866–1925)

wasteland (one word), but the poem by T. S. Eliot is '**The Waste Land**'

wastrel good-for-nothing person

'**Water, water, everywhere,/Nor any drop to drink**' are the lines from the Samuel Taylor Coleridge poem 'The Rime of the Ancient Mariner'.

Waterston, Sam (1940–) American actor; not -*son*

Watling Street Roman road between Shropshire and Dover, passing through London

Watteau, Jean-Antoine (1684–1721) French painter

Watusi African people

Waugh, Evelyn (1903–66) English novelist

Waukegon, Illinois

waver, waiver The first means to hesitate; the second is the relinquishment of a claim.

Waverley Station, Edinburgh

wavy, not -*ey*

way, shape or form Choose one.

WCTU Woman's Christian Temperance Union (US)

Wealth of Nations, The by Adam Smith (1776); formally it is *Inquiry into the Nature and Causes of the Wealth of Nations*

weasel

weather conditions is redundant, as in 'Freezing weather conditions will continue for the rest of the week.' Delete *conditions*. Similarly tiresome is the weather forecasters' fondness for 'activity', as in 'thunderstorm activity over the plains states'.

Weddell Sea, Antarctica

Wedgwood china; not *Wedge-*

weevil type of beetle

Wehrmacht German armed forces 1935–45

Weidenfeld & Nicolson for the British publisher; not -*field*, not *Nich-*

Weil, Simone (1909–43) French philosopher; pronounced *vay*

Weill, Kurt (1900–50) German-born American composer

Weimar Republic German republic 1919–33

Weimaraner (cap.) breed of dog

Weir, Peter (1944–) Australian film director
weird
Weisz, Rachel (1971–) British actress
Weizmann, Chaim (1874–1952) Russian-born Israeli scientist and statesman, President of Israel 1948–52
Welles, Orson (1915–85) American film actor and director
Wellesley College, Wellesley, Massachusetts
wellington boots (no cap.)
Weltschmerz (Ger.) sadness over the state of the world
werewolf, pl. **werewolves**
West, Nathanael pen name of Nathan Wallenstein Weinstein (1903–40), American novelist
Westchester, New York, but **West Chester**, Delaware and Pennsylvania
Western Australia for the Australian state, but the *West Australian* for its largest newspaper
Westmeath Irish county
Westmoreland, William C. (1914–2005) American general
Westmorland, not -*more*- former English county, now part of Cumbria
Westpac Banking Corporation Australian bank
West Point-Pepperell, US textiles company, is now called **WestPoint Home.**
West Virginia US state, entirely separate from neighbouring Virginia; capital Charleston (not to be confused with a more famous city of that name in South Carolina)
Westward Ho!, Devon (exclamation mark)
Westwood, Vivienne (1941–) British fashion designer
wether a castrated sheep
Weyerhaeuser Company forestry products company
whacky (alt.)/**wacky** (pref.)
whammy in the UK, a blow; in the US, a curse

wharf, pl. **wharves/wharfs**

wheedle coax

wheeze

whelk edible mollusc

whence Although there is ample precedent for writing 'from whence' – the King James Bible has the sentence 'I will lift up mine eyes unto the hills from whence cometh my help' – it is nonetheless tautological. *Whence* means 'from where'. It is enough to say 'the hills whence cometh my help'.

whereabouts is plural.

whether or not The second two words should be dropped when *whether* is equivalent to *if*, as in: 'It is not yet known whether or not persons who become reinfected can spread the virus to others.' *Or not* is necessary, however, when what is being stressed is an alternative: 'I intend to go whether or not you like it.'

whet one's appetite, not *wet* The word has nothing to do with heightened salivary flow or anything of the kind. It comes from an old English word, *hwettan*, meaning 'sharpen'. Hence also *whetstone*, for a stone used to sharpen knives.

which The belief that *which* may refer only to the preceding word and not to the whole of a preceding statement is without foundation except where there is a chance of ambiguity. The impossibility of enforcing the rule consistently is illustrated by an anecdote cited by Gowers. A class in Philadelphia had written to a local paper's resident usage expert asking him what was wrong with the sentence 'He wrecked the car, which was due to his carelessness.' Notice how the authority hoists himself with the last three words of his reply: 'The fault lies in using *which* to refer to the statement "He wrecked the car." When *which* follows a noun, it refers to that noun as its antecedent. Therefore in the foregoing sentence it is stated that the car was due to his carelessness, which is nonsense.' See also THAT, WHICH.

whim, **whimsy** A *whim* is a sudden wish or change of mind; *whimsy* is quaint behaviour or humour.

whinny the sound a horse makes

whippet breed of dog

whippoorwill North American bird, so named because of its call

whirligig for the fairground ride and beetle, but **whirlybird** for the slang term for a helicopter

whisky, **whiskey** In the UK *Scotch whisky* is written thus and *Irish whiskey* thus. In the US, both are *whiskey*.

Whistler, James Abbott McNeill (1834–1903) American painter

Whitaker's Almanack British reference book

White Friars Carmelites

Whit Sunday the seventh Sunday after Easter

whitish, not *white-*

Whittier, John Greenleaf (1807–92) American poet

whittle to pare wood; to reduce gradually

whiz, **whizzed**, **whizzing**

whiz kid, not *whizz*, is generally the preferred spelling, though most dictionaries recognize both. The same applies for *whiz-bang*, but with the addition of a hyphen.

who, **whom** *Whom* is used when it is the object of a preposition ('To whom it may concern') or verb ('The man whom we saw last night') or the subject of a complementary infinitive ('The person whom we took to be your father'). *Who* is used on all other occasions.

whodunit is the usual spelling for a mystery story. Note the single *n*.

whortleberry

Who's Who biographical reference work

Whyte & Mackay Scotch whisky

widget a gadget or other small undefined item

wield

Wien German for Vienna

Wiener, Norbert (1894–1964) American mathematician, developed the science of cybernetics

Wiener schnitzel fried breaded veal cutlet

Wiesbaden, Germany, not *Weis-*

Wiesenthal, Simon (1919–2005) celebrated hunter of Nazi war criminals

Wiest, Dianne (1948–) American actress

Wi-Fi (generally cap.) short for wireless fidelity

Wii Nintendo home video game console

Wilde, Oscar (Fingall O'Flahertie Wills) (1854–1900) Irish poet and playwright

wildebeest, pl. **wildebeeste/wildebeests**

wildflower (adj.), **wild flower** (noun) A *wildflower* garden is filled with *wild flowers*.

wilful (US **willful**)

Wilkes-Barre, Pennsylvania

Wilkes Land, Antarctica (two words, no apos.)

Willkie, Wendell L(ewis) (1892–1944) American business-man chosen by the Republican Party as its presidential candidate in 1940

will-o'-the-wisp a phosphorescent light, thus something elusive

Wills, Garry (1934–) US historian

willy-nilly regardless of feelings

Wilshire Boulevard, Los Angeles, not *Wilt-*

Wimbledon tennis club; officially, the All-England Lawn Tennis and Croquet Club

Wimpey, **Wimpy** The first is a building company; the second is a hamburger chain.

Windhoek capital of Namibia

Winger, Debra (1952–) American film actress

Winnemucca, Nevada

Winnibigoshish, Lake, Minnesota

Winnipeg capital of Manitoba, Canada

Winnipesaukee, Lake, New Hampshire

Winsor & Newton artist's supplies company; not *Windsor*

Wisbech, Cambridgeshire pronounced *wizz-beach*

wisteria, not *-staria*, for the flowering shrub, though the American scientist for whom it was named was **Caspar Wistar**

withal in addition, moreover; not *-all*

withershins/widdershins Either is acceptable for the meaning of anticlockwise; both are pronounced *widder-shins.*

withhold, **withheld** Note *-hh-*.

Wittgenstein, Ludwig (1889–1951) Austrian-born British philosopher

Witwatersrand South African region in which Johannesburg is located. The university commonly known as **Wits University** is formally **University of the Witwatersrand** (note *the*).

wizened shrivelled

Wobegon, Lake fictional town in novels by Garrison Keillor. The word itself, meaning dismal-looking, is spelled **woebegone**.

Wodehouse, P. G. (1881–1975) prolific comic novelist; formally Sir Pelham Grenville Wodehouse

Wolfe, Thomas (1900–38) American novelist, author of *Look*

Homeward, Angel (1929). Not to be confused with **Tom Wolfe** (1931–), journalist and novelist, author of *The Bonfire of the Vanities* (1987)

Wolfit, Sir Donald (1902–68) English actor-manager

Wollongong, New South Wales

Wollstonecraft, Mary (1759–97) English author, mother of Mary Wollstonecraft Shelley

Wolseley British motor car and name of a popular restaurant (housed in an old Wolseley showroom) on Piccadilly, London

Wolsey, Thomas, Cardinal (c. 1475–1530) English clergyman and statesman

Women's Institute UK women's voluntary organization

wondrous, not -*erous*

Woods Hole Oceanographic Institution, Woods Hole, Massachusetts

woofer type of loudspeaker

Woolf, Virginia (1882–1941) English novelist, founder of the Hogarth Press with her husband, **Leonard Woolf** (1880–1969)

Woollcott, Alexander (1887–1943) American journalist and critic

woollen (US **woolen**), **woolly** (US **woolly** also)

Woolloomooloo for the euphonious district of Sydney. Note the single *l* at the end.

Woolsack large cushion on which the Lord Chancellor sits in the House of Lords

Woonsocket, Rhode Island

Woosnam, Ian (1958–) British golfer

Worcester sauce (US **Worcestershire sauce**)

workaholic

World Bank officially the International Bank for

Reconstruction and Development, but that title is rarely used, even on first reference

World Court officially the International Court of Justice and that title should generally be used on first reference or soon thereafter

Worrall Thompson, Antony (1951–) British chef

worshipped, **worshipper** (US **worshiped**, **worshiper**)

worsted fabric; not *-stead*

would like 'I would have liked to have seen it' is a common construction and may be excused in conversation, but in writing it should be 'I would like to have seen it' or 'I would have liked to see it.'

wound, **scar** The two are not as interchangeable as writers sometimes casually make them. A scar is what remains after a wound heals. Thus it is always wrong, or at least stretching matters, to talk about a scar healing, including in figurative senses.

Wozniak, Steve (1950–) computer engineer, co-founder of Apple Computer (now Apple Inc.) with Steve Jobs

wrack, **rack** *Wrack* is a kind of seaweed, a cloud mass or a wreck; *rack* to strain. The expressions are *rack and ruin*, *nerve-racking* and *rack one's brain*.

WRAF Women's Royal Air Force

Wrangell Mountains, **Cape Wrangell**, **Wrangell-St Elias National Park**, Alaska

wreak havoc cause chaos

WRNS Women's Royal Naval Service; a member is a Wren

Wrocław, Poland formerly Breslau

WRVS Women's Royal Voluntary Service

wunderkind, not *wonder-* a prodigy

Wyatville, Sir Jeffry (1766–1840) British architect; note unusual spelling of both names

Wycherley, William (1640–1716) English playwright

Wyclif (or **Wycliffe**)**, John** (c. 1320–84) English religious reformer

Wykehamist student of Winchester College

Wymondham, Norfolk pronounced *win-dum*

Wynette, Tammy (1942–98) American country singer; born Virginia Wynette Pugh

Wythenshawe, Greater Manchester

Xavier, St Francis (1506–52) Spanish missionary, one of the founders of the Jesuit order

XDR TB extensive drug-resistant tuberculosis

Xenophon (c. 430–c. 350 BC) Greek historian and soldier

xerography (no cap.) photocopying process

Xerox (cap.) brand of photocopier and the copies it produces

Xerxes (519–465 BC) Persian king, defeated by the Greeks at Salamis

Xianggang Pinyin name for Hong Kong, but use **Hong Kong**

Xinhua Chinese news agency; pronounced *shin-hwa´*

Xizang Pinyin name for Tibet, but use **Tibet**

X-ray

xylophone

Y

Yablonovy Range, Russia

Yahoo! computer search engine company; note exclamation mark

yakuza (not cap.) Japanese organized crime groups

Yamaguchi, Kristy (1971–) American figure skater

Yamoussoukro capital of Côte d'Ivoire

Yangon formerly Rangoon, capital of Burma

Yangtze China's greatest river, now increasingly known by its pinyin name, Chang Jiang. Until the relationship between the two names is more generally known, however, Yangtze should also be used on first reference.

Yaoundé capital of Cameroon

Yar'Adua, Umaru (1951–) President of Nigeria 2007–

yarmulke skullcap worn by Jewish men

yashmak veil worn by Muslim women

Yerevan capital of Armenia

Yeşilköy Airport, Istanbul

Yevtushenko, Yevgeny (1933–) Russian poet

yoicks old foxhunting cry

Yoknapatawpha County fictional county in many of William Faulkner's novels

Yokohama, Japan

Yokosuka, Japan

Yom Kippur   Jewish holy day, also called the Day of Atonement

Yourcenar, Marguerite   pen name of Marguerite de Crayencour (1903–87), Belgian-born French-American writer

YouTube video-sharing website

Yushchenko, Viktor (1954–) President of Ukraine 2004– ; not to be confused with **Viktor Yanukovych** (1950–), whom he narrowly beat in a run-off election

Z

Zaandam, Zaanstad, Netherlands

zabaglione Italian dessert

Zacatecas city and state in central Mexico

Zaire since 1997, the Democratic Republic of the Congo; central African republic; capital Kinshasa

Zakinthos Greek island; also known as Zacynthos, Zakyntos and Zante

Zambezi African river

Zambia formerly Northern Rhodesia; African republic; capital Lusaka

Zanuck, Darryl F. (for **Francis**) (1902–79) American film producer and studio executive, father of **Richard Darryl Zanuck** (1934–), film producer

Zapatero, José Luis Rodríguez (1960–) Prime Minister of Spain 2004–

Zappeion Gardens, Athens

Zarathustra (Persian)/**Zoroaster** (Greek) (*fl*. 6th c. BC) Persian prophet, founder of Zoroastrianism

Zarqawi, Abu Musab al- (1966–2006) Jordanian insurgent, associated with Al Qaeda

Zatlers, Valdis (1955–) President of Latvia 2007–

Zátopek, Emil (1922–2000) Czech long-distance runner

Zeebrugge Belgian port

Zeffirelli, Franco (1923–)   Italian film, theatre and opera director

Zeil, Mount, Northern Territory, Australia

zeitgeist spirit of the age

Zell am See (no hyphens) Austrian resort

Zellweger, Renée (1969–) American actress

Zeppelin Germany military airship in the First World War

Zermatt, Switzerland

zeros

Zeus pre-eminent Greek god

Zhao Ziyang (1910–2005) Prime Minister of China 1980–7, General Secretary of Chinese Communist Party 1987–9

Zhonghua Remnin Gongheguo (Mandarin)   People's Republic of China

Zhou Enlai (Pinyin)/**Chou En-lai** (1898–1976)   Prime Minister of China 1949–76

Zia (ul-Haq), Muhammad (1924–88) President of Pakistan 1977–88

Zidane, Zinedine (1972–) French soccer player

Ziegfeld, Florenz (1867–1932) American producer of musicals

ziggurat a stepped tower

Zimbabwe   formerly Rhodesia; African republic; capital Harare

Zinnemann, Fred (1907–97) Austrian-born American film director

Zions BanCorp Utah-based banking company

Zip Code (caps) US postal code

zloty Poland's basic unit of currency; pl. **zlotys**

Zoellick, Robert (1953–)   American civil servant, made president of the World Bank in 2007 in succession to Paul Wolfowitz

zoetrope 19th-century optical toy

Zoroaster (Greek)/**Zarathustra** (Persian) (*fl.* 6th c. BC) Persian prophet, founder of **Zoroastrianism**

Zorrilla y Moral, José (1817–93) Spanish poet

Zsigmond, Vilmos (1930–) Hungarian-born American cinematographer

zucchini (US) vegetable known in France and elsewhere as courgette

Zukor, Adolph (1873–1976) Hungarian-born American film producer and studio executive

zum Beispiel (Ger.) 'for example'; abbr. *z.B.*

Zurbriggen, Purmin (1963–) Swiss skier

zut alors! (Fr.) cry of astonishment

Zvonareva, Vera (1984–) Russian tennis player

Zwelithini, Goodwill (1948–) King of the Zulu Nation in South Africa 1968–

zwieback a kind of rusk

Zwingli, Ulrich (or **Huldreich**) (1484–1531) Swiss religious zealot

Zworykin, Vladimir (1889–1982) Russian-born American scientist, one of the inventors of television

Appendix

Words ending in -*able* and -*ible*

-*able*	-*ible*
abominable	accessible
amenable	admissible
appreciable	collapsible
available	collectible (US, alt. UK)
collectable (UK, alt. US)	compatible
conformable	comprehensible
confusable	contemptible
culpable	credible
delectable	deductible
dependable	defensible
describable	digestible
estimable	discernible
execrable	divertible
expandable	exhaustible
dispensable	forcible
impassable	impassible
impressionable	incorrigible
innumerable	irresistible
inscrutable	perceptible

-*able*	-*ible*
inseparable	perfectible
knowledgeable	reprehensible
manageable	resistible
marriageable	revertible
peaceable	suppressible
perishable	
recognizable	
refusable	
reputable	
salable (US, alt. UK)	
saleable (UK, alt. US)	
separable	
sizable (US, alt. UK)	
sizeable (UK, alt. US)	
unconscionable	

Major airports

Abbr.	City	Airport Name
AMS	Amsterdam	Schiphol
ATH	Athens	Elefthérios Venizélos
ATL	Atlanta	Hartsfield Atlanta International
BCN	Barcelona	Barcelona International or El Prat
SXF	Berlin	Schönefeld
THF		Tempelhof
TXL		Tegel
BOS	Boston	Logan International

Abbr.	City	Airport Name
EZE	Buenos Aires	Ministro Pistarini (informally Ezeiza)
ORD	Chicago	O'Hare International
CPH	Copenhagen	Copenhagen Airport (informally Kastrup)
HAM	Hamburg	Hamburg-Fuhlsbüttel
HEL	Helsinki	Helsinki-Vantaa
LHR	London	Heathrow
LGW		Gatwick
LAX	Los Angeles	Los Angeles International
VNY		Van Nuys (pronounced *van nize*)
MAD	Madrid	Barajas
YUL	Montreal	Montreal-Pierre Elliott Trudeau International
YMX		Mirabel
SVO	Moscow	Sheremetyevo
VKO		Vnukovo
DME		Domodedovo
MUC	Munich	Franz Josef Strauss International
EWR	Newark	Newark Liberty International
JFK	New York	John F. Kennedy International
LGA		La Guardia
GMN	Oslo	Gardermoen
ORY	Paris	Orly
CDG		Charles de Gaulle
FCO	Rome	Leonardo da Vinci (Fiumicino)
CIA		Ciampino
GRU	São Paulo	Guarulhos International
VCP		Viracopos
CGH		Congonhas-São Paulo International
GMP	Seoul	Kimpo International

Abbr.	City	Airport Name
ICN		Incheon International
SIN	Singapore	Changi
ARN	Stockholm	Arlanda
BMA		Bromma
SYD	Sydney	Kingsford Smith
TPE	Taipei	Taiwan Taoyuan International
TLV	Tel Aviv	Ben Gurion
HND	Tokyo	Tokyo International or Haneda
NRT		Narita
YYZ	Toronto	Lester B. Pearson International
IAD	Washington, DC	Dulles International
WAS		Ronald Reagan Washington National

Temperature conversion table

Celsius*	←F/C→	Fahrenheit*	Celsius*	←F/C→	Fahrenheit*
−18	0	32	0	32	90
−15	5	41	2	35	96
−12	10	50	4	40	104
−9	15	59	7	45	113
−7	20	68	10	50	122
−4	25	77	38	100	212
−1	30	86			

*figures rounded off to the nearest whole number

Distance conversion table

km* →miles/	km←	miles*	km* →miles/	km←	miles*
1.6	1	0.6	48.3	30	18.6
3.2	2	1.2	64.4	40	24.9
4.8	3	1.9	80.5	50	31.1
6.4	4	2.5	96.6	60	37.3
8.0	5	3.1	112.7	70	43.5
9.7	6	3.7	128.7	80	49.7
11.3	7	4.3	144.8	90	55.9
12.9	8	5.0	160.9	100	62.1
14.5	9	5.6	402.3	250	155.3
16.1	10	6.2	804.7	500	310.7
32.2	20	12.4			

figures rounded off to one decimal place

Metric prefixes

Prefix	Meaning	Prefix	Meaning
deci-	one-tenth	deka-	10
centi-	one-hundredth	hecto-	100
milli-	one-thousandth	kilo-	1000
micro-	one-millionth	mega-	1 million
nano-	one-billionth	giga-	1 billion
pico-	one-trillionth	tera-	1 trillion

Monarchs of England

Saxons and Danes

802–39	Egbert
839–58	Ethelwulf
858–60	Ethelbald
860–5	Ethelbert
865–71	Ethelred
871–99	Alfred
899–924	Edward (the elder)
924–39	Athelstan
939–46	Edmund
946–55	Edred
955–9	Edwy
959–75	Edgar
975–8	Edward (the Martyr)
978–1016	Ethelred (the Unready)
1016	Edmund (Ironside)
1016–35	Canute/Cnut
1035–7	Harold (*regent*)
1037–40	Harold I
1040–2	Harthacanute
1042–66	Edward (the Confessor)
1066	Harold II

Normans

1066–87	William I (the Conqueror)
1087–1100	William II (Rufus)
1100–35	Henry I

House of Blois

| 1135–54 | Stephen |

House of Plantagenet

1154–89	Henry II
1189–99	Richard I (Coeur de Lion)
1199–1216	John
1216–72	Henry III
1272–1307	Edward I
1307–27	Edward II
1327–77	Edward III
1377–99	Richard II

House of Lancaster

1399–1413	Henry IV
1413–22	Henry V
1422–61	Henry VI

House of York

| 1461–70 | Edward IV |

House of Lancaster

| 1470–1 | Henry VI |

House of York

1471–83	Edward IV
1483	Edward V
1483–5	Richard III

House of Tudor

1485–1509	Henry VII
1509–47	Henry VIII
1547–53	Edward VI
1553–8	Mary I
1558–1603	Elizabeth I

House of Stuart

1603–25	James I (and VI of Scotland)
1625–49	Charles I
1660–85	Charles II
1685–8	James II
1689–94	William III and Mary II
1694–1702	William III alone
1702–14	Anne

House of Hanover

1714–27	George I
1727–60	George II
1760–1820	George III
1820–30	George IV (Prince Regent 1811–20)
1830–7	William IV
1837–1901	Victoria

House of Saxe-Coburg	
1901–10	Edward VII
House of Windsor	
1910–36	George V
1936	Edward VIII
1936–52	George VI
1952–	Elizabeth II

Main units of currency

Country	Currency	Country	Currency
Afghanistan	afghani	Colombia	peso
Albania	lek	Congo (DR)	franc
Algeria	dinar	Costa Rica	colon
Argentina	peso	Croatia	kuna
Australia	dollar	Czech Republic	koruna
Austria	euro	Denmark	krone
Belgium	euro	Egypt	pound
Bolivia	boliviano	El Salvador	US dollar
Bosnia-Herzogovina	marka	Ethiopia	birr
Brazil	cruzeiro	Finland	euro
Bulgaria	lev	France	euro
Canada	dollar	Germany	euro
Chile	peso	Ghana	cedi
China	renminbi	Greece	euro
	yuan	Guatemala	quetzal

Country	Currency	Country	Currency
Haiti	gourde	Panama	balboa
Honduras	lempira	Paraguay	guaraní
Hungary	forint	Peru	nuevo sol
Iceland	króna	Philippines	piso *or* peso
Indonesia	rupiah	Poland	zloty
India	rupee	Portugal	euro
Iran	rial	Puerto Rico	US dollar
Iraq	dinar	Romania	leu
Ireland	euro	Saudi Arabia	riyal
Israel	shekel	Singapore	dollar
Italy	euro	Slovakia	koruna
Jamaica	dollar	South Africa	rand
Japan	yen	Spain	euro
Korea, South	won	Sweden	krona
Korea, North	won	Switzerland	franc
Kenya	shilling	Syria	pound
Kuwait	dinar	Taiwan	dollar
Laos	kip	Thailand	baht
Lebanon	pound	Tunisia	dinar
Libya	dinar	Turkey	lira
Luxembourg	euro	Uganda	shilling
Malawi	kwacha	UK	pound
Malaysia	ringgit	Uruguay	peso
Malta	euro	USA	dollar
Mexico	peso	USSR	rouble
Morocco	dirham	Venezuela	bolívar
Netherlands	euro	Vietnam	dong
New Zealand	dollar	Yugoslavia	dinar
Nicaragua	córdoba	Zambia	kwacha
Nigeria	naira	Zimbabwe	dollar
Norway	krone		

Numerals

Arabic	Roman	Arabic	Roman
1	I	20	XX
2	II	40	XL
3	III	50	L
4	IV	60	LX
5	V	90	XC
6	VI	100	C
7	VII	500	D
8	VIII	1,000	M
9	IX	5,000	$\bar{V}$
10	X	10,000	$\bar{X}$
11	XI	50,000	$\bar{L}$